BRIDGES 1 *Neu!*

Englisch für die Erwachsenenbildung

Classroom Book

von
Linda Gallasch, Jonathan Marks,
Karl-Heinz Noetzel, Bruce Pye,
John Riach, Geoff Tranter

Ernst Klett Verlag
Stuttgart Düsseldorf Leipzig

BRIDGES 1 NEU
Classroom Book

von

Dr. Linda Gallasch, Fachbereichsleiterin Fremdsprachen an der Volkshochschule Norderstedt

Jonathan Marks, Teacher Trainer und Autor, Łeba, Polen

Karl-Heinz Noetzel, Fachbereichsleiter Sprachen an der Volkshochschule Böblingen-Sindelfingen

Bruce Pye, Fachbereichsleiter Englisch an der Volkshochschule Nürnberg

John Riach, Trainer und Autor, Calw

Geoff Tranter, Koordinator für abschluß-bezogene Bildung an der Volkshochschule Dortmund, Landesbeauftragter für die Europäischen Sprachzertifikate Englisch in Nordrhein-Westfalen

Illustrationen:
Ulrike Müller, Heidelberg
Peter Schimmel, München

Magazine-Seiten:
Jenny Richardson-Schlötter, Zirndorf
Marlene Pohle, Stuttgart (Illustrationen)

Gedruckt auf Papier aus chlorfrei gebleichtem Zellstoff, säurefrei.

1. Auflage   1 4 3 2 1 | 2004 03 02 01

Alle Drucke dieser Auflage können im Unterricht nebeneinander benutzt werden. Die letzte Zahl bezeichnet das Jahr dieses Druckes.
© Ernst Klett Verlag GmbH, Stuttgart 1993 (2001).
Alle Rechte vorbehalten.
Internetadresse: http://www.klett-verlag.de

Redaktion:
Heinke Behal-Thomsen (Projektleitung),
David Shallis, Inge Spaughton, Elizabeth Webster,
Claudia Birkhold, Edda Vorrath-Wiesenthal

Druck: Schnitzer Druck GmbH, Korb.
Printed in Germany.
ISBN 3-12-501450-6

VORWORT

Liebe Kursteilnehmer/innen!

BRIDGES 1 NEU ist der erste Band eines dreibändigen Lehrwerks für Erwachsene aller Altersstufen, die wie Sie gemeinsam mit anderen die englische Sprache systematisch und zielgerichtet erlernen möchten und dabei auch auf Abwechslung, Spaß und persönliche Horizonterweiterung Wert legen.

Grundlage des Kursunterrichts mit **BRIDGES 1 NEU** ist das vorliegende **Classroom Book**. Es gliedert sich in fünf Blöcke von je drei regulären UNITS und einem kürzeren Kapitel, PREVIEW genannt, weil es neben einer Wiederholung der vorangegangenen UNITS immer auch eine Vorschau auf den nächsten Block enthält.

In allen 15 regulären UNITS stehen am Ende die Aussprache- und Intonationsübungen. Es folgen dann jeweils eine Seite MAGAZINE und eine Seite LANGUAGE CHECKLIST. Die MAGAZINE-Seiten enthalten Texte und landeskundliche Informationen, die Sie außerhalb des Unterrichts lesen können. Die LANGUAGE CHECKLISTS geben Ihnen eine Zusammenfassung der sprachlichen Schwerpunkte jeder Unit.

Für Ihren Lernerfolg ist es wichtig, daß Sie sich auch mit den anderen Bestandteilen vom **Classroom Book** vertraut machen, die im Inhaltsverzeichnis auf den Seiten 4 – 8 aufgeführt sind.

Darüber hinaus können Ihnen das **Practice Book**, die Tonmaterialien zu **BRIDGES 1 NEU**, das zusätzliche Übungsheft **Grammar Practice** und die **CD-ROM** (siehe Werkübersicht auf der hinteren Umschlagseite), dabei helfen, Ihr Ziel zu erreichen: ***Building BRIDGES of understanding!***

Einen guten Start und viel Erfolg wünscht Ihnen

Ihr **BRIDGES**-Team

Symbole

- Kassette/CD
- Überprüfen Sie mit Hilfe der Kassette/CD
- Musik/Lied
- Partnerarbeit
- Gruppenarbeit
- Notieren Sie

BRIDGES Kurszeitschriften-Wettbewerb

Für das **BRIDGES**-Team wäre es sehr interessant zu sehen, was Sie im Verlauf der Arbeit mit **BRIDGES 1 NEU** geschrieben, gezeichnet und gestaltet haben. Wir möchten Sie deshalb einladen, ein Exemplar Ihrer Kurszeitschrift an uns zu senden:

Ernst Klett Verlag GmbH
Redaktion Weiterbildung Sprachen
Postfach 10 60 16
70049 Stuttgart

Einmal im Jahr vergeben wir für die beste Kurszeitschrift einen Preis!

INHALT

UNIT 1 · Nice to meet you — S. 9

Themen/Situationen/Texte
Begrüßung und Verabschiedung; Vorstellung; Kennenlernen; Namen; Herkunft; Vorlieben; im Unterricht

Sprechabsichten
sich selbst/jmdn. vorstellen; auf Vorstellung reagieren; jmdn. grüßen; nach dem Befinden fragen und darauf reagieren; sich verabschieden; sprachliche Hilfe erbitten; eine Frage weitergeben; das Thema wechseln; sagen, was einem gefällt

Grammatik
Persönliche Fürwörter: *I, you, he, she*
Gegenwartsformen *be: I'm, he's, she's*
Zeitwörter, 1. und 3. Person Einzahl, Present Simple: *I like, he/she likes*
Frageform *be: … are you?*
Fragewörter: *How …? What …?*

Aussprache/Intonation
Aussprache des Buchstabens i: [aɪ] – [ɪ]

Magazine / Language Checklist

UNIT 2 · Names and numbers — S. 18

Themen/Situationen/Texte
Das englische Alphabet; ABC-Reim; Buchstabieren; Europa: Länder, Sprachen, Sprachkenntnisse; Zahlen; Spiel: Personen raten; Telefonnummern; die Wochentage; Telefonieren: ein Hotelzimmer buchen

Sprechabsichten
sich bedanken; sich entschuldigen; sprachliche Hilfe erbitten; um eine Wiederholung bitten; eine Meinung mitteilen; Unwissen ausdrücken; widersprechen; zustimmen; sagen, was einem nicht gefällt; eine Bitte äußern; auf eine Bitte reagieren; etwas bestellen

Grammatik
Persönliche Fürwörter: *it, we*
Gegenwartsform *be: it's*
Zeitwörter, 1. Person Mehrzahl, Present Simple: *we think*
Zeitwörter, verneinte Form, Present Simple: *I don't like*
Grundzahlen: *0 – 10*

Aussprache/Intonation
Aussprache des englischen Alphabets: Sortierung nach Lauten

Magazine / Language Checklist

UNIT 3 · Breakfast time — S. 25

Themen/Situationen/Texte
Uhrzeiten; Tageszeiten; Mahlzeiten; Frühstücksgewohnheiten: persönlich und interkulturell; Lebensmittel; Ansagen im Supermarkt; Gedicht

Sprechabsichten
eine Frage weitergeben

Grammatik
Persönliche Fürwörter: *they*
Gegenwartsformen *have: I/we/they have; he/she has*
Zeitwörter, verneinte Form, Present Simple: *he/she doesn't eat; we/they don't eat*
Regelmäßige Mehrzahlformen: *egg – eggs; tomato – tomatoes; country – countries*
Grundzahlen: *11, 12, 20, 25*
Uhrzeiten
Umstandsbestimmungen der Häufigkeit: *always, normally, usually, often, sometimes, never*
Umstandsbestimmungen der Zeit: *in the morning/afternoon/evening*
Stellung der Umstandsbestimmungen im Satz

Aussprache/Intonation
Wörter mit 1, 2, 3 oder 4 Silbe/n; betonte und unbetonte Silben; Betonungsmuster in 2- und 3-silbigen Wörtern

Magazine / Language Checklist

PREVIEW A — S. 33

Wiederholung von Block 1 und Vorschau auf Block 2

UNIT 4 · Where do you live? — S. 36

Themen/Situationen/Texte
Bingo-Spiel; Adressen; Telefonieren: Adressenauskunft; Wohnungen und Häuser: Größe, Gegend etc.; Gebäude und Anlagen in der Stadt; Rekorde

Sprechabsichten
sich bedanken; auf Dank reagieren; um eine Wiederholung bitten; eine Bitte äußern

Grammatik
Gegenwartsformen *be*: *you're, we're*
Frageform *be*: *Is it …?*
Frageform regelmäßiger Zeitwörter: *Do you …?*
Regelmäßige Mehrzahlbildung: *church – churches*

Bestimmter/Unbestimmter Artikel: *the, a/an*
Besitzanzeigende Fürwörter: *your, their*
Grundzahlen: *13 – 100*
Ordnungszahlen: *first, second, third*
Steigerung der Eigenschaftswörter (Superlativ): *smallest, nicest, biggest, easiest*

Aussprache/Intonation
Aussprache des Buchstabens a: [æ] – [aː] – [eɪ]; Satzbetonung

Magazine / Language Checklist

UNIT 5 · Travel — S. 45

Themen/Situationen/Texte
Reiseinformationen; Verkehrsmittel; Werbeplakate; Informationsentnahme aus Fahrplänen; Informationen für Zugreise/Flug erfragen

Sprechabsichten
um eine Wiederholung bitten; Wünsche äußern; nach Wünschen fragen; etwas bestellen

Grammatik
Frageform regelmäßiger Zeitwörter: *Does it …?*
Fragewörter: *When …? Where … from? How much …? How long …? How often …?*
Uhrzeiten bei Fahrplänen

Aussprache/Intonation
Aussprache des Buchstabens r: [r]; I – I'd

Magazine / Language Checklist

UNIT 6 · Outdoors — S. 53

Themen/Situationen/Texte
Farben; Lieder über Farben; das Wetter; Informationsentnahme aus Wetterbericht; Postkarten; die Landschaft beschreiben; die Monate und die Jahreszeiten; Reime über Monate

Sprechabsichten
begründen; sagen, was einem gefällt; sagen, was einem nicht gefällt

Grammatik
Gegenwartsformen *be*, Mehrzahl: *they are, there are*
Gegenwartsform *be*, Einzahl: *there's*
Gegenwartsform *be*, Mehrzahl, verneinte Form: *there are no*
Gegenwartsform *be*, Einzahl, verneinte Form: *there's no*
Modalverb *can*: *I can*
Modalverb *can*, verneinte Form: *I can't*
Modalverb *can*, Frageform: *Can I …?*
Satzmuster Aussagesätze: *because, so*
Satzmuster Fragen: *Can you …? (How) do you …? (Where) does it …? (When) does …?*
Fragewörter: *What's … like? How many …?*

Aussprache/Intonation
Satzbetonung; Wiederholung von [iː] – [eɪ] – [uː] – [əʊ] – [aʊ] – [ʌ]

Magazine / Language Checklist

PREVIEW B — S. 62

Wiederholung von Block 2 und Vorschau auf Block 3

UNIT 7 · Family   S. 64

Themen/Situationen/Texte
Familienbeziehungen; Visumformular; über Familienfotos sprechen; Stammbaum; Gedicht über Familie; Feiertage; Kalender; Geburtstage; Geschwister

Sprechabsichten
jmdn. vorstellen; Angaben zur Person machen; gute Wünsche äußern

Grammatik
Zeitwort *have got: he's/she's got, they've got*
Zeitwort *have got*, Frageform, Einzahl: *have you got …? has he/she got …?*
Zeitwort *have got*, Frageform, Mehrzahl: *have they got …?*
Kurzform *'s: he's, she's*
Mehrzahl, regelmäßige Form: *brothers-in-law*
Mehrzahl, andere Formen: *children, wives*

Aussprache/Intonation
Aussprache und Unterscheidung von verschiedenen Vokalen; Betonungsmuster

Magazine / Language Checklist

UNIT 8 · In town   S. 71

Themen/Situationen/Texte
In der Stadt; Wegbeschreibungen; Schilder; Gebäude in der Stadt; Stadtplan; Geschäfte; Öffnungszeiten

Sprechabsichten
jmdn. ansprechen und darauf reagieren; sich bedanken; auf Dank reagieren; Hilfe anbieten; ein Angebot annehmen; nach dem Weg fragen und darauf reagieren

Grammatik
Aufforderungssätze: *go, just go*
Zeitwort *have got: we've got*
Zeitwort *have got*, verneinte Form: *we haven't got*
Gegenwartsform *be*, Einzahl, verneinte Form: *there isn't*
Gegenwartsform *be*, Mehrzahl, verneinte Form: *there aren't*
Gegenwartsform *be*, Frageform: *Is there …?*
Mehrzahl, andere Formen: *men, women*

Persönliche Fürwörter als Satzergänzung, Einzahl: *me, you, it*
Persönliche Fürwörter als Satzergänzung, Mehrzahl: *you, them*
Unbestimmte Fürwörter: *some, any*
Mengenangaben: *most, a lot of, some*
Steigerung der Eigenschaftswörter (Superlativ): *best, most expensive, most interesting*
Umstandsbestimmungen der Zeit: *at eight o'clock/lunchtime/the weekend; on Thursday/Saturday morning/weekdays; in the afternoon/evening*
Umstandsbestimmungen des Ortes: *on the left/right; at the newsagent's; in Station Road/a restaurant; opposite the café; next to the hotel*

Aussprache/Intonation
Aussprache der schwachen Form [ə] bei bestimmten Wörtern im Kontext: *can, at, a; there, a; to, the; are*

Magazine / Language Checklist

UNIT 9 · At work   S. 79

Themen/Situationen/Texte
Arbeit und Berufe; Jobanzeigen; Arbeitsbedingungen; Berufe erraten; der Weg zur Arbeitsstelle; Kurzgeschichte

Sprechabsichten
berufsbezogene Informationen erfragen und geben

Grammatik
Vergangenheitsformen *be: I/it was, we were*
Regelmäßige Zeitwörter, Past Simple: *I started, we arrived*
Unregelmäßige Zeitwörter, Past Simple: *I got/went/had, it took*
Kurzantworten: *yes, I am; no, I'm not; yes, I do; no, I don't*
Persönliche Fürwörter als Satzergänzung, Einzahl: *him, her*

Aussprache/Intonation
Aussuchen von 3-silbigen Wörtern; der schwache Vokal (Schwa): [ə]

Magazine / Language Checklist

PREVIEW C   S. 85

Wiederholung von Block 3 und Vorschau auf Block 4

UNIT 10 · Memories   S. 87

Themen/Situationen/Texte
Erinnerungen an Schule; Lieblingsfächer; Lied; Rätsel; persönliche Erfahrungen; außergewöhnliche Kinder; unsinnige Gedichte

Sprechabsichten
sagen, was einem gefällt; sagen, was einem nicht gefällt

Grammatik
Vergangenheitsformen *be*: *you were, he/she was; you were, they were*
Vergangenheitsform *be*, verneinte Form: *it wasn't*
Vergangenheitsform *be*, Frageform: *were you? was it? were they?*
Unregelmäßige Zeitwörter, verneinte Form: *I didn't, he didn't*
Kurzformen: *didn't, couldn't, wasn't, weren't*
Steigerung der Eigenschaftswörter (Superlativ): *happiest, most modern, worst*
Aussagesätze mit Bindewörtern: *but, so, when*

Aussprache/Intonation
Wörter mit dem Laut [ɔː]; Betonung und Intonation

Magazine / Language Checklist

UNIT 11 · Living in Europe   S. 94

Themen/Situationen/Texte
Europa; Rätsel (Lesetext); Beschreibung von Ländern und Städten; Partnerstädte; Briefe; Lieder über Städte; überraschende Statistiken

Sprechabsichten
sich verabschieden; eine Äußerung einleiten; ein Angebot annehmen; Gewißheit ausdrücken; Ungewißheit/Unwissen ausdrücken; zustimmen; Nichtzustimmung ausdrücken; sagen, was einem gefällt

Grammatik
Unregelmäßige Zeitwörter, Frageform: *did you?*
Persönliche Fürwörter als Satzgegenstand, Mehrzahl: *us*
Ersatzwort *one*: *(What's your favourite) one?*
Grundzahlen bis über eine Million
Steigerung der Eigenschaftswörter (Superlativ): *most*
Verstärkende oder abschwächende Umstandswörter: *very, quite*
Wortstellung in Fragen: *did you …?*

Aussprache/Intonation
Wörter mit [f] – [v]

Magazine / Language Checklist

UNIT 12 · Leisure   S. 102

Themen/Situationen/Texte
Freizeitaktivitäten und Statistiken; Gedicht; Irland; Ausgehen; Karikatur; Anzeigen für Abendunterhaltung: Theater, Kinoprogramme, Musik, Restaurants; Freizeiteinrichtungen in Ihrer Stadt

Sprechabsichten
Unzufriedenheit ausdrücken; etwas vorschlagen; einen Vorschlag annehmen; einen Vorschlag ablehnen; auf einen Vorschlag unverbindlich reagieren

Grammatik
Unregelmäßige Zeitwörter, Vergangenheitsform: *used to*
Unbestimmte Fürwörter: *both, everybody, nobody*
Umstandsbestimmung der Häufigkeit: *every day, once a week, three times a year*

Aussprache/Intonation
Aussprache von ähnlichen Wörtern und Satzteilen; Betonung und Intonation

Magazine / Language Checklist

PREVIEW D   S. 109

Wiederholung von Block 4 und Vorschau auf Block 5

UNIT 13 · Eating out — S. 111

Themen/Situationen/Texte
Beurteilungskriterien für Restaurants; Speisekarten; im Restaurant; Lieblingsgerichte; eine Geschichte ordnen; Bildgeschichte; typische europäische Lebensmittel; Gedichte; Reim

Sprechabsichten
gute Wünsche äußern; sich entschuldigen; Zeit gewinnen; etwas anbieten; eine Bitte äußern; auf eine Bitte reagieren; etwas bestellen

Grammatik
Verstärkende oder abschwächende Umstandswörter: *especially, not so*

Aussprache/Intonation
Hauptbetonung; Aussprache von Vergangenheitsendung -d, -ed: [t] – [d] – [ɪd]

Magazine / Language Checklist

UNIT 14 · Lifestyle — S. 119

Themen/Situationen/Texte
Zimmer und Möbel; Umzug; Karikatur; Ausländer in Deutschland: Lebenssituation vergleichen; moderne Kunst; Reim

Sprechabsichten
etwas vergleichen; Eindrücke beschreiben

Grammatik
Steigerung der Eigenschaftswörter (Komparativ): *nicer/bigger; easier/happier; more modern; more expensive/interesting; better, worse*
Umstandsbestimmungen des Ortes: *behind, in front of, on, between*

Aussprache/Intonation
Wörter mit den Lauten [ʒ] – [dʒ]; Wiederholung von [iː] – [əʊ] – [ɑː] – [ɔː] – [ɪ] – [ɒ]

Magazine / Language Checklist

UNIT 15 · Europeans — S. 126

Themen/Situationen/Texte
Europäische Namen; Staatsangehörigkeit; Rätsel: berühmte Charaktere

Sprechabsichten
benennen/definieren; berichten; Gewißheit ausdrücken; Ungewißheit/Möglichkeit ausdrücken; widersprechen; zustimmen

Grammatik
Bezügliche Fürwörter: *who, whose*
Unbestimmte Fürwörter: *someone, anyone*
Jahreszahlen: *twelve ten, seventy-four B.C.*
Indirekte Rede: *he says …*

Aussprache/Intonation
Aussprache eines Gedichts

Magazine / Language Checklist

PREVIEW E — S. 131

Wiederholung und Zusammenfassung des gesamten Lernstoffs von BRIDGES 1 Neu: Spiel, Kurszeitschrift

FILES	S. 133
GRAMMAR	S. 143
Irregular Verbs	S. 147
VOCABULARY	S. 159
Phonetic alphabet	S. 159
Unit Vocabulary	S. 159
Personal and place names	S. 193
Alphabetical word list	S. 194
TAPESCRIPTS	S. 200

Unit 1

Nice to meet you

1

1 Hello

Hello! I'm Bruce and this is Linda.

Hi! I'm Linda and this is Geoff.

Hello! I'm Geoff.

2 I'm from Nuremberg

Leicester.
England.
I'm from Bavaria.
Nuremberg.
Ziegelstein.

I'm from Amarillo.
Texas.
America.
Hamburg.

I'm from Texas, too.

And you?

MEMO PAD   *Germany*

3 She's from Texas, he's from Yorkshire

A

I'm Bruce. I'm from Leicester.

This is Linda. She's from Amarillo.

This is Geoff. He's from Leeds.

B Write sentences.

This is Linda. She's from Amarillo.

This is _____. She's _____ _____.

This is _____. _____ _____ _____.

_____.

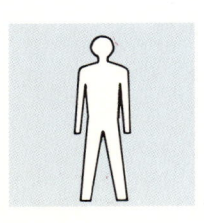

This is Geoff. He's from Leeds.

This is _____. He's _____ _____.

This is _____. _____ _____ _____.

_____.

eleven **11**

1

4 Nice to meet you

A Write the dialogue in the correct order.

△ Hello, Helga. Nice to meet you.
❑ I'm fine. By the way, this is Helga. She's from Germany.
❑ Hello, Pat. How are you?
○ Nice to meet you.   △ Fine, thanks. And you?

❑ _____
△ _____
❑ _____
△ _____
○ _____

B Listen and check. Read the dialogue aloud in groups.

C Look at File 1.

5 I am

A Read and complete.

am   are

I ____   Without "you ____"   Without "I ____"
because   "I ____"   "you ____"
you ____.   is meaningless.   is meaningless, too.

Leon Leszek Szkutnik

B Listen and check.

twelve

6 Good morning

A Read and complete.

> Good evening   Good morning
> Good afternoon

- ☐ Good evening.
- ○ _____.

- ☐ _____, Peter.
- ○ _____, John.
- ☐ How are you?
- ○ Fine, thanks.

- ☐ Mrs Irving? _____.
  Welcome to Berlin. I'm Harry Adler.
- ○ Nice to meet you, Mr Adler.
- ☐ Nice to meet you.

B Listen and check.

1

7 Goodbye

A Match the songs and the pictures.

> See you later Alligator   Goodnight Ladies
> Hello Goodbye   Bye Bye Love
> Goodnight Irene

1. _____

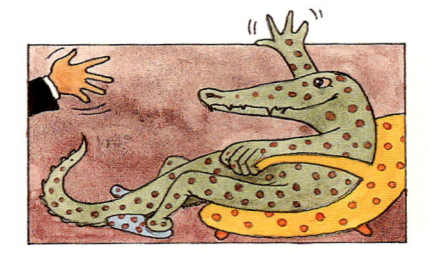

2. _____

3. _____

4. _____

5. _____

B Write one of these expressions on a card. Hold it up when you hear your expression.

Bye bye.   *Goodbye.*   *Hello.*
See you later.   *Goodnight.*

C Say goodbye.

Bye. See you next week.   *Goodbye.*   *Goodnight.*   *Bye bye.*

14   fourteen

8 I like reading

A

What's the English for Lesen?

Reading.

What's the English for Blumen?

Flowers.

MEMO PAD

Lesen = reading
Blumen = flowers

B

I'm Bruce. I like beer.

This is Linda. She likes singing.

This is Geoff. He likes gardening.

And you?

"I like your tie."

1

9 Where are they from?

A Read.

Where are they from? What do they like?

I'm Jonathan Marks.
I'm from Leeds.
I like jazz.

I'm Edda Vorrath. I'm from Hamburg. I like skiing and travelling.

I'm Karl-Heinz Noetzel.
I'm from Böblingen.
I like camping.

B Listen and fill in.

Tübingen Wales
Minnesota Toronto
music flowers
reading wine

	from	likes
Derrick		wine
Heinke	Tübingen	
John		flowers
Elizabeth	Minnesota	

C Write sentences.

Elizabeth ⇨ Elizabeth's from Minnesota. She likes _____.

Derrick ⇨ Derrick's from _____. He likes wine.

Heinke ⇨ _____

John ⇨ _____

Bruce ⇨ _____

Linda ⇨ _____

Geoff ⇨ _____

… ⇨ _____

sixteen

10 Hellos and goodbyes

Look at File 2.

| Hello. | Goodbye. |

- □ "Hello, Helga."
- △ "Hi, Maria."
- ○ "Goodbye."
- ▽ "Goodbye. See you next week."

"I hate long goodbyes."

11 PRONUNCIATION

A Write these words in the correct boxes.

dialogue English music fine goodnight I'm in is like listen nice pictures singing wine write

h<u>i</u>	th<u>i</u>s

B Listen and check.

1 magazine

Who is it? – Wer ist das?

Who is it?

He is from Liverpool.
He likes singing.
He likes the song

Hello Goodbye

Look at page 14.

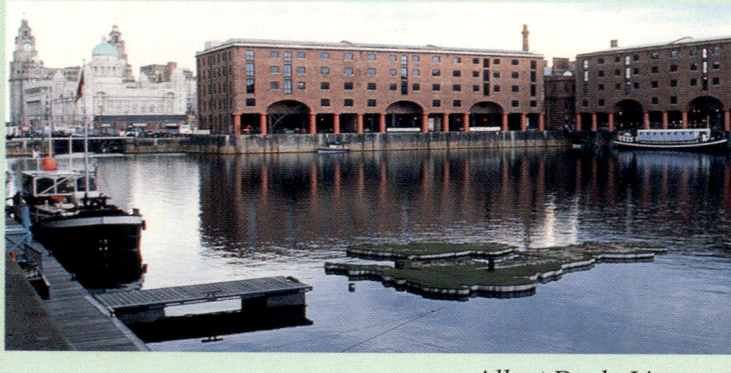

Albert Dock, Liverpool

Liverpool liegt an der Küste im Nordwesten Englands. Im 19. Jahrhundert war Liverpool eine große Industriestadt und zweitgrößter Hafen Englands. Die alten Hafenanlagen und Lagerhäuser wurden in den 1980er Jahren renoviert. Das Albert Dock beherbergt heute viele Läden, Cafés, Galerien und Museen wie The Beatles Story und das Merseyside Maritime Museum.

Jennifer

This is Jennifer.
She is from Amarillo.
She likes flowers and gardening.

Der Spanier Francisco Coronado war der erste Europäer, der 1541 die Gegend um Amarillo in Texas erkundete. 1893 zählte Amarillo ca. 500 Einwohner und 50 000 Stück Vieh. 1921 wurden die ersten Ölquellen entdeckt. Auch heute sind Rinderzucht und Ölindustrie noch sehr wichtige wirtschaftliche Faktoren neben den Touristenattraktionen, die an den Wilden Westen erinnern.

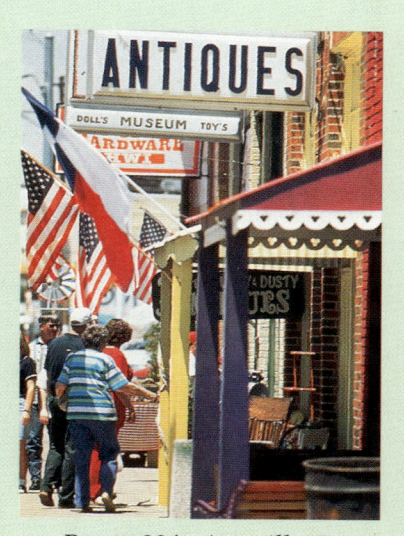

Route 66 in Amarillo, Texas

language checklist 1

Sie können jetzt:

Wendungen

sich selbst vorstellen
I'm (Bruce).
I'm from (Leicester).
(I'm from Leicester), too.

auf eine Vorstellung reagieren
Nice to meet you.

jemanden vorstellen
This is (Linda).
She's from Amarillo.

jemanden grüßen
Hello.
Hi.
Good morning/afternoon/evening.

jemanden willkommen heißen
Welcome to (Berlin).

nach dem Befinden fragen
How are you?

… und darauf reagieren
Fine, thanks. And you?
I'm fine.

sich verabschieden
Goodbye. / Bye bye. / Bye.
Goodnight.
See you (next week).

sprachliche Hilfe erbitten
What's the English for *(Lesen)*?

eine Frage weitergeben
And you?

das Thema wechseln
By the way, …

sagen, was Ihnen gefällt
I like (beer).
He likes (gardening).

Grammatik

- Persönliche Fürwörter: *I, you, he, she* → S. 151: IVa
- Gegenwartsformen *be*: *I'm, he's, she's* → S. 145: Ic, S. 149: Ie
- Zeitwörter, 1. und 3. Person Einzahl, Present Simple: *I like, he/she likes* → S. 146: Ic
- Frageform *be*: *… are you?* → S. 145: Ic
- Fragewörter: *How …? What …?* → S. 158: IXb

Hi Hello Good morning Good afternoon Good evening Goodbye Bye bye

Unit 2

Names and numbers

2

1 The alphabet

A This is an alphabet rhyme. Listen and practise.

> a b c   One, two, three
> d e f   Hi, I'm Geoff
> g h i   Hello, goodbye
> j k l   How do you spell …?
> m n o   Yes and no
> p q r   Here we are
> s t u   How are you?
> v w x   Rhymes with sex
> y, z or z   She and he

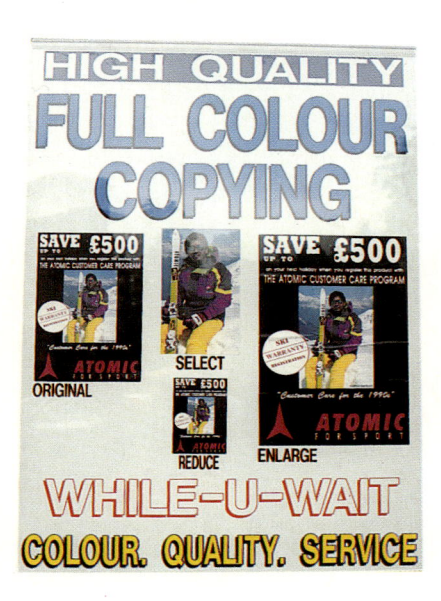

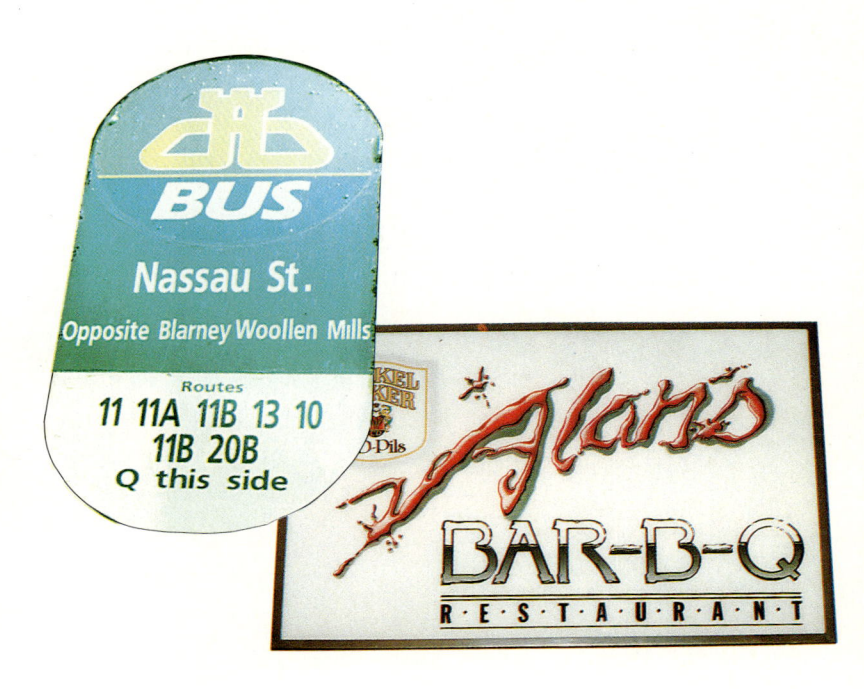

B Student A: Look at File 3.
Student B: Look at File 5.

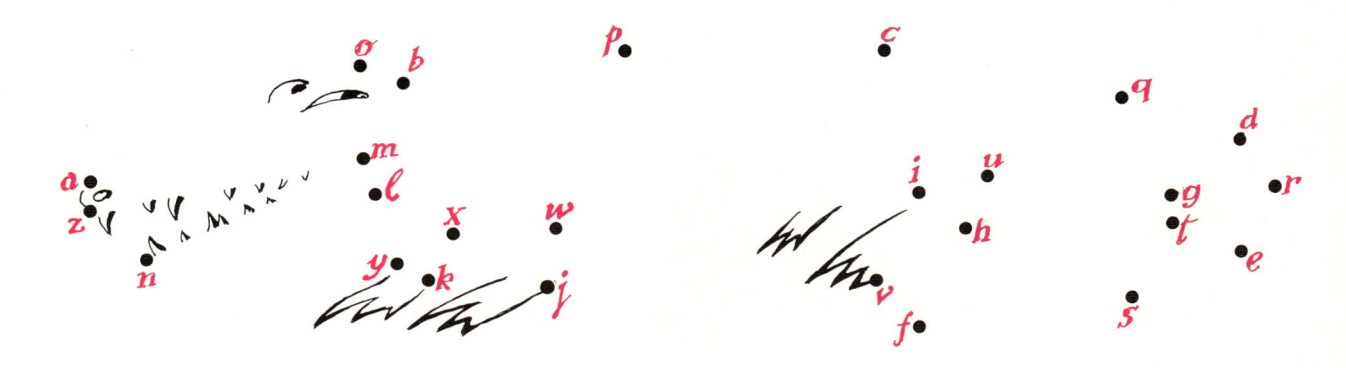

2

2 European neighbours

A Which country is it?

> France   Luxembourg   Belgium   Great Britain
> Ireland   The Netherlands   Denmark   Poland
> The Czech Republic   ~~Austria~~   Switzerland   Germany

- (A) Austria
- (B) _____
- (CH) _____
- (CZ) _____
- (D) _____
- (DK) _____
- (F) _____
- (GB) _____
- (IRE) _____
- (L) _____
- (NL) _____
- (PL) _____

"(A) is Austria."   "We think (B) is Belgium."

"(CZ) is … h'm. How do you say that?"

B Match these languages and the countries in A.

	is spoken in
Dutch	The Netherlands .
Flemish	_____ .
_____	_____ .
_____	_____ .
_____	_____ .
_____	_____ .
_____	_____ .
_____	_____ .
_____	_____ .

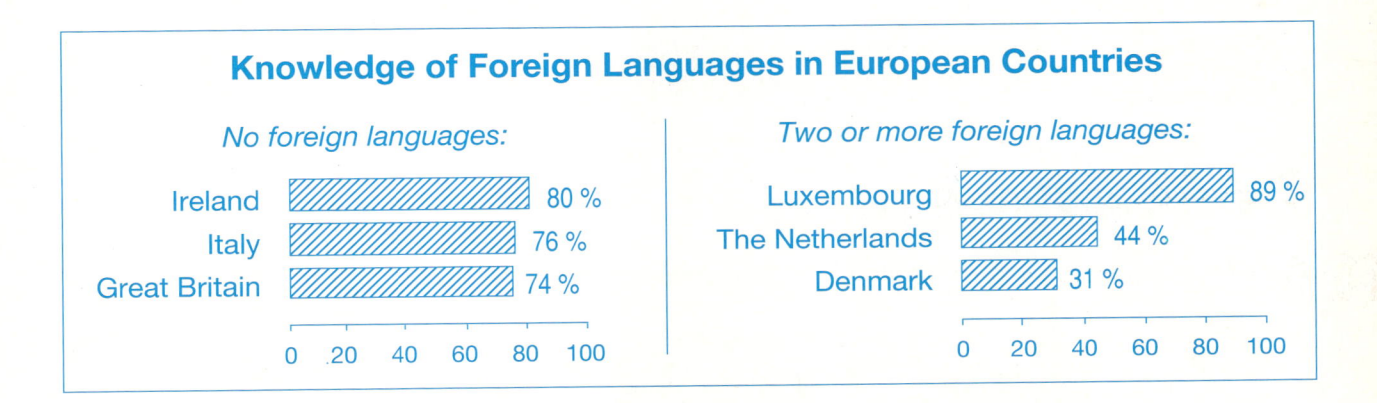

Czech   Danish
~~Dutch~~   English
    ~~Flemish~~
French   German
Italian   Polish

Knowledge of Foreign Languages in European Countries

No foreign languages:
- Ireland — 80 %
- Italy — 76 %
- Great Britain — 74 %

Two or more foreign languages:
- Luxembourg — 89 %
- The Netherlands — 44 %
- Denmark — 31 %

3 Languages

A Which language is it? Listen and write.

Czech   English
Danish   Dutch
English   French
German   English
Italian   Polish

1. _____   6. _____
2. _____   7. _____
3. _____   8. _____
4. _____   9. _____
5. _____   10. _____

B Report.

"We think number 10 is …"   "No idea!"

4 Who is it?

A Read the card.

> + I like beer.
> I like Italy and Italian food.
> I speak German and English.
> ───────────────────────────
> − I don't like swimming.
> I don't understand Italian.

B Write four or five sentences about yourself on a card. Put the card in the hat. (No name!)

C Take a card. Who is it?

"It's …"   "I think it's …"   "No idea!"   "Sorry, I don't know."

5 What's your phone number?

A

What's your phone number?
723131.

00 = double oh
22 = double two
33 = double three
etc.
4033651 = four – oh – double three – six – five – one

B Make a phone call.

522581.
Hello? 522581.
Hello, Maria. This is Helga.

6 The seven days of the week

12	Montag Lundi	Monday
13	Dienstag Mardi	_____
14	Mittwoch Mercredi	_____
15	Donnerstag Jeudi	_____
16	Freitag Vendredi	_____
17	Samstag Samedi	_____
18	Sonntag Dimanche	_____

A Ask and fill in.

"What's the English for Dienstag?"   *"How do you spell that?"*

B Listen and write down the days.

1. _____   5. _____
2. _____   6. _____
3. _____   7. _____
4. _____

> IS TODAY SUNDAY?
> NO. IT'S THURSDAY.
> THAT'S FUNNY— IT FEELS LIKE SUNDAY TO ME

7 Spelling

Think of a word and ask your partner how to spell it. Take turns.

○ *"How do you spell 'evening'?"*   ○ *"How do you spell 'Wednesday'?"*

❒ *"E-V-N-I-N-G?"*   ❒ *"W-E-D-N-E-S-D-A-Y."*

○ *"That's wrong. It's E-V-E-N-I-N-G."*   ○ *"That's right."*

2

8 Booking a room

A Complete the dialogue.

- Thank you very much.
  See you on Friday. Goodbye.
- Yes, of course. What's your name, please?
- OK, and what's your telephone number, please?
- Good morning, I'd like a double room for Friday evening, please.
- How do you spell that, please?
- Pardon?
- Thank you. Bye.

□ Good morning, Park Hotel.
○ _____
_____
_____
□ _____
_____
○ Szkopiak, John Szkopiak.
□ _____
○ Szkopiak.
□ _____
_____
○ S-Z-K-O-P-I-A-K.
□ _____
_____
○ Dover 7654382.
□ _____
_____
○ _____

B Listen and check. Read the dialogue aloud with a partner.

C Act out the dialogue. Use your own names and choose different days.

PARK HOTEL

Name of guest: _____

Phone number: _____

Day/s: _____

9 PRONUNCIATION

Find rhymes and compare results.

a, j: *k, day*

b, c: _____

i, y: _____

o: _____

q, u: _____

s: _____

24 twenty-four

magazine 2

Spelling

How do you spell *'mousetrap'*?

C-A-T

The Mousetrap von Agatha Christie ist das am längsten aufgeführte Theaterstück der Welt. Es wurde am 25. November 1952 im St. Martin's Theatre im Londoner West End uraufgeführt. Seither hat die clevere Kriminalgeschichte Menschen aus aller Welt begeistert. Das Londoner West End – ebenso wie der New Yorker Broadway – ist auf der ganzen Welt für seine Theater bekannt. In London bekommt man von Musicals bis zu modernen Theaterstücken alles geboten.

Who says what?

Read the texts and write the correct names in the *speech bubble*.

I like dog *food* and steak.
I don't like cats.

I like jogging with the dog and reading.
I like Italian food. I like Italian wine.
I like travelling.
I don't like Monday morning!

I like bananas and spaghetti.
I like swimming.
I like dogs.
I don't like babysitters.

Julie, Mum with dog Skip and Martin

I like basketball and football.
I like Germany. I don't understand German.
I like rock music and I like singing.
I like Friday night and the weekend.

mousetrap – Mausefalle
Who says what? – Wer sagt was?
speech bubble – Sprechblase
dog – Hund
food – hier: Futter

The dog Skip likes steak. Mum likes Italian wine. Martin likes singing and Julie likes swimming.

2 language checklist

Sie können jetzt:

Wendungen

sich bedanken
Thank you (very much).

sich entschuldigen
Sorry, (I don't know).

sprachliche Hilfe erbitten
How do you say that?
How do you spell that?
How do you spell ('evening')?

um eine Wiederholung bitten
Pardon?

eine Meinung mitteilen
We think (it's Belgium).

Unwissen ausdrücken
No idea!
I don't know.

widersprechen
That's wrong. (It's …)

zustimmen
That's right.
OK.

sagen, was Ihnen nicht gefällt
I don't like swimming.

eine Bitte äußern
(What's your name), please?

auf eine Bitte reagieren
Yes, of course.

etwas bestellen
I'd like (a double room).

nach dem Namen fragen
What's your name?

Grammatik

- Persönliche Fürwörter: *it, we* → S. 151, IVa
- Gegenwartsform *be: it's* → S. 145, Ic
- Zeitwörter, 1. Person Mehrzahl, Present Simple: *we think* → S. 146, Ic
- Zeitwörter, verneinte Form, Present Simple: *I don't like* → S. 146, Ic
- Grundzahlen: *0 – 10* → S. 153, VIa

UNIT 3

Breakfast time

Powers Hotel & Kildare Bar
HOT & COLD MEALS SERVED DAILY
BREAKFAST 7.30 – 10.00
LUNCH 12.30 – 2.30
AFTERNOON TEA 3.00 – 4.30

... around the clock

What do cows eat for breakfast
answer.. mooseli

Elizabeth Morris,
age 8, Wiltshire

twenty-five 25

3

1 What's the time?

A Practise with your teacher.

"What's the time?"

"It's seven o'clock."

"It's about nine o'clock."

11.00	11 a.m.	eleven o'clock (in the morning)
16.00	4 p.m.	four o'clock (in the afternoon)
20.00	8 p.m.	eight o'clock (in the evening)

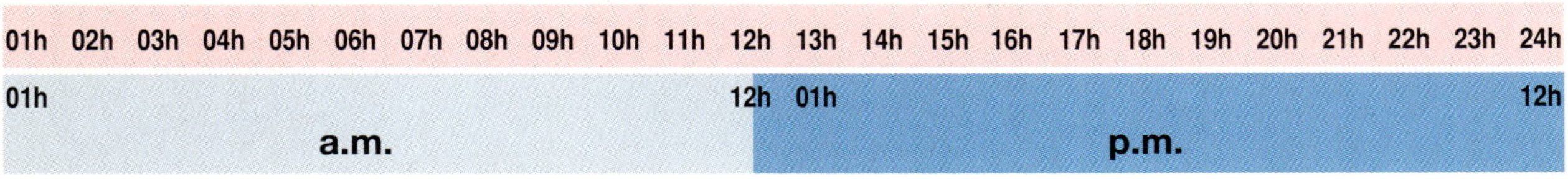

01h 02h 03h 04h 05h 06h 07h 08h 09h 10h 11h 12h 13h 14h 15h 16h 17h 18h 19h 20h 21h 22h 23h 24h

01h   12h   01h   12h

a.m.   p.m.

B Now practise these times.

11.15   quarter past eleven   11.20   twenty past eleven
11.30   half past eleven   11.35   twenty-five to twelve
11.45   quarter to twelve   11.50   ten to twelve

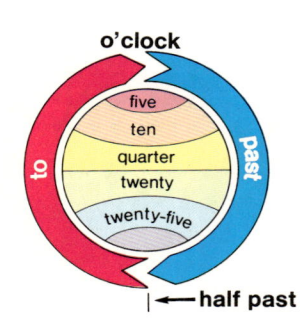

C Make four cards. Ask your partner.

2 Breakfast, lunch and dinner

A Fill in the correct times.

8.00 p.m.
12.30 - 1.30 p.m.
7.30 - 8.30 a.m.

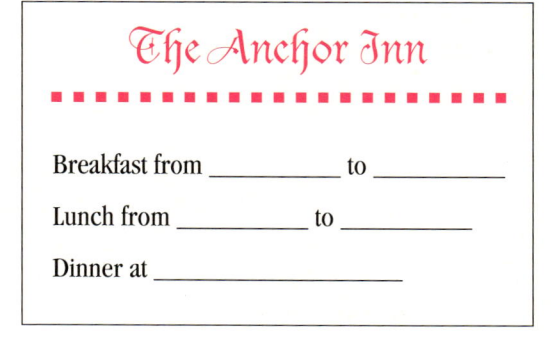

The Anchor Inn

Breakfast from _____ to _____

Lunch from _____ to _____

Dinner at _____

twenty-six

B

"We have breakfast at about 7.30. And you?"

"I normally have breakfast at 8 o'clock."

I / We	normally	have	breakfast / lunch / dinner	at	about	...

3 It's at eight o'clock

Listen and number the clocks.

☐ 18:18 ☐ 12:50 ☐ 20:00 ☐ 15:35 ☐ 07:13 ☐ 19:30

4 Breakfast

A Read this menu.

Full English Breakfast

Fruit juice or cornflakes
Fried eggs or boiled eggs
Bacon, sausages and tomatoes
Toast and marmalade
Tea or coffee

Continental Breakfast

Fruit juice or cornflakes
Rolls, butter, jam and marmalade
Tea or coffee

twenty-seven 27

3

B Now write a breakfast menu in your language. Translate it for your English-speaking guests.

✦✦✦✦✦ *Breakfast Menu* ✦✦✦✦✦

                            English

_____   _____
_____   _____
_____   _____
_____   _____
_____   _____
_____   _____
_____   _____

MEMO PAD

Joghurt = yoghurt

C Listen and match.

1. ___
2. ___
3. ___
4. ___
5. ___

a)
b)
c)
d)
e)

D Report.

Number One: He has _____

Number Two: She has _____

Number Three: They have _____

_____

Number Four: She has _____

Number Five: They have _____

5 I don't have coffee for breakfast

A Look at the menus in 4. What about your breakfast?

"I don't have … for breakfast."   "We have …"

"I have … for breakfast."   "We don't have …"

B Now ask your neighbour and report.

"What about your breakfast?"

"He has … for breakfast."   "He doesn't have … for breakfast."

"She has … for breakfast."   "She doesn't have … for breakfast."

6 What about breakfast in other countries?

"In France they have bread and jam and coffee."

"In France they don't have bacon and eggs."

In _____

_____

_____

MEMO PAD

Käse = cheese

_____

_____

twenty-nine 29

3

7 Food

A Write the words in the picture.

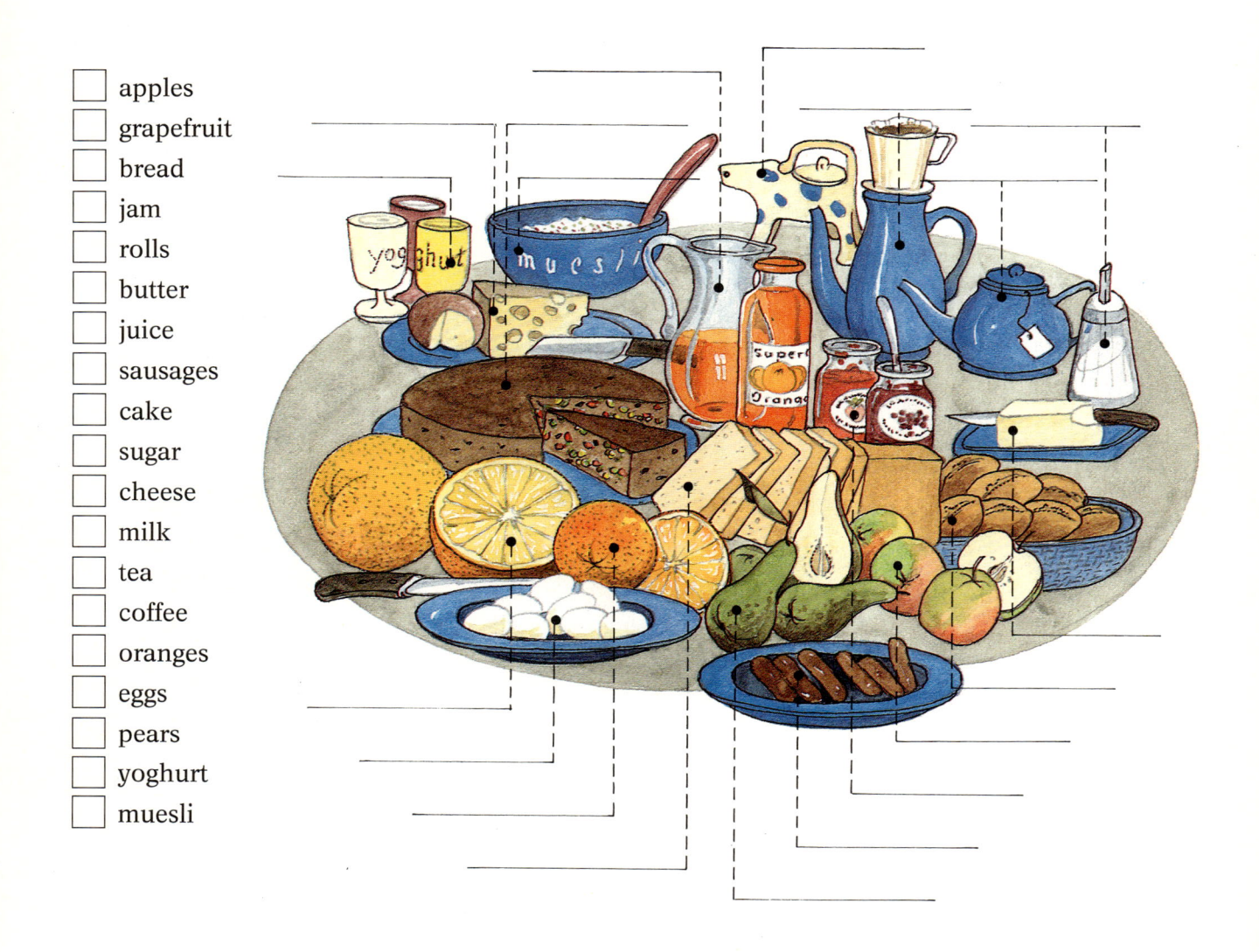

- [ ] apples
- [ ] grapefruit
- [ ] bread
- [ ] jam
- [ ] rolls
- [ ] butter
- [ ] juice
- [ ] sausages
- [ ] cake
- [ ] sugar
- [ ] cheese
- [ ] milk
- [ ] tea
- [ ] coffee
- [ ] oranges
- [ ] eggs
- [ ] pears
- [ ] yoghurt
- [ ] muesli

B How many words are the same or similar in your language? Underline them.

C You are in a supermarket.
Tick the words you hear on the list above.

30 | thirty

8 I always drink coffee in the morning

A Fill in.

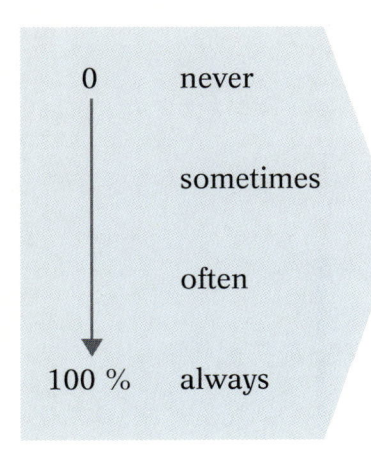

0 → never
sometimes
often
100 % always

1. I _____ eat fresh fruit in the morning.
2. I _____ have muesli for breakfast.
3. I _____ drink tea in the morning.
4. I _____ have coffee in the evening.
5. I _____ eat cake for breakfast.
6. I _____ drink milk.
7. I _____ eat eggs.
8. I _____ have cake in the afternoon.

B Find something you have in common.

We never drink tea in the morning.

We often have rolls for breakfast.

9 Poem

A Read and listen to the poem.

It's Pronoun Love

I like rock and folk songs
You think Mozart's great.
May the first's my birthday
You never know the date.

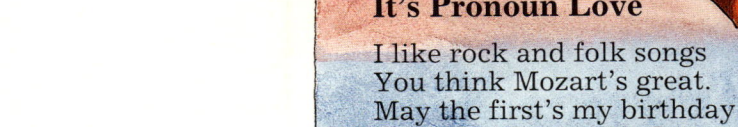

She likes wine and coffee
He drinks tea and beer.
Can she and he be they one day?
Can you and I be we?

B Complete.   ____ + ____ = they

you + I = ____

thirty-one 31

3

C Can you make a poem? Complete the sentences.

I like _____ and _____.

You like _____ and _____.

I have _____ for dinner.

You have _____ for lunch.

She doesn't like _____ or _____.

He doesn't like _____ or _____.

She never _____.

He always _____.

10 PRONUNCIATION

A Look at the lists and listen.

One syllable	Two syllables	Three syllables	Four syllables
lunch	dinner	sausages	continental
twelve	evening	tomatoes	
likes	often	marmalade	
tea	seven		
rolls	hotel		
juice	always		
	coffee		

B Which is the stressed syllable? Fill in.

Two syllables		Three syllables	
0o	o0	0oo	o0o
dinner			

C Listen and check.

magazine 3

Who is it?

She is from London.
She likes dogs and *horses*.
She usually has breakfast in Buckingham Palace.
I think she normally has tea in the morning.

What *begins* with 'T' and *ends* with 'T' and is full of tea?

A teapot.

The Teapot Cafe

Drinks
Pot of tea
English breakfast, Earl Grey, fruit tea   £1.50
Coffee   £1.20
Espresso   £1.20
Cappuccino   £1.50
Mineral Water ❖ sparkling or still   £1.50
Fruit juice ❖ orange, grapefruit or apple   £1.60
Iced Tea   £1.80

Sweets
Croissant with butter and jam   £2.10
Chocolate croissant   £1.50
Chocolate cake   £2.00
Fruit cake   £1.75

Sandwiches
Egg mayonnaise   £3.50
Cheese   £3.00
Tomato and mozzarella   £3.75

Salads
Italian salad   £5.50
French fruit salad   £3.50

Obwohl Kaffee in Großbritannien immer beliebter wird, ist Tee doch traditionell das beliebteste Getränk. Viele Briten trinken ihren Tee mit Milch und Zucker. Tee ist bei den Briten mehr als ein wärmendes Getränk. Eine Tasse Tee, die man bei Problemen oder in Krisen mit Freunden trinkt, trägt oft zur Erleichterung bei und läßt die Situation nicht mehr ganz so schlimm aussehen. Zum *afternoon tea* am Nachmittag gibt es oft *sandwiches* und Selbstgebackenes. *Tea* ist aber auch die Bezeichnung für das Abendessen um halb sechs oder sechs Uhr abends.

horses – Pferde
begins – beginnt
ends – endet
pot – Kännchen
sweets – Süßes

Queen Elizabeth II

3 language checklist

Sie können jetzt:

Wendungen

eine Frage weitergeben
What about (your breakfast)?

nach der Uhrzeit fragen
What's the time?

über Frühstücksgewohnheiten sprechen
(I have coffee) for breakfast.

Grammatik

- Persönliche Fürwörter: *they* → S. 151: VIa
- Gegenwartsformen *have*: *I/we/they have; he/she has* → S. 146: Ic
- Zeitwörter, verneinte Form, Present Simple: *he/she doesn't eat; we/they don't eat* → S. 146: Ic
- Regelmäßige Mehrzahlformen: *egg – eggs; tomato – tomatoes; country – countries* → S. 150: IIa
- Grundzahlen: *11, 12, 20, 25* → S. 153: VIa
- Uhrzeiten → S. 154: VIc
- Umstandsbestimmungen der Häufigkeit: *always, normally, usually, often, sometimes, never* → S. 155: VIIIa
- Umstandsbestimmungen der Zeit: *in the morning/afternoon/evening* → S. 156: VIIIb
- Stellung der Umstandsbestimmungen im Satz → S. 155: VIIIa, S. 156: VIIIb

PREVIEW A

1 Say it

Look at File 6.

2 Hidden dialogues

Find the hidden dialogues and act them out.

A

```
H—E  W—A—R  ?—F
|   |   |   |   |
L   O—H—E U   I
|   |       |   |
L   A—T Y—O N
|           |
O—P  A H T  E
|
O Y N K S H
|
U E R A W O
```

▢ Hello Pat, how are you?

○ F_____ ,_____

B

```
I—S C E U O Y A T S R E
|  |
T—H I I T O E T N D S G D
|
A—S N E M E L L N A E N
|
N E S N N A O E H M R U
|
N H P E A K S E N S H E
|
E S E C N A R F G D N A
|
S—H—E'S F R O M L I S H
```

▢ This is Anne. She _____.

○ _____

thirty-three 33

PREVIEW A

3 How many sentences?

A Write these words on cards.

I	this	like(s)	has	at	in
I'm	is/'s	they	doesn't	7 o'clock	evening
don't	from	for	breakfast	morning	sometimes
she	the	speak(s)	we		
he	are	have			

B Write ten more cards.

FOOD   DRINK   HOBBIES   LANGUAGES   COUNTRIES

C Now make sentences with all the cards.
How many different sentences can you make and write down in ten minutes?

she   sometimes   has   cornflakes   for   breakfast

4 Learning words

Do exercise 5 in Preview A of the Practice Book. Discuss.

34 thirty-four

PREVIEW A

5 English and German

A A lot of English words are like German words.
How many can you find in the first three units?
Can you group them?

Food and Drink:
apple/Apfel, beer/Bier,

Countries and Languages:
America/Amerika, English/Englisch,

Numbers, Times and Days:
ten/zehn, morning/Morgen, Monday/Montag,

Others:

B These words are in Units 4 to 6.
What are they in German? Can you guess?

English	German	English	German
house	Haus	postcard	
old		ninety-nine	
new		weather	
ferry		modern	
park		church	
green		Can you help me?	
May		summer	

thirty-five

UNIT 4

Where do you live?

1 Numbers

A Fill in the missing numbers.

0 oh; zero	1 one	2 two	3 three	4 four	5 five	6 six	7 seven	8 eight	9 nine
10 ten	11 eleven	12 twelve	13 thirteen	14 fourteen	15 fifteen	16 sixteen	17 seventeen	18 eighteen	19 nineteen
20 twenty	21 twenty-one	22 twenty-two							
30 thirty	31 thirty-one	32 thirty-two	33 thirty-three						
40 forty	41 forty-one	42 forty-two	43 forty-three	44 forty-four					
50 fifty	51 fifty-one	52 fifty-two	53 fifty-three	54 fifty-four	55 fifty-five				
60 sixty	61 sixty-one	62 sixty-two	63 sixty-three	64 sixty-four	65 sixty-five	66 sixty-six			
70 seventy	71 seventy-one	72 seventy-two	73 seventy-three	74 seventy-four	75 seventy-five	76 seventy-six	77 seventy-seven		
80 eighty	81 eighty-one	82 eighty-two	83 eighty-three	84 eighty-four	85 eighty-five	86 eighty-six	87 eighty-seven	88 eighty-eight	
90 ninety	91 ninety-one	92 ninety-two	93 ninety-three	94 ninety-four	95 ninety-five	96 ninety-six	97 ninety-seven	98 ninety-eight	99 ninety-nine
100 one hundred									

B Which number is it? Listen and underline the number you hear.

14 – 44   87 – 78   17 – 70   19 – 90   30 – 13
55 – 15   27 – 72   80 – 18   16 – 60   63 – 36

C Bingo!

				1– 20
				21– 40
				41– 60
				61– 80
				81–100

				1– 20
				21– 40
				41– 60
				61– 80
				81–100

				1– 20
				21– 40
				41– 60
				61– 80
				81–100

4

2 What's your address?

Ask questions and make notes.
Compare results with other groups.

"What's your first name?"

"What's your surname?"

"What's your address?"

Surname: ……
First name: ……
Address: ………

Schmidt-Oppermann *Tim*

In our group

… the longest first name is: _____

… the shortest first name is: _____

… the longest surname is: _____

… the shortest surname is: _____

… the longest street name is: _____

… the shortest street name is: _____

… the biggest house number is: _____

… the smallest house number is: _____

(number of letters)

Annekathrin *Hofweg* *Stauffenbergstraße*

"You know, most people's favourite number is 7, but mine is 6273990103648829910048253048103855722295710049274010154829477388859 17389."

thirty-eight

3 Names and addresses

A Listen and complete the addresses and phone numbers.

Name	Susan and James Wilson
Address	
	Brighton
Post code	
Phone	0273 360289

Name	MT Travel
Address	14 King Street
	Cambridge
Post code	CB2 2RU
Phone	

B Fill in.

❏ *Can you help me, please?*
❍ Yes, of course.
　　　•••

❏ _____
❍ It's 69 Granby Street.
❏ _____
　　_____
❍ G-R-A-N-B-Y.
❏ _____
❍ BN2 2BE.
　　　•••

❏ _____
　　_____
❍ Of course, 0223 467451.
❏ _____
❍ You're welcome.

Thanks very much.
What's their new address?
Can you help me, please?
Granby. How do you spell that, please?
Sorry, can you repeat that, please?
What's the post code, please?

C Now listen again and check.

main station = Hauptbh.
central

4

4 Can you help me, please?

Student A: Look at File 4.
Student B: Look at File 7.

5 I live in a small flat

A Match the words and the pictures.

why Apartments

church   flats   house   park
pub   shops   station   street

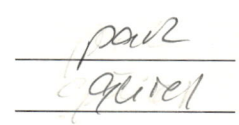

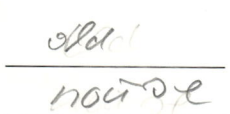

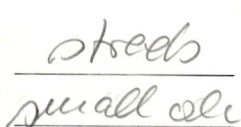

church
old

street
noisy

park
quiet

old
house

modern
flats

station
small

pubs
quiet

shops
small old

old – modern
big – small   quiet – noisy

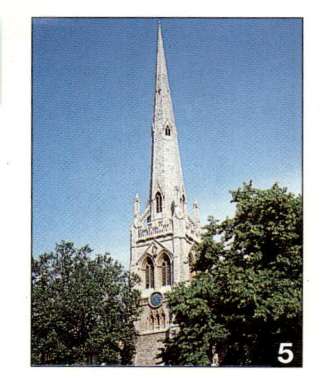

Add these words and compare results.

40 forty

B   Read.

Where do they live?

Elizabeth Webster:
I live in a noisy street, but my flat's quiet. It's a modern flat, big and with a garden, too. I like it.

Brigitte Renner:
We live in Fürstenwalde, a small town near Berlin. We live in a big, modern house near the railway station. It's quiet, we're near the woods and we like it.

Derrick Jenkins:
I live in a small flat in an old house near the Russian Church in Stuttgart. The street's noisy, but the flat's nice. I like it.

C   Three people say where they live. Listen and underline.

1. The first person lives in a <u>flat</u> / house.
   It is big / small and old / modern.
   The street is noisy / quiet.

2. The second person lives in a flat / house.
   It is big / small and old / modern.
   The street is noisy / quiet.

3. The third person lives in a flat / house.
   It is big / small and old / modern.
   The street is noisy / quiet.

D   Look at File 8.

6 Do you live near here?

A Answer the questions.

Do you live in a house or a flat?
                 In a _____.

Is it old or modern?   It's _____.

Is it big or small?   It's _____.

Do you live in a quiet street or a noisy street?
                 In a _____.

	Yes	No
Do you live near		
… a church?	☐	☐
… a park?	☐	☐
… a station?	☐	☐
… here?	☐	☐

B Find someone with similar answers.

"Do you …?"   *"Is it …?"*   *"And you?"*

7 The biggest

A Complete.

1. _____ biggest
2. _____ longest
3. new _____
4. _____ nicest
5. _____ noisiest
6. old _____
7. _____ quietest
8. _____ shortest
9. small _____

Smallest house in Britain

Oldest post office in Britain

B Make four pairs of opposites from the words in A.

big – small
_____
_____
_____   Which word is left? _____

42   forty-two

8 Records

Read and complete the sentences.

longest
oldest
youngest
biggest
smallest
shortest

1. The _____ European surname is 'O'.
   There are 28 'O's in Belgian phonebooks.
2. The _____ letters in the English alphabet are
   'j' and 'v' (from about 1630). Shakespeare has no 'j's or 'v's.
3. The _____ letter in the alphabet is O.
   It is about 3,300 years old.
4. The _____ bookshop in the world is Foyle's in
   London. It has about 50 kilometres of books.
5. The _____ church in the world is the
   Union Church, Wiscasset, Maine, USA.
   It is 2.13 x 1.37 metres.
6. The _____ street in the world is Yonge Street,
   which runs 1,185 kilometres from Toronto, Canada, to the
   US border.

9 Questions

A Write these words on cards.
Make six questions and write them down.

Do   you

Do	have	big	breakfast	morning
speak	understand	Italian	8 o'clock	house
near	a(n)	small	eat	old
you	flat	Dutch	cake	muesli
live	quiet	coffee	the	Switzerland
like	German	at	evening	supermarkets
in	street	for	Danish	here

B Choose one question. Ask other people in the class and report.

forty-three

4

10 That's a nice place

A Read the poem.

> Ten or twelve
> Houses
> And
> Two
> Streets
> A
> Name
> I
> Can't
> Even remember
>
> Pub
> Lunch
> An old
> Church
> Evening

B Now write a poem like this.
You can use the name of a person, place, or language.

11 PRONUNCIATION

A Where do the words go? Fill in.

take   pad   name   thanks   garden
park   apple   match   later

flat _____

half _____

day _____

B Listen and check.

12 Listen and mark the stressed word(s).

What's your address?   Can you repeat that, please?
What's their new address?   Do you live near here?
What's the post code?   Do you like Italian food?
Is it big or small?   Do you speak English?
Can you help me?   Do you understand French?

magazine 4

Home sweet home

Match the texts and the photos.

☐ 1. I live in an old house near the *sea*. It is very quiet. We live near a small town with four shops and a pub. The wind is noisy sometimes.

☐ 2. My home is long but small. It is very quiet. Sometimes it is near the shops and a pub. It is old, but I like it.

☐ 3. I live in an old house in London. The street is a short quiet street, but it is near a big noisy street with buses and taxis. My house, Number 10, has a private flat and *offices*. I live near St. James's Park and Big Ben. There's always a *policeman outside* my house. It is *not* my house, but I like it.

☐ 4. In the summer I live in a big garden. It is near a small tourist town with two or three pubs, a good restaurant, a café and an old church. It is very *green*. My *caravan* is small, but I like it in the summer. I like the campers and I am near my family here.

home – Zuhause, Heim
sea – Meer
offices – Büros
policeman – Polizist
outside – (draußen) vor
not – nicht
green – grün
caravan – Wohnwagen

Seit 1732 ist der Wohnsitz des britischen Premierministers in der Downing Street Nr. 10. In dem Gebäude befinden sich Büros und ein privates Appartement. 1989 wurde die Straße aus Sicherheitsgründen durch schmiedeeiserne Gitter von der Hauptstraße abgetrennt.
In Großbritannien gibt es etwa 3.200 km befahrbare Wasserwege. Bis zum 18. Jahrhundert war das Reisen auf den Wasserwegen im Allgemeinen schneller, sicherer und bequemer als auf der Straße. Heute werden die Kanäle nicht nur zu Erholungszwecken befahren, sondern dienen auch als Transportwege für 4 Millionen Tonnen Güter pro Jahr.

1.C 2.A 3.D 4.B

4 language checklist

✓ Sie können jetzt:

Wendungen

sich bedanken
Thanks.
Thanks very much.

auf Dank reagieren
You're welcome.

um eine Wiederholung bitten
Can you repeat (that), please?

eine Bitte äußern
Can you (help me), please?

Grammatik

- Gegenwartsformen *be: you're, we're* → S. 145: Ic
- Frageform *be: Is it ...?* → S. 145: Ic
- Frageform regelmäßiger Zeitwörter: *Do you ...?* → S. 146: Ic
- Regelmäßige Mehrzahlbildung: *church – churches* → S. 150: IIa
- Bestimmter/Unbestimmter Artikel: *the, a/an* → S. 151: III
- Besitzanzeigende Fürwörter: *your, their* → S. 152: IVb
- Grundzahlen: *13 – 100* → S. 153: VIa
- Ordnungszahlen: *first, second, third* → S. 154: VIb
- Steigerung der Eigenschaftswörter (Superlativ): *smallest, nicest, biggest, easiest* → S. 155: VII

"It's a cheque for a hundred thousand dollars. Do you like it?"

thousand – tausend

UNIT 5

Travel

1 Trains and planes

A Match the words and the pictures.

> train   plane   ferry
> coach   car

B Listen. What do you hear?

1. a_____
2. a_____
3. a_____
4. a_____
5. a_____

5

2 Getting information

A Which ads are about travel …

by train?	by plane?	by ferry?	by car?	by coach?

1
NATIONAL EXPRESS
LONDON
Welcome Aboard!
HEATHROW, GATWICK, LUTON & STANSTED AIRPORTS

2
The British Rail

FASTEST INTERCITY WEEKDAY JOURNEY TIMES

From	To	London	Birmingham	Bristol	Edinburgh	Manchester
Birmingham		1 hr 25				
Bristol		1 hr 32	1 hr 18			
Edinburgh		3 hrs 59	4 hrs 30	6 hrs 10		
Manchester		2 hrs 25	1 hr 30	3 hrs 15	3 hrs 55	
York		1 hr 43	2 hrs 05	3 hrs 15	2 hrs 16	1 hr 30

INTERCITY

3
Hertz
BRITISH AIRWAYS

Wherever you fly with British Airways Hertz will be there to meet you

4
Gatwick Express

FARES
between Victoria Station and Gatwick

	Standard	First class
Single	£ 7.00	£10.50
Return	£14.00	£21.00

One of the great advantages of flying from London Gatwick is the ease of getting there on InterCity's non-stop Gatwick-Express service from London Victoria. It's reliable, convenient, comfortable and very quick. The journey takes just 30 minutes.

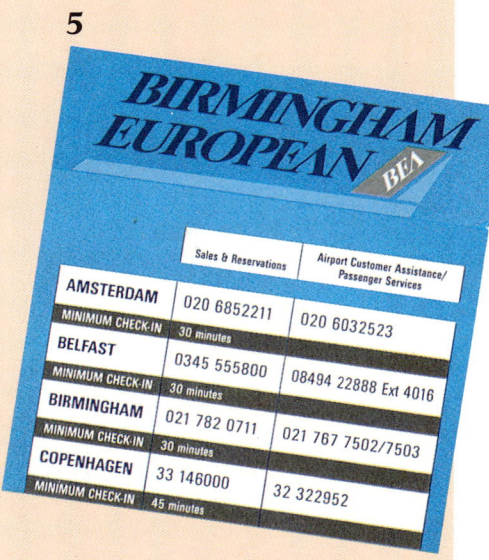

5
BIRMINGHAM EUROPEAN BEA

	Sales & Reservations	Airport Customer Assistance/ Passenger Services
AMSTERDAM	020 6852211	020 6032523
MINIMUM CHECK-IN	30 minutes	
BELFAST	0345 555800	08494 22888 Ext 4016
MINIMUM CHECK-IN	30 minutes	
BIRMINGHAM	021 782 0711	021 767 7502/7503
MINIMUM CHECK-IN	30 minutes	
COPENHAGEN	33 146000	32 322952
MINIMUM CHECK-IN	45 minutes	

6
ITALY – GREECE – ITALY
Every day from Brindisi in 9 hours.

7

From	To	Days 1234567	Depart	Arrive	Flight number	Aircraft /Class	Stops
FROM ▶	**BELFAST** **GLASGOW**	CONTINUED					
		12345--	0830	0910	BA5843	ATP/M	0
		12345--	1400	1440	BA5845	ATP/M	0
		-----67	1800	1840	BA5849	ATP/M	0
		12345--	1820	1900	BA5849	ATP/M	0

forty-six

B Answer the questions.

1. When does flight number BA 5843 arrive in Glasgow? __At 9.10.__
2. How much does the Gatwick Express cost (Standard Return)? £_____.
3. How long does the train from Gatwick to Victoria take? _____.
4. How often does the car ferry go to Greece? _____.
5. Where does the car ferry leave from? _____.

3 A flight from Birmingham to Vienna

A Listen and complete the timetable.

BIRMINGHAM TO AMSTERDAM			AMSTERDAM TO VIENNA		
Flight no.	Departure	Arrival	Flight no.	Departure	Arrival
VB 400	8.30	_____	VB 401	_____	_____
Price from Birmingham to Vienna: £ _____					

The flight leaves Birmingham at eight thirty in the morning.

B Listen again and complete the sentences.

1. How long _____?
2. When _____?
3. How much _____?

forty-seven 47

5

4 A trip from Finland to Germany

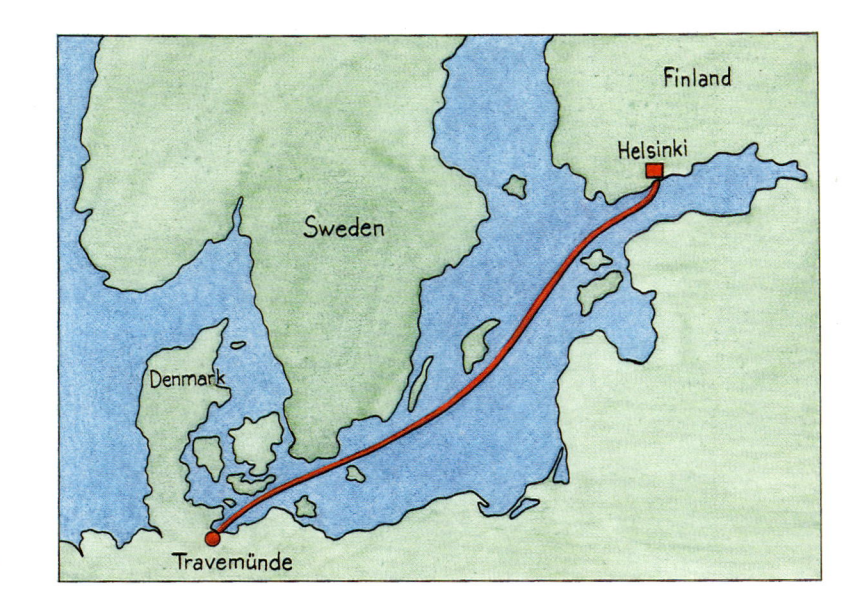

A You are in a travel agent's in Helsinki and want to go by ferry to Germany. What questions do you ask?

Questions: Answers:

B Listen. How many of your questions can you answer now?

5 A railway station

48   forty-eight

A Make a poem from these lines.

WAY IN
But where to?
What for?
A railway station?
Where am I?
Travel?
Not today
WAY OUT
No, thank you.
So the way out.
But where to?

A Railway Station

B The original poem is in File 9. Compare.

順 路
THIS WAY

6 Bikes and trams

A How do you get here? Match the words and the pictures.

underground   bike
tram   bus

1
by _____

2
by _____

3
by _____

4
by _____

MEMO PAD

Motorrad = motorbike

forty-nine 49

5

B Interview two people. Ask these questions.

	Person 1	Person 2
How do you get here?		
How long does it take?		
How much does it cost?		
How do you get to work?		
How long does it take?		
How much does it cost?		

"By tram."   "I walk."   "It takes 20 minutes."

"It costs 5 Marks 30."   "I work at home."

C Report the results and make a class survey.

	gets to class	gets to work
by car		
by public transport	Martin (bus)	
by bike		
walks		Maria

Martin gets here by bus.

Maria walks to work.

7 I'd like to go to London

A Fill in.

> Oh, 23.50.   When does the night train leave?
> Good afternoon.   I'd like to go to London.
> Thank you.   23.15?

- ❐ British Rail, Glasgow Central. Good afternoon.
- ○ *Good afternoon.* _____
- _____
- _____

- ❐ 23.50 from Glasgow Central.
- ○ _____

- ❐ No, madam. 23.50.
- ○ _____

- ❐ You're welcome.

B Listen and check.

8 When would you like to go?

A Write the dialogue in the correct order.

> ❐ On Monday morning. When does the first flight leave?
> △ When, sir?   △ British Airways. Good morning.
> △ When would you like to go?   ❐ Sorry?
> ❐ Good morning. I'd like to go to Dublin.

△ _____
❐ _____
△ _____
❐ _____
△ _____
❐ _____

B Listen and check.

5

9 A trip from Norway to Germany

ROLE PLAY

A Student A: Look at File 11.
   Student B: Look at File 14.

B Student A: Look at File 17.
   Student B: Look at File 12.

10 Word map

Draw your own word map of this unit.

(ticket) — **travel** — (How long … ?)
              |
           (station) — (arrive)

PRONUNCIATION

11 Listen to the 'r' sound and practise.

railway	return	Greece	price	travel
reading	ferry	Friday	train	public transport
report	arrive	three	tram	return trip
results	breakfast			

12 Listen. Do you hear 'I like' or 'I'd like'?

	1.	2.	3.	4.	5.	6.
I like	✓					
I'd like						

52 fifty-two

magazine 5

Your Travel Agent ABC

- **A**rrivals
- **B**y bus or bike,
- **C**ar or coach
- **D**epartures
- **E**very day to cities and countries
- **F**lights
- **G**ood food and good prices
- **H**ow much does it cost? Not much.
- **I**'d like to go to …
- **J**azz festivals
- **L**ong *walks*
- **M**any traditional hotels
- **N**ice breakfasts
- **O**ld *pubs*
- **P**lanes or trains
- **Q**uiet cafés
- **R**eturn ticket or *one-way ticket*
- **S**kiing, swimming and sports
- **T**owns and cities
- **U**nderstanding the country and the people
- **V**ery good restaurants
- **W**hen would you like to leave?
- **X**-*cellent* service 7 days a week.
- **Y**our trip:
- **Z**ero work for you!

**Call your travel agent now!
We can help you with your trip.**

Open from 9 a.m. to 9 p.m. Monday to Friday
Saturday and Sunday from 9 a.m. to 6 p.m.

walks – Spaziergänge
pubs – Kneipen
one-way ticket – Einfachfahrkarte
X-cellent = excellent – ausgezeichnet
open – geöffnet

Which bus goes to the USA?

Colum-bus.

5 language checklist

Sie können jetzt:

Wendungen

um eine Wiederholung bitten
Sorry?

Wünsche äußern
I'd like to (go to London).

nach Wünschen fragen
(When) would you like to (leave)?

etwas bestellen
I'd like (a return ticket), please.

über Verkehrsmittel sprechen
(I'd like to go) by train/plane/car/ ...

über Häusliches sprechen
(I work) at home.

Grammatik

- Frageform regelmäßiger Zeitwörter: *Does it ...?* → S. 146: Ic
- Fragewörter: *When ...? Where ... from? How much ...? How long ...? How often ...?* → S. 158: IXb
- Uhrzeiten bei Fahrplänen → S. 154: VIc

"Hi! I'm on the train!"

UNIT 6

Outdoors

1 Colours

A Match the colours and the balloons.

blue
yellow
red
orange
dark green
light green
brown
white
black
pink
purple

B Listen to the songs and fill in the colours.

1. We all live in a _____ submarine.

2. Again I'll touch the _____, _____ grass of home.

3. _____ rain.

4. I'm dreaming of a _____ Christmas.

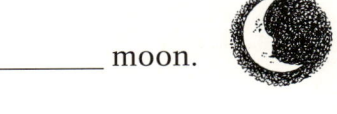

5. _____ moon.

6. Lady in _____.

She's the black sheep of the family.

fifty-three 53

6

C Choose a colour. What do you think of when you see this colour? Make a list.

"I think of ..."

D Find someone with the same colour. Compare your lists.

2 Weather

A What do the colours mean?

"I think light blue means very cold."

very cold   cold   cool   warm   hot   very hot
−40° C ⟵   ⟶ +40° C

B Match the words and the symbols.

1. _____
2. _____
3. _____
4. _____
5. _____

foggy
windy
sunny
cloudy
rainy

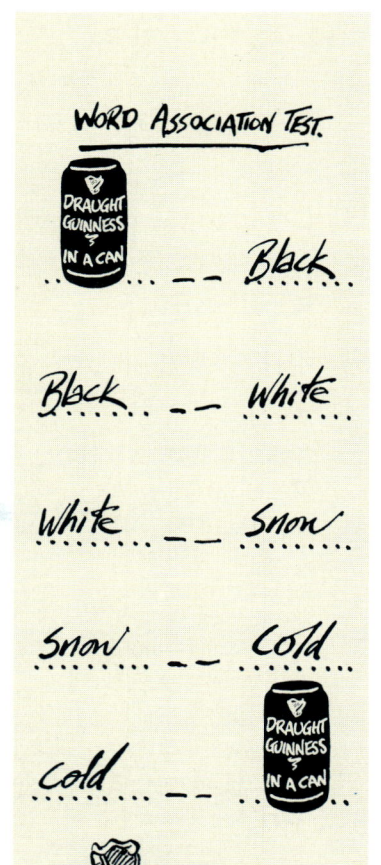

WORD ASSOCIATION TEST.

.... -- Black

Black ... -- White

White ... -- Snow

Snow ... -- Cold

Cold ... -- ....

PURE GENIUS.

54   fifty-four

C Look at the weather map.

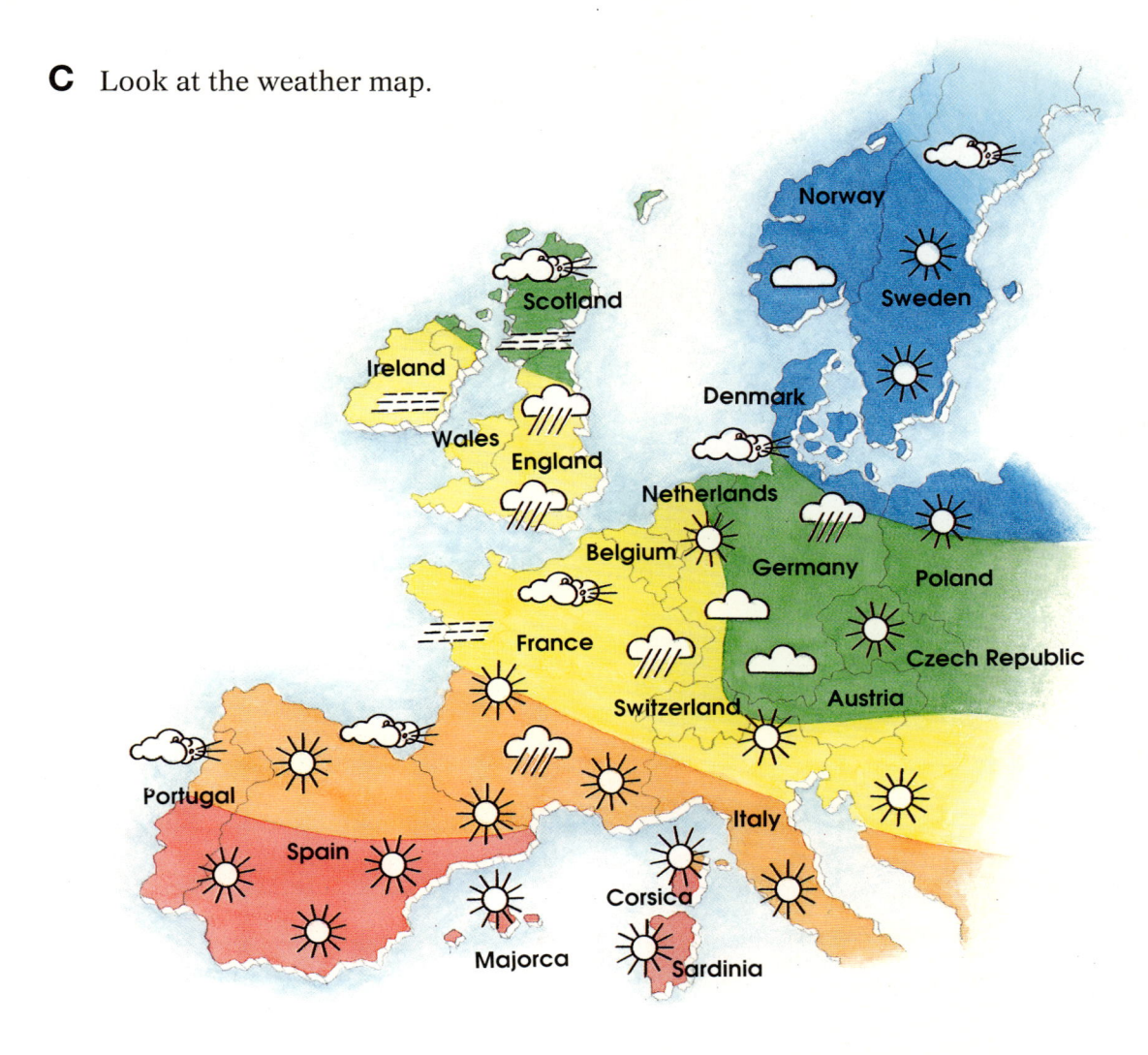

What's the weather like in southern Sweden? It's sunny and cold.
in eastern Spain? _____
in Ireland? _____
in northern France? _____
in western Germany? _____
in The Netherlands? _____

3 Where am I?

One of you chooses a country on the map.
The others can ask three questions to find out which country it is.
You can only answer with 'yes' or 'no'.

"Is it sunny?"   "Is it in the green area?"   "Are you in …?"

6

4 What would you like to do?

A It is May. You are on holiday on the French Riviera. What would you like to do?

"I'd like to …"

Mediterranean holiday

- ☐ read the newspaper
- ☐ go jogging
- ☐ play cards
- ☐ write some postcards
- ☐ go swimming
- ☐ lie on the beach
- ☐ go for a walk
- ☐ go to a museum
- ☐ go for a meal
- ☐ play tennis
- ☐ go shopping
- ☐ go to a café
- ☐ hire a bike

B Now listen to the weather report. Make notes.

C What are your plans now?   *"I'd still like to …"*   *"Now I'd like to …"*

5 Wish you were here

A Positive (+) or negative (–)?

- ☐ … so we can't go swimming.
- ☐ Our hotel room's quiet with a great view of the sea.
- ☐ The restaurants are very expensive.
- ☐ The weather's terrible.
- ☐ There's a disco next door so we can't sleep.
- ☐ … so the children can play on the beach all day.
- ☐ It's warm and sunny, …
- ☐ It's rainy and cold, …
- ☐ The restaurants are cheap but good.
- ☐ The weather's beautiful.

B Complete the two postcards.

(+)

Dear Susan,
Well, here we are in Monaco.
_____
_____
_____
_____
_____
_____
_____

Wish you were here.
Love, *Ann + Stephen*

(−)

Dear Pat and John,
Well, here we are in Monaco.
_____
_____
_____
_____
_____
_____
_____

Back home next week, thank goodness!
Tom + Rebecca

6

6 The countryside

A Write these words in the correct boxes.

sky
forest
fields
tree
mountains
clouds
flowers
garden
river

B Look at the two pictures. Which group can find the most differences between the two pictures?

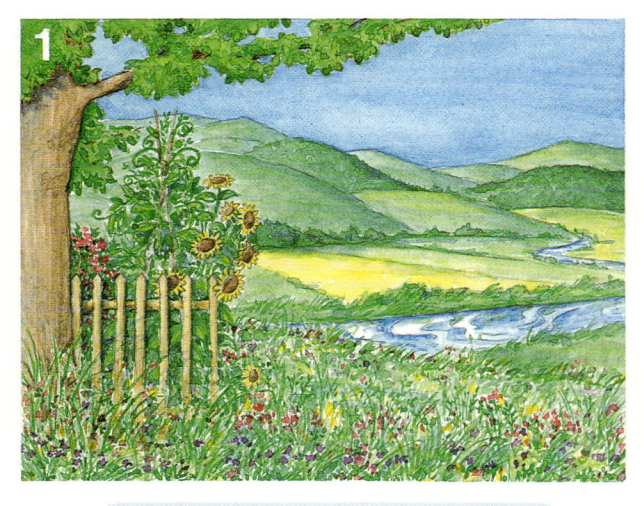

"The sky's blue in picture 1."   "There are no flowers in picture 2."

"There's …"   "The mountains are …"   "There are …"   "There's no …"

58   fifty-eight

7 The months of the year

A Ask.

"What's the English for Februar?"

"How do you spell that?"

January   J
F   A
M   S
A   O
M   N
J   D

B Choose a month. Now listen to the song. How often can you hear your month? _____

C Read and complete.

Thirty days have September, April, June and November.
All the rest have thirty-one, except _____.

How many months have 30 days? _____

No fruits, no flowers, no leaves, no birds,
No_____.

Thomas Hood

8 Seasons

Which season is it? Listen.

- spring
  - summer
    - autumn *Hall*
      - winter

1. _____
2. _____
3. _____
4. _____

fifty-nine 59

9 I love winter

A Fill in the seasons and the months.

autumn leaves fall

"There are only two seasons in Scotland: June and winter."
Billy Connolly

B Make a class poster of the seasons.
Write a sentence or draw a picture for each season.

I	love ♥ like ♡ don't like ♤ hate ♠	winter spring summer autumn	because	you can go swimming. it's cold. you can't go skiing. it's often foggy. it's often sunny. I like gardening. ...

Spring

I hate spring because I don't like flowers.

Summer

I love summer because it's often sunny.

10 PRONUNCIATION

A Listen and mark the stressed words.

- I'd like to go skiing in February.
- I don't like skiing.

- We can't sleep – there's a disco next door.
- You can go to the disco and sleep later.

- Why do you go for a walk every day?
- I don't go for a walk every day.

- I'd like to play tennis with Karen.
- She can't play tennis.
- Yes, she can.

- I'd like to go swimming.
- But the weather's terrible.
- I'd still like to go swimming.

B Practise with a partner.

11 How many words with each sound can you find in this unit?

gr<u>ee</u>n	dr<u>ea</u>ming
r<u>ai</u>n	l<u>a</u>dy
bl<u>ue</u>	c<u>oo</u>l
yell<u>ow</u>	c<u>o</u>ld
m<u>ou</u>ntain	fl<u>ow</u>er
c<u>o</u>lour	s<u>u</u>nny

6 magazine

A postcard from Melanie

Where is Melanie on holiday: in Scotland, in Denmark or in Gibraltar?

> November 20
> Dear Pat,
> The weather is beautiful here in autumn. It's sunny and warm every day. I love the beach because we can still go swimming. You can go for a meal to an African restaurant or an English pub! The 'Rock' is great!
> See you next week.
> Love, Melanie

rock – Felsen
peanuts – Erdnüsse
nightmares – Alpträume

Gibraltar ist seit 1704 eine Englische Kolonie. Es ist eine kleine Halbinsel an der Südspitze Spaniens und nur 17 km von Afrika entfernt. Die Menschen sprechen dort Englisch und Spanisch. Das Klima ist das ganze Jahr über mild. Gibraltar ist für seine Vielfalt an Pflanzen und Tieren bekannt und wegen seiner einzigartigen Geschichte berühmt.

End of a holiday

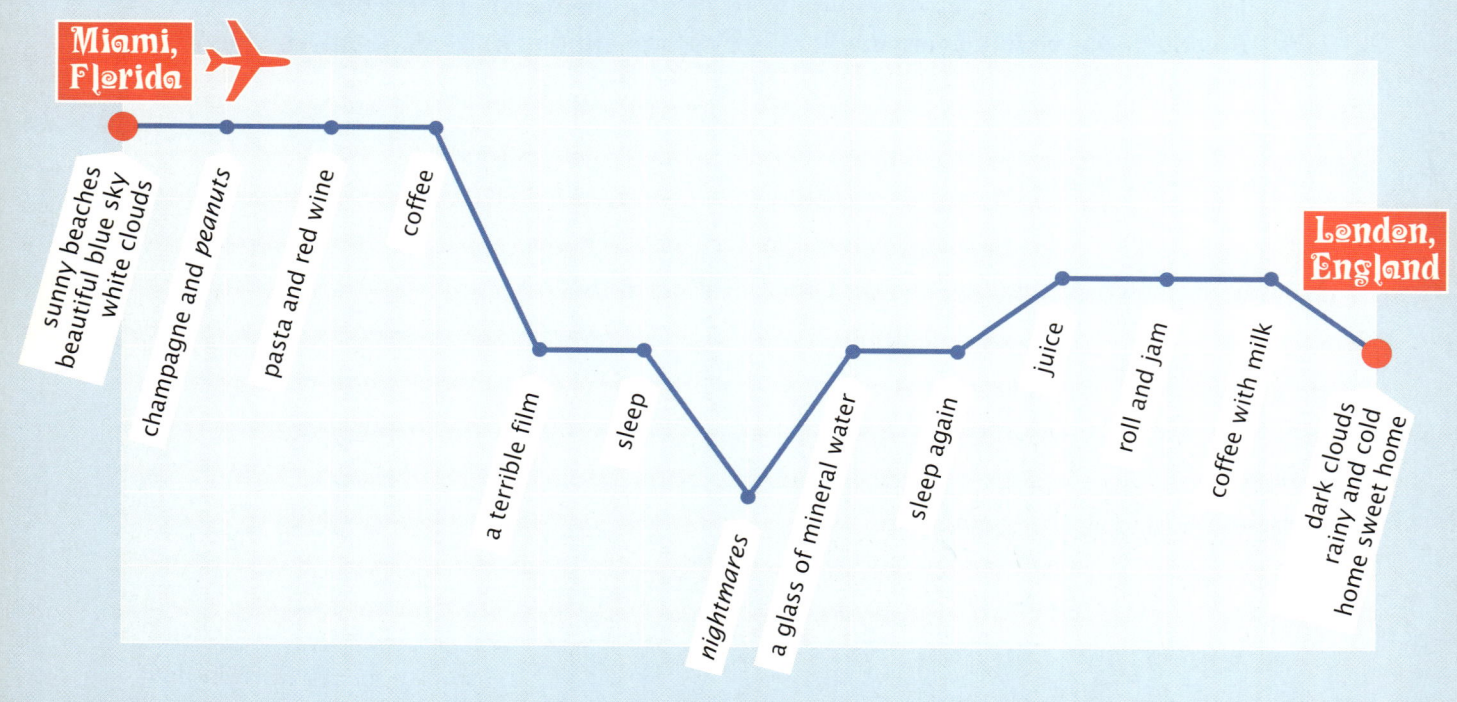

Miami, Florida → sunny beaches, beautiful blue sky, white clouds → champagne and peanuts → pasta and red wine → coffee → a terrible film → sleep → nightmares → a glass of mineral water → sleep again → juice → roll and jam → coffee with milk → dark clouds, rainy and cold, home sweet home → **London, England**

Melanie is (on holiday) in Gibraltar.

language checklist 6

Sie können jetzt:

Wendungen

etwas begründen
… because (it's often foggy).
… so (the children can play on the beach).

sagen, was Ihnen gefällt
I love (winter).

sagen, was Ihnen nicht gefällt
I hate (summer).

sagen, woran Sie denken
I think of (snow).

ausdrücken, was Sie vermuten
I think (blue) means (cold).

einen Wunsch äußern
Wish you were here.

Erleichterung ausdrücken
Thank goodness!

Grammatik

- Gegenwartsformen *be*, Mehrzahl: *they are, there are* → S. 145: Ic
- Gegenwartsform *be*, Einzahl: *there's* → S. 145: Ic
- Gegenwartsform *be*, Mehrzahl, verneinte Form: *there are no* → S. 145: Ic
- Gegenwartsform *be*, Einzahl, verneinte Form: *there's no* → S. 145: Ic
- Modalverb *can*: *I can* → S. 149: Id
- Modalverb *can*, verneinte Form: *I can't* → S. 149: Id
- Modalverb *can*, Frageform: *Can I …?* → S. 149: Id
- Satzmuster Aussagesätze: *because, so* → S. 157: IXa
- Satzmuster Fragen: *Can you …? (How) do you …? (Where) does it …? (When) does …?* → S. 157 – 158: IXb
- Fragewörter: *What's … like? How many …?* → S. 158: IXb

"I can't come to work today. I'm in bed with a nasty bug."

nasty bug – böse/r Wanze/Bazillus

PREVIEW B

1 Planning a class trip

Tariff

Standard Rooms	2 Jan – 15 May	16 May – 25 Sep	26 Sep – 20 Dec
Double B & B	£25	£31	£28
Single B & B	£28	£34	£31

All prices are per person per day and include VAT. @ 17,5 %

Terms include:
- Colour TV / Teamakers
- Full English Breakfast

A You would like to go to London with your class. What would you like to know about your hotel?

_____'s the name of the hotel?   _____ it a quiet street?

_____'s the hotel?   _____'s the telephone number?

_____'s the address?   _____ does a single room cost?

_____ I have dinner in the hotel?   _____?

B How much information about a hotel can you get from your partner in five minutes?

Student A: Look at File 10.
Student B: Look at File 15.

2 Negative sentences

A Complete the sentences.

I can't speak Italian.

I can't _____.

I _____.

He/She doesn't go to work by bus.

He doesn't _____.

She _____.

There isn't a good hotel near here.

There isn't _____.

There _____.

They don't get to evening class by car.

They don't _____.

They _____.

PREVIEW B

B Make a negative sentence ending with one of the following words and phrases.

~~August~~   by bus
near here   poems
tennis   winter

It isn't foggy here in August.
_____

C Can the others guess the beginning of your sentence?

3 Grammar game

A Think of some words for these four topics.

Food   *milk, eat, cold,* _____
Outdoors _____
Places   _____
Travel   _____

B Compare lists with your neighbour.

C Now play the game. It is in File 24.

4 Word pictures

Take one of the words from Units 1 to 6 and try to make a word picture.

5 Preview ⇨ ⇨ ⇨ ⇨ ⇨ ⇨ ⇨ ⇨ ⇨ ⇨ ⇨ ⇨ ⇨ ⇨ ⇨

Can you guess which unit the following words are in?

father   bank   engineer   birthday
chemist's   children   colleague   expensive
regular working hours   married   buy

UNIT 7   **Family**   _____
UNIT 8   **In Town** _____
UNIT 9   **At Work** _____

UNIT 7

Family

1 Her name is Faith Desai

Faith Desai needs a visa for a visit to the United States. This is her form:

VISA APPLICATION FORM

① Surname or family name:	Desai	⑩ Sex:	Male / <u>Female</u>
② First name and middle name:	Faith	⑪ Marital status:	<u>Married</u> Single Divorced Widowed Separated
③ Date of birth: (Day, Month, Year)	26/8/64	⑫ Name(s) of child(ren):	June, Philip
④ Place of birth: (City, Country)	New Delhi	⑬ Purpose of visit:	Holiday
⑤ Nationality:	Indian	⑭ Address in the U.S.A.:	c/o Brenda Reeves, 3412 Hollywood Drive, Los Angeles, CA 90052
⑥ Passport number:	J 579212		
⑦ Home address:	74, Highland Gardens, Glasgow, Scotland, G10 4BU		
		⑮ Date of application:	25th June 1993
⑧ Home telephone number:	041 493782	⑯ Signature:	F. Desai
⑨ Business telephone number:	041 284693		

Read the form and complete the sentences.

① ② Her name is _____.
④ She was born in _____.
⑤ She is _____.
⑥ Her _____.
⑦ She lives in _____.
⑧ Her _____.
⑪ She is _____.
⑫ She has got _____.
    Her daughter's name is _____.
    Her son's _____.
⑭ Her friend lives in _____.

2 On the way from London to L. A.

A Listen to the dialogue and fill in.

	Faith	Allan
From?	Glasgow	
How many children?	2	
How many sons?	1	
How many daughters?	1	
Their names	June, Philip	
Their ages		

B Compare.

"How many children has Faith got?"

"She's got two children."

3 Which picture is it?

A Read the text. Which picture is it? _____

"This is Aimee and Claude Dubois. Aimee was born in Dublin. She's Irish and Claude's French. They've got two daughters, twelve and ten years old, and a small son called Jean. They live in a small town in northern France. They've got a small house with a big garden. They like long bike trips and in summer they often go to the mountains for their holidays."

B Choose one of the other pictures and write a similar text.

_____
_____
_____
_____
_____

C Read your text to the class. Can they guess which picture it is?

4 This is my father

A Here are pictures of Linda's family and Bruce's family.

Fill in. daughter son husband wife mother father   Her His

1. This is Linda's _____. _____ name is Lena.

2. This is Linda's _____. _____ name is Immo.

3. This is Linda's _____. _____ name is Hillery.

parents in law = Schwiegereltern
relationship

4. This is Bruce's _____. _____ name is Alec.

5. This is Bruce's _____. _____ name is Peggy.

6. This is Bruce's _____. _____ name is Martin.

B Listen and check.

5 Family trees

A This is Bruce's family tree.

Martin — Caroline
Ian
Bruce ∞ Peggy
Alec ∞ Edna

Answer the questions.

1. Who is Alec and Edna's grandson? _____
2. Who is Martin's sister? _____
3. Who is Bruce's brother? _____
4. Who are Caroline's parents? _____
5. Who are Martin's grandparents? _____
6. Who are Alec's grandchildren? _____
7. Who is Alec's wife? _____
8. Who is Peggy's brother-in-law? _____

sixty-seven 67

B Draw your own family tree. Show photos of your family and introduce the people to your group.

This is ...

6 Sons and daughters

Read and listen to the poem.

Children

We are the
Sons and daughters of
Our parents.

Our parents are the
Sons and daughters of
Our grandparents.

Our grandparents are the
Sons and daughters of
Their parents.

We are all
Sons and daughters.

We are all children.

7 Holidays and special days

A Complete the sentences with the English names for special days of the year.

Boxing Day
New Year's Eve
Christmas Day
New Year's Day
Christmas Eve

Christmas Eve is December the twenty-fourth.
Christmas Day is December the twenty-fifth.
December the twenty-sixth is _Boxing Day_.
December the thirty-first is _New Years Eve_.
January the first is _New Years Day_.

1st = first	10th = tenth	20th = twentieth
2nd = second	11th = eleventh	21st = twenty-first
3rd = third	12th = twelfth	22nd = twenty-second
4th = fourth	13th = thirteenth	23rd = twenty-third
5th = fifth	14th = fourteenth	
6th = sixth	15th = fifteenth	30th = thirtieth
7th = seventh	16th = sixteenth	31st = thirty-first
8th = eighth	17th = seventeenth	
9th = ninth	18th = eighteenth	
	19th = nineteenth	

B What other holidays or special days are there in your country?
What holidays or special days do you know in other countries?

sixty-eight

8 **HAPPY BIRTHDAY**

A Today is this man's tenth birthday!

Can you guess why?

His birthday is _____

B Mark your birthday and the birthdays of your family and friends on this calendar.

	January	February	March	April
Mon	4 11 18 25	1 8 15 22	1 8 15 22 29	5 12 19 26
Tue	5 12 19 26	2 9 16 23	2 9 16 23 30	6 13 20 27
Wed	6 13 20 27	3 10 17 24	3 10 17 24 31	7 14 21 28
Thu	7 14 21 28	4 11 18 25	4 11 18 25	1 8 15 22 29
Fri	1 8 15 22 29	5 12 19 26	5 12 19 26	2 9 16 23 30
Sat	2 9 16 23 30	6 13 20 27	6 13 20 27	3 10 17 24
Sun	3 10 17 24 31	7 14 21 28	7 14 21 28	4 11 18 25

	May	June	July	August
Mon	3 10 17 24 31	7 14 21 28	5 12 19 26	2 9 16 23 30
Tue	4 11 18 25	1 8 15 22 29	6 13 20 27	3 10 17 24 31
Wed	5 12 19 26	2 9 16 23 30	7 14 21 28	4 11 18 25
Thu	6 13 20 27	3 10 17 24	1 8 15 22 29	5 12 19 26
Fri	7 14 21 28	4 11 18 25	2 9 16 23 30	6 13 20 27
Sat	1 8 15 22 29	5 12 19 26	3 10 17 24 31	7 14 21 28
Sun	2 9 16 23 30	6 13 20 27	4 11 18 25	1 8 15 22 29

	September	October	November	December
Mon	6 13 20 27	4 11 18 25	1 8 15 22 29	6 13 20 27
Tue	7 14 21 28	5 12 19 26	2 9 16 23 30	7 14 21 28
Wed	1 8 15 22 29	6 13 20 27	3 10 17 24	1 8 15 22 29
Thu	2 9 16 23 30	7 14 21 28	4 11 18 25	2 9 16 23 30
Fri	3 10 17 24	1 8 15 22 29	5 12 19 26	3 10 17 24 31
Sat	4 11 18 25	2 9 16 23 30	6 13 20 27	4 11 18 25
Sun	5 12 19 26	3 10 17 24 31	7 14 21 28	5 12 19 26

C Now report to the class.
Are there any birthdays on the same day?

"My sister's birthday's May the 25th."

"That's my aunt's birthday, too."

"My father's birthday's January the 2nd."

"That's my uncle's birthday, too."

sixty-nine

7

9 Have you got any brothers and sisters?

A Interview two people and fill in the answers.

1. Have you got any children? How many?
2. Have you got any brothers and sisters? How many?
3. Have you got any grandchildren? How many?
4. Have you got any relatives in another country? Where?
5. Have you got any friends in another country? Where?
6. Have you got any friends from another country? Where from?

Name: _____	Name: _____
1. _____	_____
2. _____	_____
3. _____	_____
4. _____	_____
5. _____	_____
6. _____	_____

B Report.   *"Martin's got three children."*   *"Claudia's got relatives in America."*

PRONUNCIATION

10 Listen. In each group one word has a different vowel sound. Which one is it?

1. s<u>o</u>n – h<u>u</u>sband – m<u>o</u>ther – d<u>au</u>ghter – br<u>o</u>ther
2. s<u>ur</u>name – f<u>ir</u>st – b<u>ir</u>th – div<u>or</u>ced
3. W<u>e</u>dnesday – <u>e</u>vening – T<u>e</u>xas – h<u>e</u>llo – t<u>e</u>n
4. b<u>ee</u>r – h<u>e</u>re – th<u>ir</u>ty – n<u>ea</u>r – w<u>e</u>'re
5. p<u>ea</u>rs – wh<u>e</u>re – th<u>ei</u>r – th<u>e</u>re – f<u>e</u>rry

11 Look through this unit and find examples of words with these stress patterns.

oO _____   Oo _____

Ooo _____

12 Practise. Say these lines with a steady rhythm.

surname, first name and middle name
first name, surname and middle name
middle name, first name and surname

sons, daughters and grandchildren
daughters, sons and grandchildren
grandchildren, daughters and sons

magazine 7

An American wedding

Jim and Bertha are married. They live in California. Jim and Bertha have got big families. Here is a picture of their *wedding* in August.

The church is modern, but the wedding is traditional. All the people are very elegant. The ladies have long dark red *dresses*. You can see the *bride* and *groom* in the middle. *On the left* you can see the bride's sisters and friends and *on the right* you see the groom's brother and friends. The bride has got three sons, they are fourteen, eleven and seven years old. They are in the middle of the picture. They like their new *step-father*.

After the wedding there is a party for the family and friends. Sometimes there is a dinner. There is always a wedding cake. The bride and groom *cut* the cake and *serve* the guests. After the party they go on a holiday, the *honeymoon*.

In den USA ist es Tradition, daß vor der Hochzeit eine Party *(shower)* für die Braut stattfindet. Die Freundinnen der Braut und die Frauen aus beiden Familien finden heraus, was die Braut benötigt und feiern eine Party, die unter einem Motto steht, z. B. a *kitchen shower*. Die Braut bekommt dann von allen Gästen entsprechende Geschenke *(presents)*. Meistens gibt es ein kleines Essen; danach werden Gesellschaftsspiele gemacht. Am Abend vor der Hochzeit findet eine Generalprobe *(rehearsal)* der ganzen Hochzeitszeremonie mit allen Beteiligten statt. Danach wird gemeinsam gegessen *(rehearsal dinner)*.

wedding – Hochzeit
dresses – Kleider
bride – Braut
groom – Bräutigam
on the left – links
on the right – rechts
step-father – Stiefvater
cut – schneiden
serve – bedienen
honeymoon – Hochzeitsreise

7 language checklist

Sie können jetzt:

Wendungen

Angaben zur Person machen
She was born (in Dublin).
She's (Irish).
They've got (two daughters).
They live (in a small house).

jemandem zum Geburtstag gratulieren
Happy birthday!

Grammatik

- Zeitwort *have got*: *he's/she's got, they've got* → S. 146: Ic, S. 149: Ie
- Zeitwort *have got*, Frageform, Einzahl: *have you got …? has he/she got …?* → S. 146: Ic
- Zeitwort *have got*, Frageform, Mehrzahl: *have they got …?* → S. 146: Ic
- Kurzform *'s*: *he's, she's* → S. 149: Ie
- Mehrzahl, regelmäßige Form: *brothers-in-law* → S. 150: IIa
- Mehrzahl, andere Formen: *children, wives* → S. 150: IIa

"Mirror, mirror on the wall, who's got the best face-lift of them all?"

mirror – Spiegel
wall – Wand
face – Gesicht

UNIT 8

In town

1 Shops and things

A Complete the sentences.

bank
café
chemist's
garage
museum
newsagent's
tourist information
   centre
post office
supermarket
restaurant
station
pub

1. You can buy a train ticket at the _____.
2. You can see interesting old things in a _____.
3. You can get petrol at a _____ or a petrol station.
4. You can cash cheques at a _____.
5. A _____ sells food and household goods.
6. A _____ sells newspapers.
7. You can buy aspirin at a _____.
8. In a _____ you can have a meal (lunch, dinner).
9. In a _____ you can have a drink, and sometimes food.
10. In a _____ you can have a cup of coffee or tea.
11. You can get stamps at a _____.
12. You can get information about a town at the _____.

B How many of the things above are near your school?

"There's a post office in Königstraße."   "The station's near here."

seventy-one 71

8

2 Opposite the station

A Complete the map.

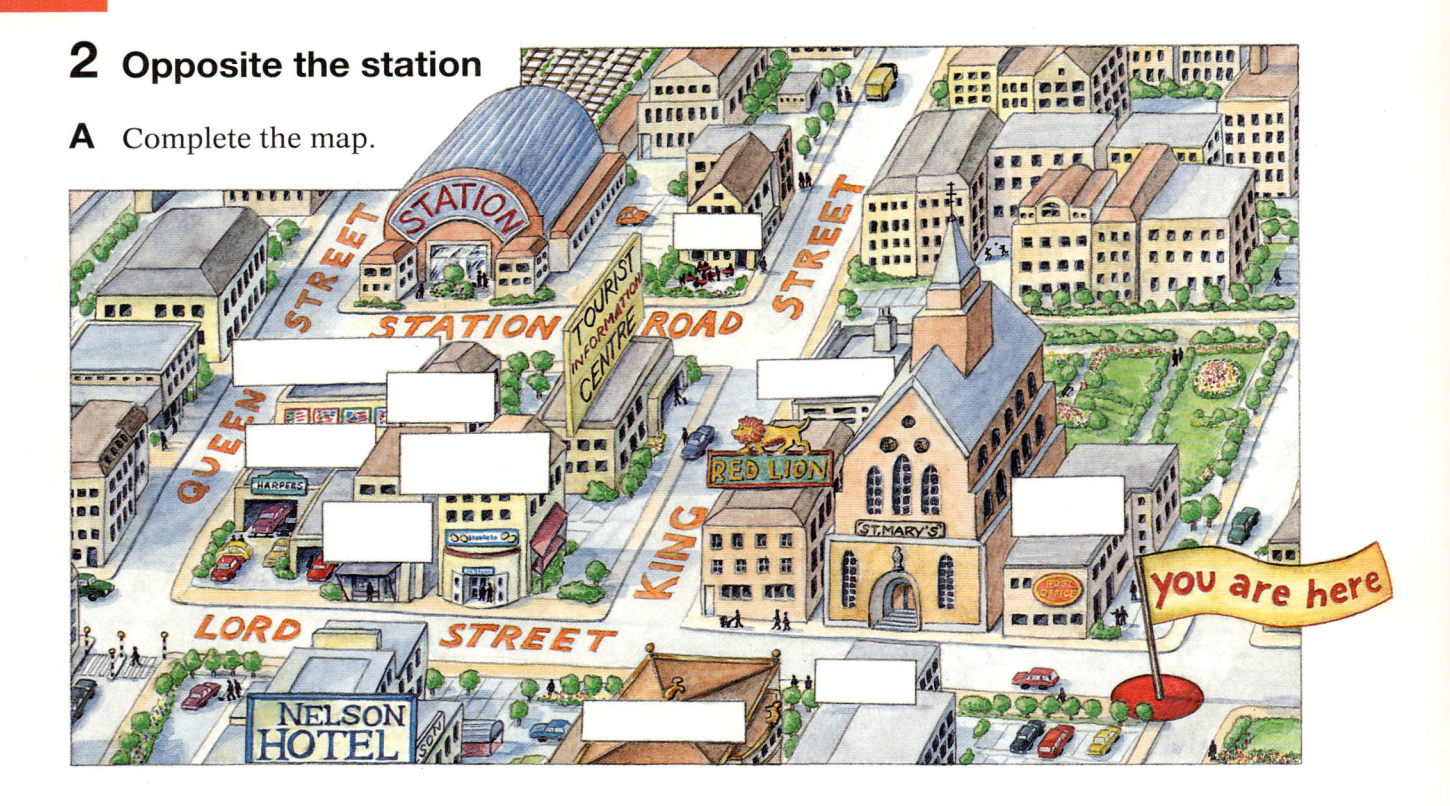

1. The EB Supermarket is in Station Road, opposite the station.
2. The post office is next to St. Mary's Church.
3. The Good Egg restaurant is in Lord Street, opposite the Nelson Hotel.
4. There's a newsagent's next to the EB supermarket.
5. There's a café opposite the Tourist Information Centre in Station Road.
6. There's a chemist's next to the Red Lion pub.
7. There's a bank opposite St. Mary's Church.

From ● You are here go down Lord Street and …

8. … the museum is on the left, opposite the Red Lion.
9. … there's a bookshop on the right, next to the Good Egg.
10. … Queen Street is on the right. There's a garage on the corner.

B What can you say about these places?

The Red Lion: *It's next to the chemist's. / It's next to St. Mary's Church. / It's opposite the museum. / It's in Lord Street. / It's on the corner. / Go down Lord Street and it's on the right.*

The Nelson Hotel:

The station: _____

St. Mary's Church: _____

The Tourist
Information Centre: _____

3 Where's the post office, please?

Student A: Look at File 20.
Student B: Look at File 22.

4 Asking for directions

A Write the dialogues in the correct order.

Dialogue 1

○ Thanks a lot.
❐ Yes, just go down this street. It's not far. It's on the left.
○ Excuse me.
❐ You're welcome.
○ Is there a garage near here?
❐ Yes?

8

Dialogue 2

- ○ Not at all. Goodbye.
- ❏ Bye.
- ○ Can I help you?
- ❏ Of course, I can see it now. Thank you very much.
- ○ Oh. That's in Minster Road, just over there on the right.
- ❏ That's very kind of you. Where's the town museum, please?

_____
_____
_____
_____
_____
_____

B Listen and check.

C Read the dialogues in A again. What do the people answer?

Excuse me. – _____

Can I help you? – _____
_____

Thanks a lot. – _____

Thank you very much. – _____

Goodbye. – _____

D Where's the nearest bank / church / supermarket / post office / … in your town / area? Ask your partner for directions. Take turns.

MEMO PAD   record shop
_____
_____

Where's the nearest bank, please?

It's in …

74   seventy-four

5 Open and closed

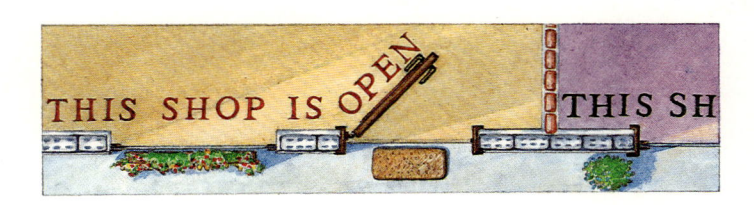

A When are shops, banks and pubs open and closed in your area?

Most shops are open from about _____ to about _____ o'clock.

Most banks are open from about _____ to about _____ o'clock.

Most pubs are open from about _____ to about _____ o'clock.

B Read the text about Britain and complete the sentences.

Banks:	Shops:	Pubs:
On weekdays (Monday to Friday) most banks open at 9.30 and close at 4 o'clock. Some banks are open on Saturday morning, but most of them are closed at the weekend.	In Britain most shops are open from 9 in the morning to 5.30 in the afternoon, Monday to Saturday. A lot of supermarkets are open till 8 in the evening on Thursday, and some food shops are open till 8 o'clock every day, including Sunday.	Most pubs are closed in the afternoon, but some are open all day. They usually close at about 11 in the evening. A lot of pubs serve meals at lunchtime but not in the evening.

In Britain …

some
a lot of
most

1. … _____ pubs are closed in the afternoon, but some are open all day.
2. … _____ banks are open on Saturday morning, but most of them are closed at the weekend.
3. … _____ supermarkets are open till 8 o'clock in the evening on Thursday.
4. … _____ shops are open from 9 in the morning to 5.30 in the afternoon.
5. … _____ pubs serve meals at lunchtime but not in the evening.
6. … _____ food shops are open till 8 o'clock every day.

8

C Collect time phrases from B and write them in the correct boxes.

at	at 9.30	on	
in		...	

D Make a poster with useful information for visitors to your town or area.

6 Which shop is it?

baker's
butcher's
clothes shop
department store
greengrocer's
shoe shop

1. _____
2. _____
3. _____
4. _____
5. _____
6. _____

76 seventy-six

7 We've got some good shops

A Listen to these people talking about the villages they live in.
Tick the things they say they have got.

	The woman	The man
	☐ good shops ☐	
	☐ a school ☐	
	☐ pubs ☐	
	☐ cafés ☐	
	☐ a supermarket ☐	
	☐ a station ☐	
	☐ a bus service ☐	

B Write sentences about where you live.

We've got some …	We haven't got any …
We've got a …	There aren't any …
We'd like …	We haven't got a …
	There isn't a …

C Report to the class.

"We haven't got any good restaurants."

"We'd like some more shops."

"We've got some good supermarkets."

We'd like some more shoe shops.

8 The best and the cheapest

A Which is the best pub in your town or village? Discuss.

| Which is the | best
smallest
cheapest
nearest
nicest
most expensive
most interesting | pub?
café?
garage?
hotel?
museum?
restaurant?
supermarket? |

B Tell the other groups what you think.

"The best pub's ..."

"We think the smallest pub's ..."

"We think the most expensive hotel's ..."

9 Find the 'b'

A How many words in this unit can you find which begin with 'b'?

B Choose five of these words and make sentences with them.

PRONUNCIATION

10 First listen and say the words. Then listen and say the sentences.

can, at, a	You can cash cheques at a bank.
there, a	There's a post office near here.
to, the	It's next to the bank.
are	Some pubs are closed in the afternoon.

11 Which word do you hear first, the German one or the English one? Tick the 'G' for German or the 'E' for English. Then practise.

	1	2	3	4	5	6	7	8	9	10	11	12	13
G													
E													

magazine 8

St. David's, an interesting place to visit

St. David's is the smallest city in Britain. It is *really* a village on the southwestern *coast* of Wales. It is a city because it has a cathedral, St. David's Cathedral. In Britain, towns with cathedrals are called cities.

▶ The village is full of tourists in the summer because they like the beautiful walks near the sea, the quiet village, and, of course, the cathedral. There is a small park in the middle of the village. *Around* the park there are shops, a newsagent's, a chemist's, a butcher's and a nice old hotel. There are also cafés, pubs, galleries and *craft shops nearby*. There are some expensive restaurants in town, but the cheapest place is the Fish and *Chip* Shop.

▶ St. David's is in the Pembrokeshire Coast National Park. There are 290 km of *paths* in the National Park with the most beautiful views.

▶ The best beach is Whitesand Bay. You can lie on the beach, surf or go swimming, but the sea is very cold. Every year in August there is a Sand Church *Contest*. People have a lot of *fun* making and looking at the different sand churches.

St. David ist der Schutzheilige von Wales. Der 1. März ist St. David's Day. In Wales trägt man an diesem Tag einen Lauch oder eine Osterglocke. Beides sind walisische Symbole. Der Lauch war ursprünglich eine der wichtigsten Nahrungsquellen, weil er auf dem kargen Boden wuchs. Die Osterglocke ist in Wales weit verbreitet und wächst dort wild. Es sieht wunderschön aus, wenn im Frühjahr die Osterglocken überall blühen.

really – eigentlich
coast – Küste
around – um … herum
craft shops – kunstgewerbliche Geschäfte
nearby – in der Nähe
chips – Pommes frites
paths – Wanderwege
contest – Wettbewerb
fun – Spaß

8 language checklist

Sie können jetzt:

Wendungen

jemanden ansprechen
Excuse me?

… und darauf reagieren
Yes?

sich bedanken
Thanks a lot.
That's very kind of you.

auf Dank reagieren
Not at all.

Hilfe anbieten
Can I help you?

ein Angebot annehmen
That's very kind of you

nach Orten fragen
Is there a (garage) near here?
Where's the (town museum), please?
Where's the nearest (bank), please?

… und Ortsauskünfte geben
It's opposite (the station).
It's next to (the church).
Go (down Lord Street).
It's on the left/right.
It's on the corner.
It's over there.

über Öffnungszeiten sprechen
(Some pubs are open) all day.
(Some food shops are open) every day.

Grammatik

- Aufforderungssätze: *go, just go* → S. 145: Ib
- Zeitwort *have got*: *we've got* → S. 146: Ic, S. 149: Ie
- Zeitwort *have got*, verneinte Form: *we haven't got* → S. 146: Ic
- Gegenwartsform *be*, Einzahl, verneinte Form: *there isn't* → S. 145: Ic
- Gegenwartsform *be*, Mehrzahl, verneinte Form: *there aren't* → S. 145: Ic
- Gegenwartsform *be*, Frageform: *Is there …?* → S. 145: Ic
- Mehrzahl, andere Formen: *men, women* → S. 150: IIa
- Persönliche Fürwörter als Satzergänzung, Einzahl: *me, you, it* → S. 151: IVa
- Persönliche Fürwörter als Satzergänzung, Mehrzahl: *you, them* → S. 151: IVa
- Unbestimmte Fürwörter: *some, any* → S. 152: IVe
- Mengenangaben: *most, a lot of, some* → S. 153: V
- Steigerung der Eigenschaftswörter (Superlativ): *best, most expensive, most interesting* → S. 155: VII
- Umstandsbestimmungen der Zeit: *at eight o'clock/lunchtime/the weekend; on Saturday morning/weekdays; in the afternoon/evening* → S. 156: VIIIb
- Umstandsbestimmungen des Ortes: *on the left/right; at the newsagent's; in a restaurant; opposite the café; next to the hotel* → S. 156: VIIIc

UNIT 9

At work

1 What is important in a job?

Choose three points that are important to you.

flexible	pay
good	working hours
regular	colleagues
friendly	office
interesting	work
long	holidays
nice	boss

1. _____
2. _____
3. _____

MEMO PAD

sichere Stelle = a safe job

SECRETARY

required for boss of busy office in central Bristol. Must be flexible. Good pay for the right person.

For more information contact Jill Baynes on 0272-339065 or write to

J&G Designs,
96 Portman Rd, Bristol

FLIGHT ATTENDANTS

Athens, Rio, LA, Singapore, Sydney …
these are just some of the fascinating places we fly to …
and you can, too!

Interesting work? *Yes!*
Friendly colleagues? *Yes!*
Fair pay? *Yes!*

If you are 20 – 35, fit, and like working with people, call us now on:
081-515151-3040

GERMAN TEACHER

required by exclusive international school near Ascot. Regular working hours and long holidays.
£11,500 pa.

Write with curriculum vitae to
   The Headmaster,
   Grange Park School,
   Old Windsor Road,
   Ascot, Berks.

seventy-nine 79

9

2 I like my job

Listen. Do you think the five people like their jobs?
Listen again and write down reasons.

| Carolyne Barton, secretary | Nick Smith, footballer | Anne Temple, flight attendant | Gill Stileman, teacher | Janet Wright, artist |

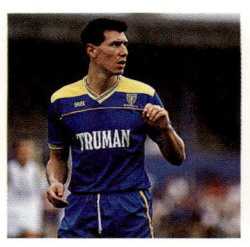

	Do they like their jobs?	Why? Why not?
secretary	Yes	regular working hours
footballer		
flight attendant		
teacher		
artist		

3 A job I'd like to do

A Write down a job you would like to do.

_____

B Tick the words and phrases that describe it.

- [ ] I work with other people.
- [ ] I work alone.
- [ ] I work in a building.
- [ ] I work outdoors.
- [ ] I work in an office.
- [ ] I work at home.
- [ ] …
- [ ] I make things.
- [ ] I help people.
- [ ] I sell things.
- [ ] I work regular hours.
- [ ] I work flexible hours.
- [ ] I only work weekdays.
- [ ] I do shiftwork.
- [ ] I'm my own boss.
- [ ] I'm not my own boss.
- [ ] I travel a lot.
- [ ] I don't travel very much.
- [ ] The pay is good.
- [ ] The pay isn't very good.

MEMO PAD

Arzt = doctor

80 eighty

C Read out your sentences from B.
Can the other people in the class guess what job it is?

"Are you a bus driver?"

"Are you an engineer?"

"No, I'm not."

"Yes, I am."

4 "Guess my job"

A Match the pictures and the jobs.

policewoman
shop assistant
secretary
bus driver
dentist Zahnarzt
housewife
flight attendant
teacher
travel agent
artist
writer
waiter
nurse Krankenschwester/pflege

B Try to guess what jobs other people in the class have. Collect questions.

1. *Do you work in an office?*
2. *Do you work regular hours?*
3. _____?
4. _____?
5. _____?

C Compare and make a class list of questions.

eighty-one 81

9

D Look at File 16.

- Do you work in an office?
- Yes, I do.

5 The big jam

A Read about how and when these people normally get to work.

a) It takes about thirty minutes to get to the office.

b) I usually get to work at about half past eight.

c) I start work at about nine o'clock.

d) We're normally the first people in the office.

e) We arrive at the office at about quarter to nine.

f) The tram's always on time.

g) I normally go to work by car.

h) I have breakfast in the office.

i) I'm never late for work!

There's a traffic jam today …

B In the evening the same people talk about the traffic jam. Read what they say.

1. We were the last people in the office this morning.
2. I had breakfast in the car.
3. I got to work at half past nine.
4. The tram was fifteen minutes late this morning.
5. It took two hours to get to the office this morning.
6. I was on time for work as usual.
7. I went to work by tram today, not by car.
8. We arrived at the office thirty minutes late this morning.
9. I started work at half past nine.

C Who says what?

a) _5_   d) _____   g) _____
b) _____   e) _____   h) _____
c) _____   f) _____   i) _____

6 "Round the block" – a language game

Look at File 26 and play the game.

7 A short story

A Read this 50-word story and choose a title.

On Monday morning he saw her in the bus.
On Tuesday he saw her again.
On Wednesday he wanted to speak to her,
   but he didn't know what to say.
On Thursday he decided to say hello – on Friday.
On Friday she wasn't there.
Well, that's life!

B Write your own story.

On Monday morning she saw him

PRONUNCIATION

8 A Which ten words have three syllables? Underline them.

important	colleagues	footballer	engineer	terrible
holidays	interesting	evenings	assistant	arrived
regular	cassette	sentences	secretary	minutes

B Listen and check.

9 A Listen to the sentences on the cassette and mark the places where you hear the same weak vowel as in 'husb<u>a</u>nd', 'aut<u>u</u>mn' and 'mod<u>e</u>rn'.

I'm fine, thanks. And you?   Can you help me?   I'd like to book a flight.
How do you spell that?   How much does it cost?   Do you work in an office?
Of course.   What's the weather like?   You can go swimming.

B Listen again and practise.

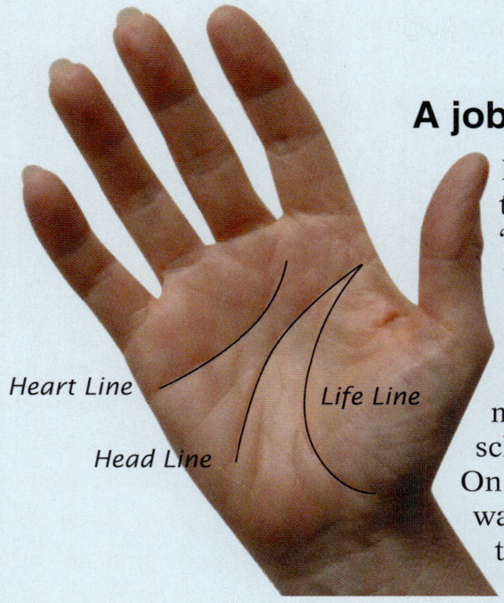

magazine 9

A job at home

Linda Spears is 35 and lives in Worcester. She looks like a typical housewife and mother – but at work she's a *palmist*. "I was a professional photographer till my son and daughter were born.

I wanted to be at home with my children. I was always interested in *palmistry*, so I learned to be a palmist. Now I can be with my children more, because I have my office in my home. My working hours are very flexible and I have school holidays.

On a typical day I see a lot of different people. Most people want *advice* about their love lives. Other people have questions about their children. I love meeting different people, that is the most interesting *part* of this job."

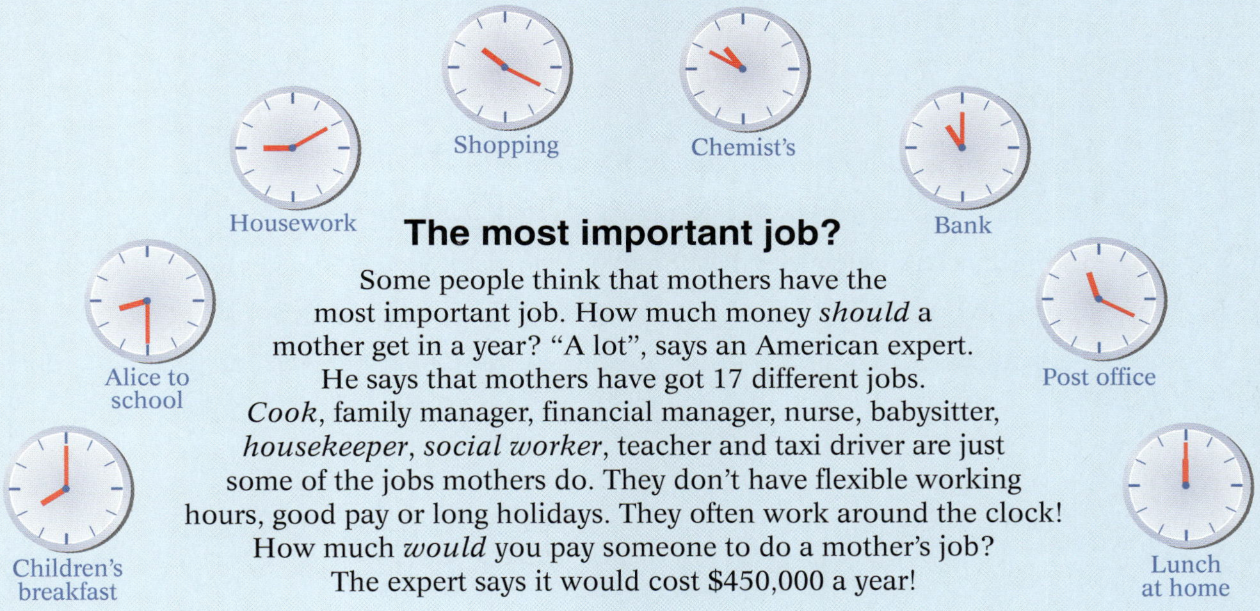

Heart Line
Life Line
Head Line

Housework
Shopping
Chemist's
Bank
Alice to school
Post office
Children's breakfast
Lunch at home

The most important job?

Some people think that mothers have the most important job. How much money *should* a mother get in a year? "A lot", says an American expert. He says that mothers have got 17 different jobs. *Cook*, family manager, financial manager, nurse, babysitter, *housekeeper*, *social worker*, teacher and taxi driver are just some of the jobs mothers do. They don't have flexible working hours, good pay or long holidays. They often work around the clock! How much *would* you pay someone to do a mother's job? The expert says it would cost $450,000 a year!

In Großbritannien gibt es nicht so viele Feiertage wie in manchen anderen europäischen Ländern, sondern nur folgende: den 1. und 2. Weihnachtsfeiertag, den Neujahrstag, Karfreitag, Ostermontag, einen Bankfeiertag *(bank holiday)* im Frühjahr und einen Bankfeiertag im August. Die meisten Arbeitnehmer/innen haben vier bis fünf Wochen Urlaub im Jahr.

palmist – Handleserin
palmistry – Handlesekunst
advice – Rat(schlag)
part – Teil
should – sollte
cook – Köchin
housekeeper – Haushälterin
social worker – Sozialarbeiterin
would – würde

9 language checklist

Sie können jetzt:

Wendungen

berufsbezogene Informationen erfragen
Do you work (in an office)?

berufsbezogene Informationen geben
I work (regular hours).
I do (shiftwork).
It takes (about thirty) minutes to get to the office.

Ihren Beruf nennen
I'm my own boss.
I'm a (secretary).
I'm an (engineer).

über Pünktlichkeit sprechen
(The tram's always) on time.

sich über regelmäßige Abläufe äußern
(I started work at nine) as usual.

Lebenserfahrung ausdrücken
That's life!

Grammatik

- Vergangenheitsformen *be*: *I/it was, we were* → S. 146: Ic
- Regelmäßige Zeitwörter, Past Simple: *I started, we arrived* → S. 147: Ic
- Unregelmäßige Zeitwörter, Past Simple: *I got/went/had, it took* → S. 147–148: Ic
- Kurzantworten: *yes, I am; no, I'm not; yes, I do; no, I don't* → S. 149: Ic
- Persönliche Fürwörter als Satzergänzung, Einzahl: *him, her* → S. 151: IVa

"It's spring, the sun is shining, it's a beautiful day, let's put the siren on!"

PREVIEW C

1 Reading

A Look quickly at the three texts. Which text is …

… a poem? ☐   … from a dictionary? ☐   … from a story? ☐

B Read the texts again quickly and match them to the topics.

☐ Family (Unit 7)   ☐ In town (Unit 8)   ☐ At work (Unit 9)

C Can you think of good titles for texts 1 and 2?

D What are these words in your language?

family name _____
family planning _____
family tree _____

1.

_____

_____

On
a dark December
morning
half way
between rain
and snow,
a long way away
from reality   *Realität*
I heard
your voice: *Stimme*
"Excuse me,
how do I get
to Piccadilly Circus?"
I told you.
"Thank you",
you said
and
that was all.
I never saw
you
again.
Who are you?
I wonder.

        L.L. Szkutnik

2.

_____

[…] The work at Friendship International was hard. Every day, Max and Frank received lots of letters. These letters wanted 'FSI products'. But FSI products had no names. They only had numbers and letters: X3Ys, L7Ks, A5Os. What did these strange numbers and letters mean? Max and Frank did not know!

Each day, they opened hundreds of these orders. They put the orders into groups for 'L' products, and one group for 'A' products. The orders came from all over the world. Some of the orders were very big.

"We're working very hard", said Max to Frank one day.

"Yes", replied Frank. "Letters, letters, letters! Hundreds of them! What do they mean, Max? What do they want? What are they asking for?"

"I don't know", said Max. "Don't ask so many questions, Frank!"

"OK!" said Frank. "OK." […]

3.

fami·ly name, family names. Your **family name** is your surname. EG … *a tomb with our family name inscribed on it.*	N COUNT
fami·ly plan·ning is the practice of using contraception to control the number of children in a family. EG … *family planning clinics.*	N UNCOUNT, = birth control
fami·ly tree, family trees. A **family tree** is a chart that shows all the people in your family over many generations and their relationships with one another.	N COUNT

PREVIEW C

2 "What do you say?" – a card game

Look at File 13.

3 "Be a verb!"

Look at File 27.

4 Word pairs

Look at File 31 and play the game.

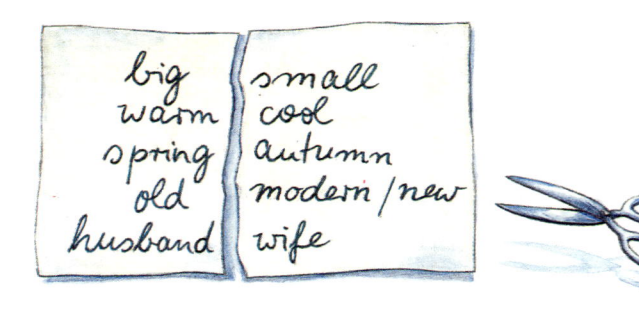

5 Preview ⇨ ⇨ ⇨ ⇨ ⇨ ⇨ ⇨ ⇨ ⇨ ⇨ ⇨ ⇨ ⇨ ⇨ ⇨

These are the topics of the next 3 units: Memories (Unit 10), Living in Europe (Unit 11), and Leisure (Unit 12).
Which unit do you think these sentences are from?

		Unit
1.	Fred was good at Art and bad at German.	____
2.	How many twin towns has your town or area got?	____
3.	I love Paris in the springtime, I love Paris in the fall.	____
4.	Let's go out tonight.	____
5.	More than 8 million cats and dogs watch television.	____
6.	My first job was washing dishes in an Italian restaurant.	____
7.	The most important industry is tourism.	____
8.	There are too many discos.	____
9.	When you were 15: What was your favourite music?	____

UNIT 10

Memories

Report	
Subject	**Grade**
English	C+
French	A
History	B–
Geography	B+
Art	B
Physical Education	C

1 School

A Here are some school subjects. Write down the words in your language. Which ones are similar? _Englisch_

- [ ] French _____
- [ ] English _____
- [ ] maths _____
- [ ] history _____
- [ ] geography _____
- [ ] German _____
- [ ] music _____

- [ ] science _Wissenschaft_
- [ ] biology _____
- [ ] chemistry _Chemie_
- [ ] physics _____
- [ ] art _Kunst_
- [ ] PE (Physical Education) _Sport_

B Listen to the song and tick the subjects you hear.

MEMO PAD

Religion
= RE (Religious Education)

2 Favourite subjects

A Answer the questions for yourself.

When you were at school:

1. What were your favourite subjects?
   _____
2. What were the most boring subjects?
   _____
3. What were you good at?
   _____
4. What were you bad at?
   _____

When you were 15:

5. What was your favourite food?
   _____
6. What was your favourite drink?
   _____
7. What was your favourite music?
   _____

10

B Ask your teacher the same questions. Write down the answers.

C Interview two other students. Write down the answers.

	Name: _____	Name: _____
• favourite subjects?		
• most boring subjects?		
• good at?		
• bad at?		
• favourite food?		
• favourite drink?		
• favourite music?		

D Report something interesting.

> "I spoke to Christine. Her favourite subjects were maths and PE."

> "Fred was good at art and bad at German."

3 "Don't know much about history"

A Listen to the song from Step 1 again and tick the correct statement.

1. The singer is ☐ bad at most school subjects.
   ☐ good at most school subjects.

2. The singer is in love with a girl who ☐ loves him.
   ☐ doesn't love him.

3. If the singer wins the girl he thinks ☐ the world will be wonderful.
   ☐ maths will be easy.

4. The singer would like to get good marks because of ☐ the girl.
   ☐ his parents.

B Can you think of a good title for the song?

_____

10

4 Then and now

A Listen to the interview with Bruce. Write down his answers.

At school:
- favourite subjects?
  _____
- most boring subjects?
  _____
- good at?
  _____
- bad at?
  _____

When he was 15:
- favourite food?
  _____
- favourite drinks?
  _____
- favourite music?
  _____

B Listen again. Match the beginnings of the sentences and the ends.

1. At school he didn't like classical music … *d*
2. At school he thought art was boring … *c*
3. When he was at school he couldn't sing … *e*
4. When he was young he ate three or four eggs a day … *a*
5. When he was 15 he started to drink beer …
6. When he was 15 he liked rock music … *f*

a) … but he doesn't eat so many now.
b) … and he still likes it.
c) … but he likes it now.
d) … but today he's very interested in it.
e) … and he still can't.
f) … and he still likes the old songs.

1.	
2.	
3.	
4.	
5.	
6.	

C What about you? Write four sentences.

1. _____
   but _____
2. _____
   and _____
3. _____
   but _____
4. _____
   and _____

eighty-nine 89

10

5 What they remember

A Here are some memories of school, jobs, learning experiences and holidays. Listen and number the pictures.

B Match the texts and the pictures.

1. I remember the school theatre group and things like that, and friends.
   (Heinke) **d**

2. School wasn't very exciting.
   (Linda) **g**

3. I didn't like school very much. I spent most of my time playing hockey and baseball.
   (John) **i**

4. Because of my father's job my parents moved several times and I went to several different schools. It was a bit difficult sometimes. The worst move was from Wales to England.
   (Derrick) **h**

5. My first job was in my father's office. It was very boring. My best job was teaching English in a prison. I learned a lot of things there which you don't learn in the outside world.
   (Linda) **a**

6. My first job was washing dishes in an Italian restaurant.
   (Derrick) **e**

7. I started to learn German when I was 22 or 23. I'm proud of that because I was never good at languages at school and I thought German was impossible to learn.
   (John) **f**

8. I learned to swim quite late – when I was twelve – and I'm very proud of my running dive.
   (Heinke) **b**

9. I remember the holidays best. We usually spent two weeks in Paignton in Devon with my grandmother. She lived in this fantastic house with a panoramic view and a beautiful garden. She was a great gardener. Those were really happy times, and of course it was always hot and sunny and it never rained.
   (Jonathan) **c**

C Read the texts again. What belongs together?

beautiful – _____
boring – _____
fantastic – _____
hot and sunny – _____
impossible to learn – _____
not very exciting – _____
proud of – _____

> first job
> German
> garden
> holiday weather
> house
> running dive
> school

D Find ten past tense forms in the texts, five regular and five irregular.

Regular	Irregular
moved	spent
learn	learned
think	thought
do – did	take/was
to start	started
to go/went	

E Write three true sentences and three false sentences about the texts in B. Then read your sentences aloud. The other groups say which sentences are true and which are false.

Derrick's parents moved several times.   "That's true."
Derrick liked his first English school.   "That's false."

_____
_____
_____
_____
_____

6 Who is it?

A Write down six sentences about yourself on a card. (No name!)

B Put the card in a hat. Take a card from the hat and read it out. Who is it?

> I went to school in
> At school I didn't like
> At school I was good at
> When I was 15
> My first job was
> I spent my first holiday
> I learned to

ninety-one 91

10

7 Brilliant children

A Complete the following text. Fill in the verbs.

> went   got   could   wrote   started   learned   won

Wolfgang Amadeus Mozart __wrote__ music from the age of five, and there are many modern examples of brilliant children.

In 1981 *Ruth Lawrence*, 10, __won__ a place at Oxford University to study mathematics.

Another mathematician, the British chess player *John Nunn*, learned to play chess when he was three. He __went__ to Oxford University at 15 and __got__ a doctorate at 21.

In 1991 three-year-old *Seth Kinast* from Kansas could say the Greek alphabet, count in German and Spanish. He __could__ also read books.

But don't worry – *Ray Kroc* was over 60 when he started a business called MacDonald's.

The American painter *Grandma Moses* __started__ to paint when she was over 70 and my grandmother __learned__ to swim when she was 84.

B Write five sentences about yourself or other people you know.

learned to started to could	drive play chess read use a computer ride a bike swim walk	when

I learned to swim when I was seventeen.
My sister could drive when she was seventeen.

ninety-two

8 Nonsense

Illustrate something from the poems.

1.
> It was in the month of Liverpool
> In the city of July
> The moon lay thick upon the ground
> The snow shone in the sky
> The flowers were singing sweetly
> The birds were in full bloom
> I went down to the cellar
> To clean an upstairs room

2.
> Said she to me, "Was that you?"
> Said I, "Who?"
> Said she, "You."
> Said I, "Where?"
> Said she "There."
> Said I, "When?"
> Said she, "Then."
> Said I, "No."
> Said she, "Oh ..."

3.
> I remember – I remember well –
> The first girl that I kissed.
> She closed her eyes, I closed mine,
> And then – worst luck – we missed!

9 What can you remember?

Answer the questions as quickly as you can.

1. What are the names of five school subjects?
2. What school subjects was your teacher bad at?
3. What was your teacher's favourite music at 15?
4. Why did the singer in Step 1 want to be an "A student"?
5. What did John play at school?
6. What was Derrick's first job?
7. What was Linda's best job?
8. Who did Jonathan spend his holidays with?
9. How old was Grandma Moses when she started to paint?
10. What did Ruth Lawrence win in 1981?

PRONUNCIATION

10 Mark the words with the same vowel sound as 'course'.

sport   history   boring   favourite   worst   thought   information   world

11 Practise these sentences with the same intonation as on the cassette.

1. At school he didn't like classical music but today he's very interested in it.
2. At school he thought art was boring but he likes it now.
3. When he was at school he couldn't sing and he still can't.
4. When he was young he ate three or four eggs a day but he doesn't eat so many now.
5. When he was fifteen he started drinking beer and he still likes it now.
6. When he was fifteen he liked rock music and he still likes the old songs.

10 magazine

- *Guy Fawkes Night* ist ein nationales Ereignis, das nur in Großbritannien gefeiert wird. Am 5. November gibt es Feuerwerk und riesige Scheiterhaufen bzw. Feuer *(bonfires)*, in denen große Guy-Fawkes-Puppen verbrannt werden. Guy Fawkes war ein Rebell, der 1605 die Parlamentsgebäude in London sprengen wollte.
- *Hallowe'en* ist der Name des Abends bzw. der Nacht vor Allerheiligen. Die ursprünglich irischen Bräuche dieser Geisternacht am 31. Oktober sind schon seit langem in den USA sehr populär und haben sich inzwischen auch in vielen anderen Ländern durchgesetzt.
- Zur Erinnerung an das erste Erntedankfest der englischen Siedler in Amerika im 17. Jahrhundert wird in den USA am vierten Donnerstag im November *Thanksgiving* gefeiert. Es ist ein wichtiges Familienfest, dessen Höhepunkt das traditionelle Festessen mit einheimischen indianischen Zutaten wie Truthahn *(turkey)*, Mais *(corn)*, Preiselbeeren *(cranberries)* und Kürbis *(pumpkin)* ist.

Memories of favourite special days

Read the texts and fill in the special days.

- Christmas
- Hallowe'en
- Guy Fawkes Night
- Thanksgiving (Day)

1. I always liked _____ because we went to my grandmother's house. Of course, I liked the dinner, but I didn't eat turkey. I was a vegetarian when I was a child. The *pumpkin pie* was my favourite food. The best thing was playing with my cousins.

2. My favourite holiday was _____. One year I was a black cat. My mother made me a beautiful costume. She is good at that. I loved the *jack-o-lanterns* and I liked going from house to house at night in the dark. Of course, I liked the sweets, too.

3. _____ was always the best holiday for me: the tree, the music, presents, the stories of Father Christmas, the cake and lots of good food and, of course, the school holidays!

4. I liked _____ because of the *fireworks* and the bonfires. We always spent our *pocket money* on lots of fireworks. My parents made a bonfire with some of their friends and we cooked *potatoes* in the fire and made *taffy*.

pumpkin pie – (eine Art) Kürbiskuchen
jack-o-lanterns – ausgehöhlte Kürbisse
fireworks – Feuerwerk
pocket money – Taschengeld
potatoes – Kartoffeln
taffy – Karamel

1. Thanksgiving 2. Hallowe'en 3. Christmas 4. Guy Fawkes Night

language checklist 10

Sie können jetzt:

Wendungen

sagen, was Ihnen gefällt
(Her) favourite (subjects were maths and PE).

sagen, was Ihnen nicht gefällt
(He) didn't like (classical music).
(Her first job) was boring.

sagen, was Sie interessiert
(He's) interested in (art).

über Zeit sprechen
(He ate three or four eggs) a day.

Grammatik

- Vergangenheitsformen *be*: *you were, he/she was; you were, they were*
  → S. 146: Ic
- Vergangenheitsform *be*, verneinte Form: *it wasn't* → S. 146: Ic
- Vergangenheitsform *be*, Frageform: *were you? was it? were they?* → S. 146: Ic
- Unregelmäßige Zeitwörter, verneinte Form: *I didn't, he didn't* → S. 147: Ic
- Kurzformen: *didn't, couldn't, wasn't, weren't* → S. 149: Ie
- Steigerung der Eigenschaftswörter (Superlativ): *happiest, most modern, worst*
  → S. 155: VII
- Aussagesätze mit Bindewörtern: *but, so, when* → S. 157: IXa

"Oh, I can't sing. I can only eat like him."

impersonator – Imitator

UNIT 11

Living in Europe

1 Which country is it?

Read the following text. Which country do you think it is?   _Malta_

With a population of only 345,418, ***** is a fairly small country. It is not really an industrial country, but because land is cheap and wages are low, a number of large European companies now have factories and offices here.

The most important industry is tourism and ***** offers a lot of attractive and interesting places for the tourist to visit. There are beautiful historical buildings in the old parts of the towns, clean beaches, pleasant modern hotels, and the local people are very friendly.

***** has a healthy climate with long hot dry summers and short cool winters. The people have their own language, but most of them speak very good English, and this is why so many people now visit the country to learn English.

2 What's hot, dry and historical?

A How many of these words do you know?
How many can you guess? Mark the words.

[+] I know what it means.

[?] I'm not sure.

[−] I don't know what it means.

	hot		dry		historical
	healthy		important		industrial
	short		modern		interesting
	attractive		old		cheap
	friendly		expensive		clean
	new		dirty		boring
	beautiful		quiet		noisy
	small		pleasant		large
	cool		long		

ninety-four

B Put some of the words from A into the following groups.

Town: _____
_____
_____

Countryside: _____
_____
_____

Climate: _____
_____
_____

C What could it be? Guess.

What's hot, dry and historical?

Is it a country?

Yes, it is.

Is it Turkey?

No, it isn't.

3 Describing places

A Listen and guess the country. It's _____

B Listen again and write down the first two or three words at the beginning of the sentences.

It's a

C Choose a European country and write some sentences about it. The other groups try to guess which country it is.

11

4 I don't agree

A Write three sentences about your town or area.

It's	(very) (quite)	interesting pleasant clean noisy …

Tübingen lies on the river Neckar south of Stuttgart and is world famous for its ancient university.

This friendly little city, home to numerous writers and philosophers over the centuries, is still an important academic centre today.

Twinned with Durham in northeastern England and Ann Arbor, Michigan, among other cities, Tübingen's south German charm makes it a magnet for visitors from all over the world.

B Read the sentences out and talk about them.

"I don't think that's true."

"I'm afraid I don't agree. I think …"

"It depends."

"I agree (with that)."

"Yes, that's right."

5 Last year's holidays

A Find someone who

… went abroad last year.
… went camping.
… had bad weather.
… stayed at home.
… went to an English-speaking country.
… visited a lot of museums.
… stayed in a large city.
… stayed on an island.

"Did you go abroad last year?"

"Yes, I did."

"Where did you go?"

"I went to Poland."

B Report something interesting.

6 Coventry's twin towns

Many towns around the world have got twin towns in other countries. Coventry in England has got twenty-six – probably more than any other town or city. In the following interview Lorraine Ford, International Relations Officer for the City of Coventry, talks about some of Coventry's contacts.

A Listen to the interview and tick the towns and countries she mentions.

☐	Volgograd, Russia	___
☐	Jinan, China	___
✗	Nicaragua	6.
☐	St. Etienne, France	___
☐	Arnhem, The Netherlands	___
☐	Kiel, Germany	___
☐	Kecskemet, Hungary	___
☐	Ostrava, Czech Republic	___
☐	Coventry, Connecticut/USA	___
☐	Dresden, Germany	___
☐	Bologna, Italy	___
☐	Graz, Austria	___

B Listen again and match each place and the reasons she gives.

1. Language learning contacts
2. Coventry's first twin town
3. Coventry's newest twin town
4. Sporting contacts
5. Business contacts
6. Political contacts
7. Contacts for young people

7 Your twin towns

How many twin towns has your town or area got?
What do you know about them?

Name(s) of twin town(s): _____
When the contact(s) started: _____
How far from our area: _____
Other details: _____

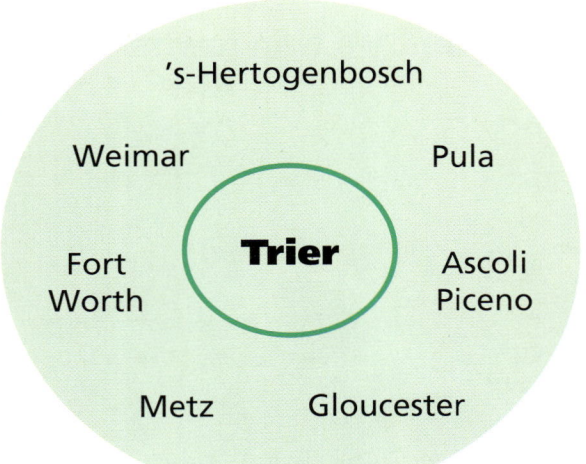

's-Hertogenbosch
Weimar
Pula
Fort Worth
Trier
Ascoli Piceno
Metz
Gloucester

8 I'm looking forward to the visit

A A group of people from Britain plan to visit your town or area.
Read this letter to one of the host families.

2 Banks Road
Rochester
Kent ME1 1EW   31 August 1993

Dear Mr and Mrs Nolde,

Thank you very much for your letter. I'd love to stay with you when our group comes to visit next month.
As you know we plan to stay a week and I would like to see and do a lot. I really enjoy walking around a town and looking at the buildings. Are there lots of interesting old buildings or are most of them modern? Are there any museums in the area?
In the evenings I'd like to try the local restaurants. What's your favourite one?
That's probably enough questions already, but just one more. What's the weather usually like in September? Is it still warm and sunny then?

Thank you again for your invitation.
I'm really looking forward to the visit.
Yours sincerely,

Angela Frewin

B Now help the Noldes to answer the letter.

```
Dear Ms Frewin,

Thank you for your letter. Here's a little information for you.
There are lots of things to see and do in and around _____.
There are some interesting _____ buildings near where
we live, for example the _____. There are some muse-
ums too, but we think the _____ is the best one. I
think you would like to visit the _____, too.
You wanted to know about restaurants in the area. There is a
nice Italian one near here and a very good _____
one, but our favourite is a _____ restaurant called
_____.

Oh yes, you asked us about the weather. It's
usually _____, but you never know!

Looking forward to meeting you next month,

Yours sincerely,
```

MEMO PAD

Schloß = castle

_____

9 Which city is it?

Amsterdam   Dublin   Glasgow
London   Paris

A Fill in.

1.
In _____'s fair city
Where the girls are so pretty
I first set my eyes on sweet Molly Malone.

2.
When it's spring again, I'll bring again
Tulips from _____.

3.
I love _____ in the springtime.
I love _____ in the fall.
I love _____ in the winter – when it drizzles,
I love _____ in the summer – when it sizzles.

4.
I belong to _____,
Dear old _____ town.
Oh, what's the matter with _____?
For it's going round and round.

5.
_____ Bridge is falling down, falling down, falling down
_____ Bridge is falling down, my fair lady.

B Listen and check.

C What other English songs do you know with the names of cities?

11

10 Surprising statistics

A Can you guess?
Fill in the correct numbers.

> 221,000   1,478   140   3
> 74,991   4,050   421

- The person with the most first names lives in Barrow Hill in England. Tracey Nelson has _____ names because her parents did not know which name they wanted to give her, so they gave her all the names in the book.

- Berlin is the city with the most dogs in Germany. _____ dogs were registered there in 1988.

- The highest waterfall in Europe is near Lourdes in France and is _____ m high.

- The people of Cyprus smoke more cigarettes than any other people in the world: _____ cigarettes per person per year.

- The largest wine barrel in the world is in Heidelberg and holds _____ litres.

- The person with the longest first name in the world is Dr. Brahmatma of New Delhi. It takes him about _____ minutes to say all the _____ letters of his name – on a good day!

B Listen and check

C Match the numbers.

> ~~140~~
> 3
> 421
> 4,050
> 74,991
> 221,000
> 1,478

_____ seventy-four thousand nine hundred and ninety-one

____140____ one hundred and forty

_____ four thousand and fifty

_____ three

_____ one thousand four hundred and seventy-eight

_____ four hundred and twenty-one

_____ two hundred and twenty-one thousand

100   one hundred

11 Large numbers

A Listen. Underline the numbers you hear.

a) 418   480
b) 626   662
c) 1,837   18,037
d) 4,050   4,500
e) 7,223   7,233
f) 16,995   60,995
g) 74,991   47,991
h) 221,000   220,100
i) 345,418   34,518
j) 1,659,400   1,695,040

B Round off the following numbers.

3,921	4,000
195	
59,654	
21,877	
402	
3,954,261	
8,008	
79,611	
6,001,001	

"That's about four thousand."

Number of Hotels in European Countries

	1988
B	2,105
DK	945
D	38,871
GR	6,129
E	10,477
F	20,378
IRL	889
I	38,114
L	388
NL	2,150
P	1,634
GB	40,501

12 PRONUNCIATION

A Listen to the words on the cassette and mark [f] or [v], according to the sound in the word.

	1.	2.	3.	4.	5.	6.	7.	8.	9.
[f]									
[v]									

	10.	11.	12.	13.	14.	15.	16.	17.
[f]								
[v]								

B Now practise the words.

one hundred and one

11 magazine

A Christmas pantomime

Amy is an 18-year-old girl who lives in Germany. Her father is German and her mom is American. Here is an e-mail she wrote to her grandmother in California.

From: Amy
To: Grandma
Date: January 5, 2001
Subject: Christmas pantomime

Dear grandma,

Thank you for the computer *bag*. I love it! :-)
I really needed one for my new laptop!
I *hope* you had a nice Christmas. I had a fantastic Christmas! You know, I am in an English-speaking theatre group. This year we did the Christmas pantomime *Cinderella*. I was Cinderella! It was so exciting.
Pantomimes are traditional in Britain around Christmas time. The story is always a *fairy tale* and there are lots of *jokes*.
In the picture you can see Cinderella's step-mother and her two terrible step-sisters. The step-sisters were two men. It is normal that men play the step-sisters and a woman plays the prince. The step-sisters were very *funny*. :-D
The panto always has a happy ending. Here you see Cinderella (me) at her wedding with the prince (my friend Samantha). You can see the costumes are beautiful and my hair is very attractive. ;-)
Well, now you know what a panto is. After our last *performance* we had a party and I was a little *sad* because now all the fun is over. :-(
I really enjoy the group because it is international. There are people from many different countries: Ireland, Scotland, England, Italy, Sri Lanka, the US, and, of course, Germany.
I hope you can visit us at Christmas *sometime* and see a Christmas panto.

Love, Amy
***

:-)	= I'm happy.
:-(	= I'm sad.
;-)	= That's a joke.
:-D	= That's very funny.
***	= kisses

Pantomimes sind besondere Theaterstücke, die in der Weihnachtszeit an vielen Orten in Großbritannien aufgeführt werden. Sie basieren auf traditionellen Märchen wie z. B. *Cinderella*. Witzige Dialoge, auch aktuelle politische Witze, Musik und Tanz gehören dazu. Das Publikum stellt einen wichtigen Teil des Weihnachtsmärchens dar: je nach Situation werden die Schauspieler und Schauspielerinnen mit lautem Buh oder Hurra unterstützt. Der Prinz wird traditionell von einer Frau gespielt, und eine witzige ältere Frau wird von einem Mann dargestellt.

Christmas pantomime/panto – eine Art Weihnachtsmärchen
bag – Tasche
hope – hoffen
Cinderella – Aschenputtel
fairy tale – Märchen
jokes – Witze
funny – lustig, witzig
performance – Vorstellung
sad – traurig
sometime – irgendwann

language checklist 11

Sie können jetzt:

Wendungen

sich verabschieden
See you soon.

eine Äußerung einleiten
As you know, …

ein Angebot annehmen
I'd love to (stay with you).

Gewißheit ausdrücken
I know (what it means).

Ungewißheit/Unwissen ausdrücken
I'm not sure.
It depends.

zustimmen
I agree (with that).
(Yes.) That's right.

Nichtzustimmung ausdrücken
I'm afraid I don't agree.
I don't think that's true.

sagen, was Ihnen gefällt
I enjoy (walking).

Vorsicht/Zweifel ausdrücken
You never know.

Grammatik

- Unregelmäßige Zeitwörter, Frageform: *did you?* → S. 147: Ic
- Persönliche Fürwörter als Satzgegenstand, Mehrzahl: *us* → S. 151: IVa
- Ersatzwort *one: (What's your favourite) one?* → S. 153: IVe
- Grundzahlen bis über eine Million → S. 154: VIa
- Steigerung der Eigenschaftswörter (Superlativ): *most* → S. 155: VII
- Verstärkende oder abschwächende Umstandswörter: *very, quite* → S. 157: VIIIe
- Wortstellung in Fragen: *did you …?* → S. 157: IXb

"You didn't answer a single question … well done son!"

exam – Prüfung
fail – durchgefallen
Well done! – Gut gemacht!

UNIT 12

Leisure

1 Leisure activities

A Tick the things you do regularly in your free time.

- [ ] go dancing
- [ ] read the newspaper
- [ ] go jogging
- [ ] work in the garden
- [ ] go for a meal
- [ ] play cards
- [ ] have a lie-in
- [ ] watch TV
- [ ] relax at home
- [ ] go for a walk
- [ ] get some exercise
- [ ] play tennis
- [ ] play the piano
- [ ] listen to music
- [ ] read a book

B Interview your neighbour and make notes.

"How often do you …?"

"I never play cards."

"I go for a meal twice a month."

every	day
once a	week
twice a	month
three or four times a	year

C Report. What do you both do?   "We both go jogging every day."

2 Leisure statistics

Here are some results from a survey about leisure activities in Britain.
Fill in the numbers.

7
12
33
66
43
50

____ per cent do absolutely nothing for three hours a week.

____ per cent spend no time on exercise.

____ per cent watch television for 11 hours a day or more.

Only ____ per cent read for 10 hours a week or more.

More than eight million cats and dogs watch television.

____ per cent of British people could not live happily without a television, ____ per cent without radio.

More than two million make love in front of the television.

Check your answers in File 18.

102 one hundred and two

3 Céad mílle fáilte

*Talking all the day
With true friends who try to make you stay
Telling jokes and news
And singing songs to pass the time away
We watched the Galway salmon run
Like silver, darting, dancing in the sun
Living on your western shore
Saw summer sunset, asked for more
Stood by your Atlantic sea
And sang a song for Ireland*

*Drinking all the day
In old pubs where fiddlers love to play
Saw one touch the bow
And he played a reel that seemed so grand and gay
Stood on Dingle beach and cast
In wild foam we found Atlantic bass
Living on your western shore
Saw summer sunset, asked for more
Stood by your Atlantic sea
And sang a song for Ireland*

12

A Read the following text and answer the questions.

> Ireland, ▨▨▨ ▨▨▨ in pubs ▨▨ drink
> ▨▨ strong Celtic traditions, ▨▨▨ ▨▨ talk ▨▨▨ sing and
> ▨▨▨ love of music. ▨▨▨ play music together. "Singing pubs" are
> ▨▨▨ singing, dancing ▨▨▨ more than ▨▨▨ tourist attractions.
> playing instruments ▨▨▨ People ▨▨▨ like singing
> fiddle, ▨▨ Uilleann pipes ▨▨ and others ▨▨▨ don't ▨▨
> harp, which is the national symbol. watch and listen, ▨▨ sing along or
> ▨▨▨ It's easy to find ▨▨▨ play an Irish ballad.
> tradition in Ireland. ▨▨ look at ▨▨▨ ▨▨▨ kind of music ▨▨
> list of events in the ▨▨▨ ▨▨▨ ? ballads are happy,
> ▨▨▨ Press under "music session" ▨▨▨ sad, ▨▨ very fast
> ▨▨ "ceól", ▨▨ Irish word ▨▨▨ slow. ▨▨ love
> music. songs, drinking songs, ▨▨▨
> ▨▨▨ ▨▨▨ concerts and music hard work and hard times and,
> festivals but the most Irish of institutions ▨▨▨ ▨▨▨ against the English.
> ▨▨ the fiddler in the pub.

1. What are some Celtic traditions? _____

2. What do people do in pubs in Ireland? _____

3. What are Irish ballads like? What are they about? _____

B Read the whole text in File 29.

4 Going out

A Put the dialogue in the correct order.

> OK, let's go to the cinema, then.
>
> That's a good idea. Shall we go to O'Reilly's?
>
> Well, I'd rather go to the cinema. It's always so noisy at O'Reilly's.

Mary: George, let's go out tonight.

George: _____

Mary: _____

George: _____

12

B Listen and check.

C Write these expressions in the correct boxes.

> Shall we …?   I don't mind.   Let's …
> That's a good idea.   Well, I'd rather …

?!	😊	😐	😐

D Listen and complete.

Harry: What shall we do at the weekend?

Claudia: Well, there's a music festival in Dublin.

Harry: Great! _____ go to that, then.

Claudia: _____ go on Saturday or Sunday?

Harry: _____. What about you?

Claudia: Well, _____ go on Saturday, then we can have a lie-in on Sunday.

E Act out one of the dialogues.

THE BORN LOSER by Art Sansom

one hundred and five 105

5 What's on?

A Match the titles and the ads.

Music: Folk & Jazz
Eating & Drinking
Theatre
Cinema

Abbey Theatre, Lower Abbey St., D1.
Moving
Opens Tuesday 21 April. Hugh Leonard's new play is a winner! Directed by Joe Dowling and featuring a superb cast. Book now!

Andrew's Lane Theatre Andrew's Lane, D2
The Odd Couple
8pm nightly. An energetic production with fine performances all round.
Late Night Comedy
25 April, Midnight. Mark LaMarr and Dermot Carmody.

Traditional Music Session
The Auld Dubliner
12.30pm Free

Hot City Orchestra Royal
Howth Hotel 8pm

East Coast Jazz
The Waterside Inn 9pm

Ballad Session
Maples House (Glasnevin)
8pm £1

Ante Room Seafood Restaurant,
20 Lower Baggot St, D2.
Open Mon-Fri 12.30-10.30pm, Sun 6pm-9pm.
Seafood and country cuisine.

Brown's Café,
9 Crown Alley, D2.
Mon-Sun 11.30am-11.30pm.
Pizza, pasta specialities.

Chandni Indian Restaurant,
174 Pembroke Rd, D4.
Mon-Fri 12.30-2.30pm,
Mon-Sun 6pm-12am.

Cinderella
Disney cartoon. Classic, Harold's Cross (Sat/Sun 2, 4pm)

Star Trek VI
The crew of the Enterprise end the war with the Klingons. Not bad at all. Santry Ominplex (11.35am, 2.00pm)

The Rocky Horror Picture Show
Classic, Harold's Cross (Fri/Sat 11.45pm)

Silence of the Lambs
Not for the nervous. Carlton, O'Connell St (2.35, 5.20, 8.05pm)

B You are on a class trip to Dublin. It's your last evening.
Look at the ads and make a list of things you would like to do.

C Discuss a programme for an evening out with one or two other people.
Make notes.

"Let's …"

"Shall we …"

"That's a good idea."

"Well, I'd rather …"

6 Our evening out

You are now on the plane back home.
Tell the others what you did on your last evening in Dublin.

"Yesterday we went …"

"We listened …"

"We watched …"

7 Leisure facilities

A What do you think of the leisure facilities your town/area has got? Tick.

	There are too many	There are enough	There aren't enough	There aren't any
discos	☐	☐	☐	☐
museums / art galleries	☐	☐	☐	☐
video rental shops	☐	☐	☐	☐
swimming pools	☐	☐	☐	☐
youth clubs	☐	☐	☐	☐
restaurants	☐	☐	☐	☐
cinemas	☐	☐	☐	☐
fitness clubs	☐	☐	☐	☐
theatres	☐	☐	☐	☐
tennis courts	☐	☐	☐	☐
cycle paths	☐	☐	☐	☐
pubs	☐	☐	☐	☐
parks	☐	☐	☐	☐
children's playgrounds	☐	☐	☐	☐

B Compare results and report.

"One person in our group thinks there are too many discos."

"Two people think …"

"Nobody thinks …"

"Everybody thinks …"

MEMO PAD

8 Mind mapping

Make a word map from this unit.

for a meal — go — jogging
go — to the theatre — comedy

9 Before there was TV

A What did people do before there was TV? Write six sentences.

Before there was TV people used to ...

... _____
... _____
... _____
... _____
... _____
... _____

B Read out your sentences.

PRONUNCIATION

10 Listen to the cassette and underline the word or phrase you hear.

a)	any	many	g)	eighteen million	eighty million
b)	play	played	h)	four hours	for four hours
c)	play	played	i)	for ten hours	fourteen hours
d)	have	haven't	j)	isn't expensive	isn't too expensive
e)	walk	work	k)	do you	did you
f)	start	started			

11 Practise these dialogues. Be careful about the intonation.

1. ▪ We haven't got many discos where I live.
   ○ We haven't got any discos in our town.

2. ▪ I played a lot of football when I was at school.
   ○ I played tennis.

3. ▪ I'd like to go out tonight.
   ○ Well, I'd rather stay at home.

4. ▪ I started school in 1955.
   ○ Did you? I started in 1953.

5. ▪ I waited for four hours.
   ○ I waited for five.

magazine 12

To watch TV or to read? That is the question.

J. K. Rowling and Delia Smith are two of the most *well-known* people in Britain. Read more about them both.

J. K. Rowling

J. K. Rowling is the *author* of the Harry Potter books. She says that she got the idea for the book on a long train *journey* from Manchester to London. It took her five years to write the first Harry Potter book. She wrote it in a café in Edinburgh, Scotland, when her young daughter slept. She says she can write *any time*, *any place* and she writes by hand – not on a computer. She spends her free time with her daughter and friends and she enjoys travelling. She loves reading and writing. Writing is her full-time job, but it is also her greatest *pleasure*.

▶ Who is Harry Potter? Harry is an eleven-year-old boy who goes to a school for *wizards* called Hogwarts. The story is about how Harry learns to be a wizard.

▶ Why do people read Harry Potter? "Muggles" (Rowling's word for normal people) of all ages enjoy reading the stories because they are exciting, *humorous* and the wizard world is full of fantastic details.

Delia Smith

DELIA SMITH is Britain's best-selling cookbook author. Her most *popular* book is called "Delia Smith's Complete Cookery Course". She started her cooking programme on BBC TV in 1975. Delia loves cooking and she wants to teach people that good cooking can be easy.

Today people do not learn how to cook at home. Working people have no time to cook so children do not learn cooking and baking from their mothers and fathers. Someone has to teach people how to cook and how to enjoy good *simple* food everyday.

Delia is married and lives in Suffolk, England.

---

well-known – bekannt
author – Schriftstellerin
journey – Fahrt
any time – jederzeit
any place – an jedem beliebigen Ort
pleasure – Freude
wizard – Zauberer
humorous – humorvoll
popular – beliebt
simple – einfach

12 language checklist

Sie können jetzt:

Wendungen

Unzufriedenheit ausdrücken
There are too many (pubs).
There aren't enough (cinemas).
I don't think there are enough (libraries).
(It's) too (loud).

etwas vorschlagen
Let's (go to that, then).
Shall we (go on Saturday or Sunday)?

einen Vorschlag annehmen
That's a good idea.

einen Vorschlag ablehnen
Well, I'd rather (stay at home).

auf einen Vorschlag unverbindlich reagieren
I don't mind.

sich nach Veranstaltungen erkundigen
What's on?

Grammatik

- Unregelmäßige Zeitwörter, Vergangenheitsform: *used to* → S. 148: Ic
- Unbestimmte Fürwörter: *both, everybody, nobody* → S. 153: IVe
- Umstandsbestimmung der Häufigkeit: *every day, once a week, three times a year* → S. 155: VIIIa

*"Come on, it's a Saturday night.
Let's go find a drunk and have a good time."*

a drunk – ein/e Betrunkene/r

PREVIEW D

1 Ask and tell

Look at File 30 and play the game.

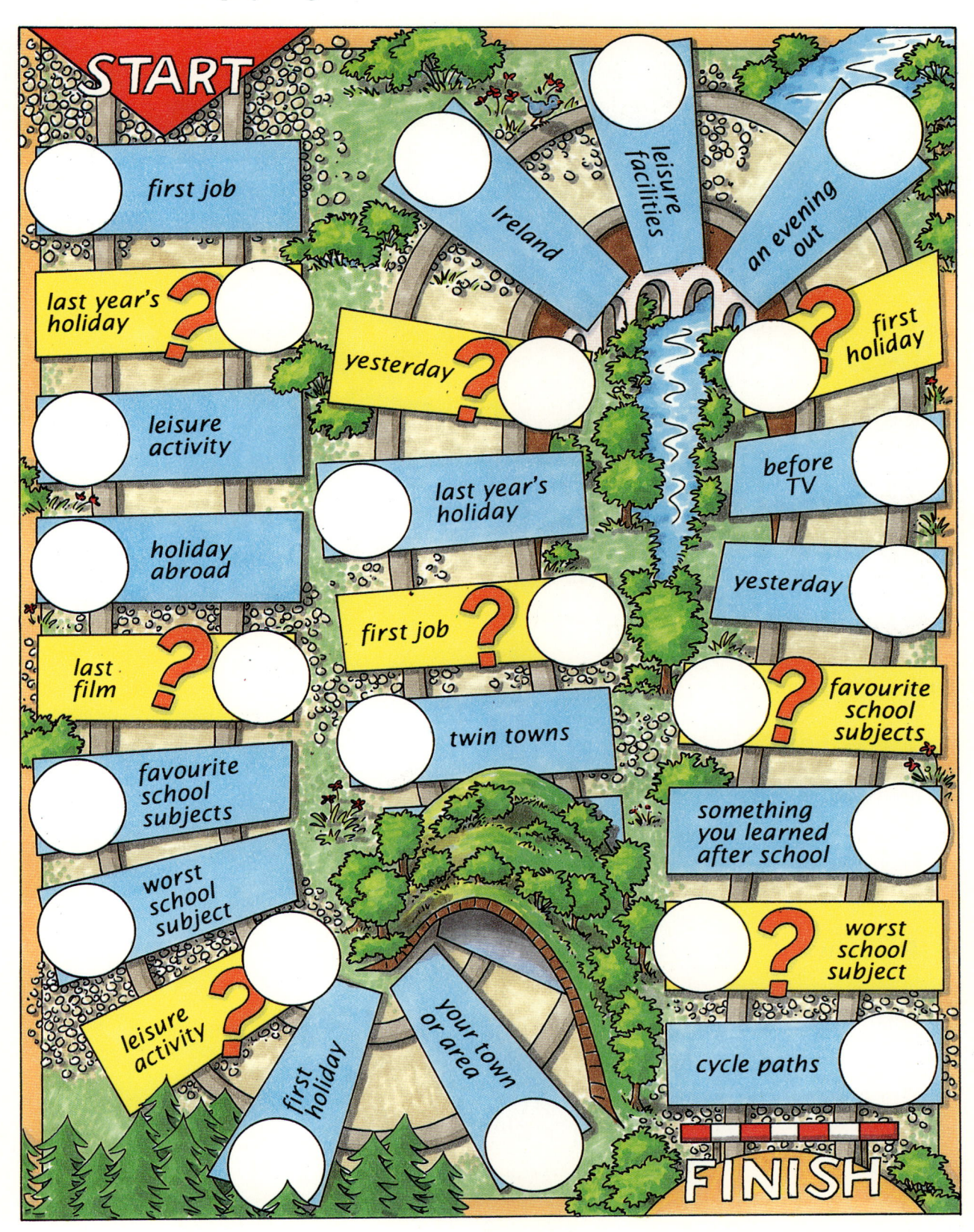

START

- first job
- last year's holiday ?
- leisure activity
- holiday abroad
- last film ?
- favourite school subjects
- worst school subject
- leisure activity ?
- first holiday
- your town or area
- twin towns
- first job ?
- last year's holiday
- yesterday ?
- Ireland
- leisure facilities
- an evening out
- first holiday ?
- before TV
- yesterday
- favourite school subjects ?
- something you learned after school
- worst school subject ?
- cycle paths

FINISH

one hundred and nine 109

PREVIEW D

2 Chain story

Look at File 32 and tell a story.

When I was 15 ...

(blackboard: can, sing, work, start, go – went, like – liked, learn, play)

3 Write a nonsense poem

Look at File 28 and write a nonsense poem.

(rainy, music, walked)

4 Preview ⇨ ⇨ ⇨ ⇨ ⇨ ⇨ ⇨ ⇨ ⇨ ⇨ ⇨ ⇨ ⇨ ⇨

The topics of the next three Units are
- **Eating out** (13),
- **Lifestyle** (14),
- **Europeans** (15).

Listen and decide which unit each extract is from.

1.	2.	3.	4.

110 one hundred and ten

UNIT 13

Eating out

EATING OUT IN *the Garden of England & Sussex*

IL VATICANO *Pasta Parlour*

Il Vaticano, 35 St Margarets Street, Canterbury. Tel: (0227) 765333. Healthy eating, value for money and fast service is the promise at Il Vaticano, probably the longest established pasta restaurant in Canterbury. The atmosphere here is informal. Prices range from between £2 and £10.

The Mad Chef's Bistro

The Harbour, Broadstairs, Kent. Tel: (0843) 69304. The Mad Chef's Bistro actually boasts its own trawler, so with fish and seafoods being a speciality, quality and freshness are absolutely guaranteed. The menu is vast and varied. The Mad Chef has to be one of the finest fish restaurants on the south coast. A meal will cost £4 – £15 for one course or £15 – £21 for three.

GREEK TAVERNA

The Greek Taverna, 13 Church Street, St. Paul's. Tel: (0227) 464931/evenings, (0843) 293624/day. Enjoy the atmosphere of the Greek Islands and sample authentic Greek dishes at their very best. English & vegetarian dishes are also available. Prices are very reasonable & portions are generous, but you can pop in for just a starter or a dessert.

1 Good restaurants

A What makes a good restaurant for you? Write the items in order of importance.

Price
Atmosphere
Quality of food
Quantity of food
Service
Cleanliness

Most important 1 _____
                2 _____
                3 _____
                4 _____
                5 _____
Least important 6 _____

B Compare.

one hundred and eleven 111

13

2 What's for lunch?

A Complete the menu.

Carrots   Ham   Green   Pie   Chips
Pie   Soup   Green   Steak   Juice

STARTERS
- [ ] Fruit _____
- [ ] _____ of the Day
- [ ] Egg Mayonnaise

MAIN DISHES
- [ ] Fillet _____
- [ ] Roast Chicken
- [ ] Steak & Kidney _____
- [ ] Fried Plaice
- [ ] Cheese Omelette
- [ ] _____ Omelette

VEGETABLES
- [ ] _____ or Boiled Potatoes
- [ ] _____ or Peas

SIDE SALADS
- [ ] _____ Salad
- [ ] Tomato Salad

DESSERTS
- [ ] Ice Cream
- [ ] Apple _____
- [ ] Fruit

B Now listen to an announcement in a department store. Tick the items you hear on the menu.

C Choose your lunch.

_____

_____

3 Can we have the menu, please?

A Complete the dialogues.

> there you are   to start with   We'd like
> Can we have   I'll have   what shall we have
> Can we have   I'll have

1. ❐ Excuse me. _____ the menu, please?
   ▽ Oh, I'm sorry … _____.
   ❐ Thank you.

2. ❐ Well, _____?
   ○ I'd like steak and kidney pie with boiled potatoes and carrots. And a soup _____.
   △ I think _____ an egg mayonnaise and then plaice with chips and peas. What about you, Christine?
   ▷ Er … I'd like steak and kidney pie, too, with boiled potatoes. No starter. And you, Richard?
   ❐ Let's see … ah, chicken, my favourite! _____ that. And soup for me, too.

3. ▽ Are you ready to order yet?
   ❐ Yes, please. _____ two soups and one egg mayonnaise, and then, er … one plaice, two steak and kidney pies, and one chicken.
   ▽ Thank you. And the vegetables?

4. ❐ _____ the bill, please?
   ▽ Certainly. One moment, please.

B Listen and check.

C Look at File 33.

13

4 Favourite dishes

What dishes do you like best?

Starter: _____
Meat: _____
Fish: _____
Vegetable: _____
Dessert: _____
Fruit: _____

MEMO PAD

Lammkotelett
= lamb chop

B Make a group survey.

C Report.

5 The chef's special

Put the parts of the story in the right order.

☐ In the end we asked, "Well, what have you got?" "The chef's special." So of course we ordered two of those. I don't know what it was – a mixture of everything the chef found in the kitchen, I think - but we didn't finish it.

☐ We agreed that the price and quality of the food, the atmosphere and the service were all much better there.

☐ It was dark and quiet inside and there was nobody else there. We sat down and studied the menu, which had lots of exotic dishes on it, and in a few minutes a waiter came to our table. We tried to order from the menu, but the answer was always, "I'm sorry, it's off tonight."

☐ On the way home, and still hungry, we stopped at a fish and chip shop.

☐ One night a few years ago I went out for a meal with a friend of mine. We wanted to go to our favourite restaurant in the old town, but when we got there it was full. It was a rainy, windy night in November and we didn't want to walk a long way, so we decided to try a new place called Ali Baba's, which was in the same street.

6 The disappointing dish

A Put the pictures in the correct order.

B Tell the story.

C Can you remember any good or bad experiences in restaurants?
Tell the group.

7 What do you say?

A These questions are about British pubs and restaurants.
What do you think the answers are?

1. You go for a meal.
   What do people say before they start eating?

   a) "Good appetite."
   b) "Enjoy your meal."
   c) Nothing.

2. A British friend buys drinks for you both in a pub.
   What do you say when he gets up to buy some more?

   a) "It's my round."
   b) "It's my turn."
   c) "Are you still thirsty? Let me buy you a drink."

"OK. Dig in!"

B What do you say in your country in these two situations?

8 Eating in Europe: North and South

A Match the words and the pictures.

beans
red meat
peas
garlic
fish
seafood
fried potatoes
oranges
cheese
lemons
butter
rice
pasta
olive oil

B Which of these foods are more typical of northern Europe, and which of southern Europe?

North: _____

South: _____

C Which of these items are especially healthy, and which are not so healthy?

Healthy: _____

Not so healthy: _____

D Now compare your lists with the text.

Which is the healthiest diet in the world? Well, some health experts say the Spanish diet is one of the healthiest. And Spain's traditional low-fat diet, with a lot of beans, fish, fruit, vegetables, salads, bread, rice, pasta and olive oil, is an important reason for the Spaniards' long and healthy lives. But a lot of Spaniards now eat more and more red meat, fried potatoes and dairy products like cheese, butter, and full-fat milk, which are more typical of northern Europe.

9 Food game

Student A: Look at File 21.
Student B: Look at File 23.

10 Food poems and pictures

Write a food poem
or make a word picture.

My favourite dish: fish!

Some soup for the group.

Write a ballad about salad.

spaghetti

tomatoes

tomatoes cheese oregano tomatoes cheese oregano cheese oregano tomatoes seafood oregano cheese cheese oregano seafood oregano tomatoes seafood cheese oregano oregano

Sing a song of sixpence
A pocket full of rye
Four and twenty blackbirds
Baked in a pie

When the pie was opened
The birds began to sing
Wasn't that a dainty dish
To set before a king?

13

PRONUNCIATION

11 Listen to the dialogues and mark the main stress on the underlined sections.

1. ◻ I think I'll have a steak.
   ○ I think I'll have a steak, too.

2. ◻ It's my round.
   ○ No it's not, it's my round!

3. ◻ This pie's really good.
   ○ Hm, I like apples, but I don't like apple pie.

4. ◻ I'll have a cheese omelette.
   ○ I think I'll have a ham omelette.

5. ◻ Which is the healthiest diet in the world?
   ○ Well, the Spanish diet is one of the healthiest.

12 A The past tense form of regular verbs ends in '-d' or '-ed'.
This can be pronounced in three different ways.
Listen to these examples and notice the differences.

liked   lived   started

12 B Where do these words go? Fill in. Then listen and check.

> moved   rained   visited   stayed   played
> watched   stopped   wanted   studied
> decided   ordered

liked	lived	started
_____	_____	_____
_____	_____	_____
_____	_____	_____
_____	_____	_____
_____	_____	_____

An unusual place for lunch

Last summer I was on holiday in Scotland with my family. It was a beautiful sunny day and we decided to take a day trip to *Loch Ness*. Of course, the children were interested in the Loch Ness *Monster*. Our first stop was the Tourist Information Office near Inverness.
- Where's the best place to see Loch Ness, please?
- Well, there's a little village called Dores; they've got a beach and a nice pub there. Oh, and a boy saw *Nessie* there just last year. It's a good place to look.
- Oh! Well, thank you.

I was surprised – and shocked.
- Mom, did she really say someone saw the monster?
- Well, yes, she did, but I'm not sure …
- *Hurry*, mom, let's go! This is exciting!

We arrived in Dores at lunchtime and stopped at the pub. I saw people outside having lunch; they all had large cameras and were ready for the Loch Ness Monster!

We were very hungry so we ordered our meals quickly: Scottish *salmon* with some brown bread and a salad for my husband, a cheese omelette for me, a salad for my daughter and chicken and chips for my son. We listened to a local man telling stories about Nessie to the tourists. We enjoyed our lunch but we couldn't take our eyes *off* the *calm* Loch Ness.

After lunch we decided to go swimming. The *water* was very cold.

Then we saw a caravan on the beach. An ice cream shop? We walked over and saw a man with a large camera and a table with some *hand-made* Loch Ness Monsters. The man's name was Steve; he told us that he wanted to take a good picture of Nessie and that's why he lived on the beach in this old caravan, waiting for the monster.

We bought a souvenir of the Loch Ness Monster and walked back to the car.
- Do you believe in Nessie now, mom?
- Well, who knows, maybe there **is** something in there.

Im aufgeklärten 21. Jahrhundert gibt es kaum noch etwas, das nicht erklärt werden kann. Allerdings gehören Ungeheuer normalerweise in den Bereich der Phantasie. Nessie, das Ungeheuer von Loch Ness, scheint eine Ausnahme zu sein: Viele Menschen – nicht nur in Schottland – sind von seiner Existenz überzeugt.

Loch Ness – (See in Schottland)
monster – Ungeheuer
Nessie – (Spitzname des Ungeheuers von Loch Ness)
Hurry! – Beeile dich!
salmon – Lachs
off – weg von
calm – ruhig
water – Wasser
hand-made – handgemacht

13 language checklist

Sie können jetzt:

Wendungen

gute Wünsche äußern
Enjoy (your meal).

sich entschuldigen
(Oh,) I'm sorry.

Zeit gewinnen
Let's see.
One moment, please.

etwas anbieten
Let me (buy you a drink).
It's my turn.
It's my round.

eine Bitte äußern
Can we (have the menu), please?

auf eine Bitte reagieren
Certainly.

etwas bestellen
We'd like (two soups).

über typische Dinge sprechen
(These foods are) typical of (northern Europe).

etwas feststellen
(The Spaniards now eat) more and more (red meat).

etwas höflich übergeben
There you are.

Grammatik

- Verstärkende oder abschwächende Umstandswörter: *especially, not so*
  → S. 157: VIIIe

"I like to think of myself as a tourist trap."

trap – Falle

UNIT 14

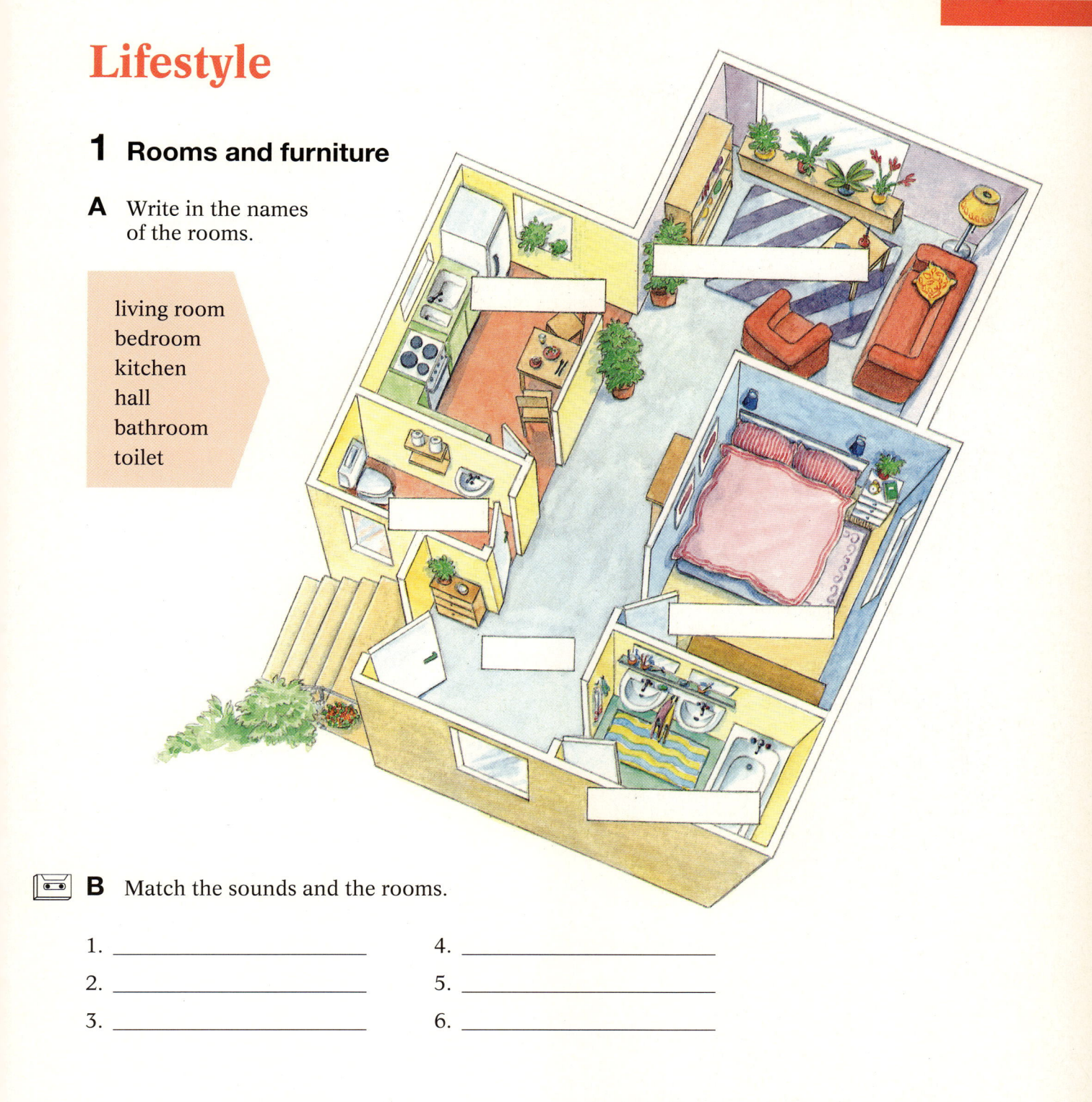

Lifestyle

1 Rooms and furniture

A Write in the names of the rooms.

> living room
> bedroom
> kitchen
> hall
> bathroom
> toilet

B Match the sounds and the rooms.

1. _____
2. _____
3. _____
4. _____
5. _____
6. _____

C How many clocks have you got at home? Where are they?

MEMO PAD

Eßecke = dining area

14

2 Moving

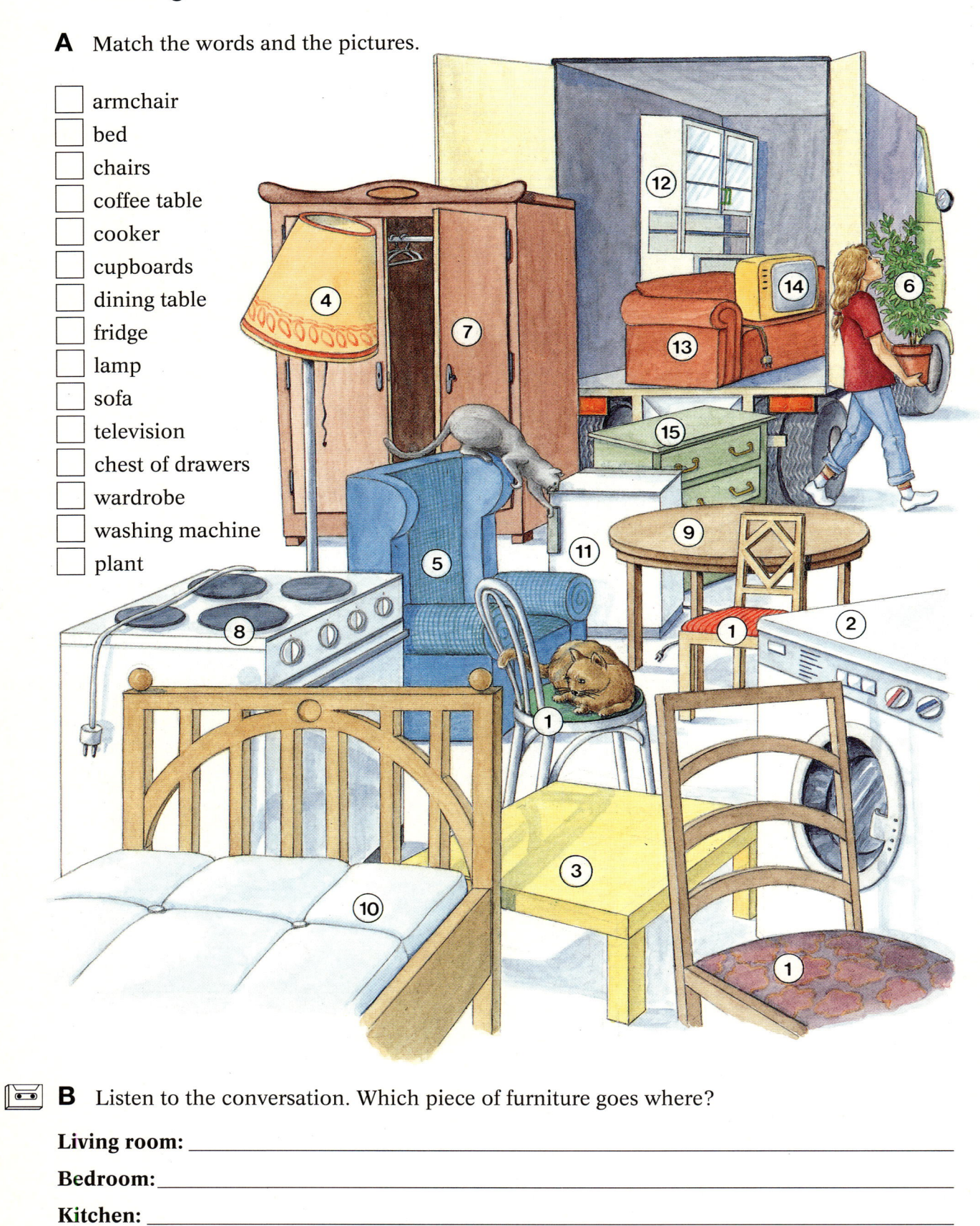

A Match the words and the pictures.

- [ ] armchair
- [ ] bed
- [ ] chairs
- [ ] coffee table
- [ ] cooker
- [ ] cupboards
- [ ] dining table
- [ ] fridge
- [ ] lamp
- [ ] sofa
- [ ] television
- [ ] chest of drawers
- [ ] wardrobe
- [ ] washing machine
- [ ] plant

B Listen to the conversation. Which piece of furniture goes where?

Living room: _____

Bedroom: _____

Kitchen: _____

120   one hundred and twenty

3 Where is it?

Look at these pictures and fill in the sentences.

in front of — behind — next to — between — on — opposite

1. The sofa was __opposite__ the window but now it is _____ the window.
2. The coffee table was _____ the sofa but now it is _____ the sofa and the armchair.
3. The plant was _____ the door but now it is _____ the coffee table.
4. The dining table was _____ the window but now it is _____ the window.
5. The TV was _____ the dining table but now it is _____ the armchair.
6. The lamp was _____ the television but now it is _____ the dining table.

4 Home sweet home

Now talk about this cartoon.

"Dammit, Teresa – not again!"

5 Life here is more interesting

A Read this text.

Another interview in our series "FOREIGNERS IN GERMANY"

We talked with John Wood and Moira Wardlaw. John and Moira both live in Stuttgart now. John comes from Toronto, the largest city in Canada. Moira used to live in Moffat, a small village in the south of Scotland.

B How do you think these two people compare their lives in Stuttgart to their home towns? Make comparisons for both John and Moira.

John
Toronto: more exciting
Stuttgart: cheaper

Moira
Moffat: quieter
Stuttgart: more interesting

C Now read the newspaper interview and compare it with your notes. How many of your guesses were correct?

Interviewer: When did you come to Stuttgart, John?
John: About 15 years ago.
Interv.: What about you, Moira?
Moira: I came here two years ago.
Interv.: And how do you like it here?
Moira: It was a big change for me. Moffat's a very small place and there isn't much to do. It's more interesting here: I can go to the theatre and the opera, look at the shops ... in Scotland it took two hours just to get to the nearest town.
Interv.: What about you, John? Living here's probably very different for you, isn't it?
John: Right. Toronto's a large city. The population's about three million and there are hundreds of cinemas, clubs and places to eat. Stuttgart's smaller and quieter. I found it a bit boring at first.

Interv.: Was it difficult to find a flat?
John: Well, it was easier then than it is now, but I was lucky: I found one in an old villa near the woods. It was nicer than my last place in Canada; that was on the 43rd floor of an apartment building!
Moira: I had a house in Moffat. They're cheaper in Scotland than they are here. Now I live in a small flat in the city centre; it's very expensive.
Interv.: What do you miss most here, Moira?
Moira: Oh, my family and friends, of course, and the quiet country life. It's much noisier here in Stuttgart. My flat's near a busy road and I can hear the traffic all night. The air's better in Moffat, too.
John: Yes, the air's not very good in Stuttgart, but I don't find it noisy after Toronto. Life's slower and more old-fashioned here. Sometimes it's too quiet for me. I miss the excitement of a big city.

D Read the text again and underline the comparative forms.

E Complete.

large	larger		noisy	noisier
nice	_____		quiet	_____
small	_____		busy	_____
cheap	_____		easy	_____
old-fashioned	more old-fashioned		good	better
exciting	_____		bad	worse
interesting	_____			

6 A tale of two towns

Compare two towns you know. Find five differences.

7 Art

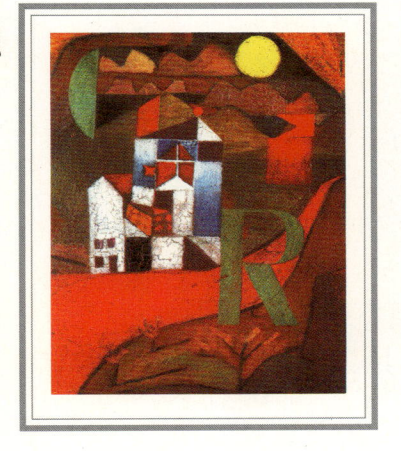

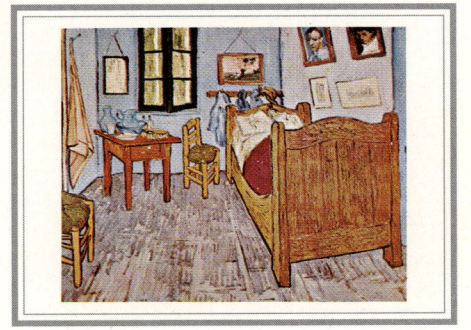

A Compare two of the paintings.

nicer   better
more attractive   more modern
more colourful   more exciting
more romantic   worse
more interesting
more old-fashioned

MEMO PAD

realistic
→ more realistic

B Choose a painting for your classroom.

14

8 Draw a room

Think of a room that is important to you. Describe it to your partner. Your partner draws it. Check the drawing.

9 The Key of the Kingdom

This is the Key of the Kingdom:
In that Kingdom there is a town;
In that town there is a street;
In that street there is a garden;
In that garden there is a house;
In that house there is a room;
In that room an empty bed;
And on the bed a basket -
A basket of sweet flowers:
    Of flowers, of flowers;
    A basket of sweet flowers.

Flowers in a basket;
Basket on the _____;
Bed in the _____;
Room in the _____;
House in the _____;
Garden in the _____;
Street in the _____;
Town in the _____ –
This is the Key of the Kingdom,
    Of the Kingdom this is the Key.

10 Things that make you feel good

Find ten items in this unit that make you feel good.

11 PRONUNCIATION

A Look at these words. Listen to the different sounds.

televi<u>s</u>ion   fri<u>dg</u>e

B Put these words in the correct list.

page   Germany   usually   language
June   leisure   geography

televi<u>s</u>ion   fri<u>dg</u>e

_____   _____
_____   _____
_____   _____
_____   _____
_____   _____

C Listen and check.

D Practise.

12 In this unit, find:

1. a preposition containing the sound of the letter 'E'. _____
2. a piece of furniture containing the sound of the letter 'O'. _____
3. a piece of furniture containing the sound of the letter 'R'. _____
4. a part of a house or flat containing the sound of the word 'or'. _____
5. an adjective containing the sound of the letter 'O'. _____
6. three prepositions containing the same vowel sound. _____
_____

The simple life or the rat race?

Graham: Country life! I used to live in London. There's nothing – absolutely nothing to do here in Wales. It's boring!

Rose: Look around you! Enjoy the countryside. The mountains are beautiful! It's spring and the fields are full of wild flowers.

Graham: It's OK for a weekend or a short holiday, but … Well, I *miss* the different restaurants, the theatres, the busy streets, the big shops and all the people.

Rose: I don't. I like the simple life. I enjoy life in a small village. I think it's nice to know all your neighbours.

Graham: Yes, but I **don't** know my neighbours.

Rose: Well, that's why I invited you to get to know some of the neighbours! But you could also go to one of the church activities or help at the *charity shop*.

Graham: I usually don't go to church. But that's an idea, I could work at the charity shop in the village.

Joe: I love country life, especially the *peace and quiet*. The *stars* are beautiful at night.

Rose: That's right. The city's noisy, dirty and everything's expensive. A small flat really costs a lot!

Joe: Yes, my wife and I both had full-time jobs, but we couldn't pay the bills **and** go on holiday. Now my wife only works part-time and we can still go on holiday abroad.

Rose: Right, I work from home and I have lots of time to spend with my children. And, of course, the countryside's wonderful for them.

Joe: It's safer, cleaner and healthier. They can play outside all day.

Graham: True.

Rose: We wanted to be *self-sufficient*, so we built our own house. We have our own vegetable garden and some chickens. Most of our food is fresh. I don't buy much at the shop.

Joe: That's a lot of hard work! I was happy to get out of the rat race – getting up at 5 a.m., travelling 2 hours to work, 8 to 10 hours at the office and then 2 hours to get home. I was too tired to enjoy life. We have less *money* now, but I'm happier here.

Rose: I am, too. We live in a beautiful place, we have good friends and lots of time to spend with the family.

Joe: What more could you want?

Graham: I understand why you're happy, but I still miss the *choice* you have in the city – the chance to eat and see and do different things. …

---

rat race – erbarmungsloser Konkurrenzkampf
miss – vermissen
charity shop – Laden einer karitativen Organisation
peace and quiet – Ruhe und Frieden
stars – Sterne
self-sufficient – selbständig
money – Geld
choice – Wahl

In Großbritannien gibt es viele Läden von karitativen Organisationen *(charity shops)*. In diesen Läden werden gespendete Gebrauchtwaren verkauft; die Einnahmen kommen der karitativen Organisation zugute. Selbst in kleinen Orten gibt es diese Läden, die gebrauchte Bücher, Bekleidung und anderes verkaufen.

language checklist 14

Sie können jetzt:

Wendungen

etwas vergleichen
(Toronto is) more exciting.
(Stuttgart is) cheaper.

Eindrücke beschreiben
I found it (a bit boring) at first.

sagen, was Ihnen gut tut
(The quiet country life) makes me feel good.

Grammatik

- Steigerung der Eigenschaftswörter (Komparativ): *nicer/bigger; easier/happier; more modern; more expensive/interesting; better, worse* → S. 155: VII
- Umstandsbestimmungen des Ortes: *behind, in front of, on, between* → S. 156: VIIIc

"This is our first TV-dinner party."

UNIT 15

Europeans

1 European names

A What can you guess about these European names? Complete the table.

Names	Country of origin	First name	Family name	Male	Female
1. Penelope					
2. O'Brian					
3. Llewellyn					
4. Lesley					
5. Oquendo					
6. MacDonald					
7. April					
8. István					

"Perhaps it's Greek."

"That could be a man's name."

"That's probably a family name."

"That must be a Spanish name."

"I'm sure that's Scottish."

"Yes, perhaps."

"I think you're right."

"Are you sure?"

"No, I don't think so."

"I'm not sure."

B Check your answers in File 25.

2 What's in a name?

A Interview your partner.

1. Do you know where your family name comes from?
2. How many names have you got?
3. Have you got a nickname?
4. Do you like your names?
5. Do you know what your name means?

B Report.

"She's got three names."

"She doesn't know where her name comes from."

"He says he doesn't like his family name."

"He says his name means ..."

C How many English words can you make from the letters of your name?

GEOFF TRANTER
tea great off for
far eat near
free are

3 Nationalities

A Listen and make notes.

	1	2	3	4
He/She was born in …	Hamburg			
He/She grew up in …				
He/She speaks …				
He/She lives in …				
Her/His passport is …				
Her/His parents are/were …				
He/She feels she is …				

B Compare.

4 I know someone who was born outside Europe

A Tick the boxes. Do you know anyone …

- ☐ … who was born outside Europe?
- ☐ … who grew up abroad?
- ☐ … whose parents were born abroad?
- ☐ … who speaks two or more languages?
- ☐ … who has got two passports?
- ☐ … whose name is of foreign origin?
- ☐ … who used to live abroad?
- ☐ … whose car was made abroad?

B Compare and report.

"Helmut knows someone who speaks seven languages."

"Inge knows three people who grew up abroad."

"Christel doesn't know anyone whose parents were born abroad."

5 Famous characters

A Who are they? Read the texts and write in the names.

1. I was born in about 1210 in Yorkshire. I don't know the date for certain.
My friends and I lived in a forest near Nottingham and helped poor people. I never married but I had a girlfriend. There are many stories about me which are still very popular today.

   Who am I?

   _____

2. I was born in about 74 B.C. and I lived in a little village in northwestern France. My friends and I fought against Julius Caesar and his Roman army.
Napoleon, Joan of Arc and I are France's most popular heroes.

   Who am I?

   _____

3. They say I'm 118 but I don't feel so old. When I woke up this morning there was a young man in my room. The room was dirty and the window was full of wild roses.

   Who am I?

   _____

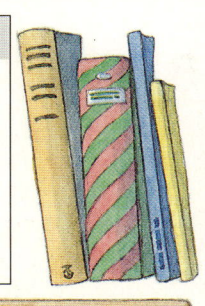

4. My father's a sailor, so he's away most of the time. I live alone in the house and I only go to school when I want to. I've got red hair and I'm a very strong girl!

   Who am I?

   _____

B Compare.

15

6 Who were you?

One of you writes down the name of a historical person.
(Don't show it to the others!) The others try to guess who you were.
Each person asks a question in turn. You can only answer with 'Yes' or 'No'.
Use questions like these:

1. Were you European?
2. Were you born in this century?
3. Did you live in Germany?
4. Were you a woman?
5. Were you a nice person?
6. Were you successful?
7. Were you rich?
8. Did you help people?
9. Did you travel a lot?
10. Did you die young?
11. Were you a politician?
12. Did you die naturally?

7 Review

How many words in this unit begin with the first letter of your name? Can you put them into different categories?

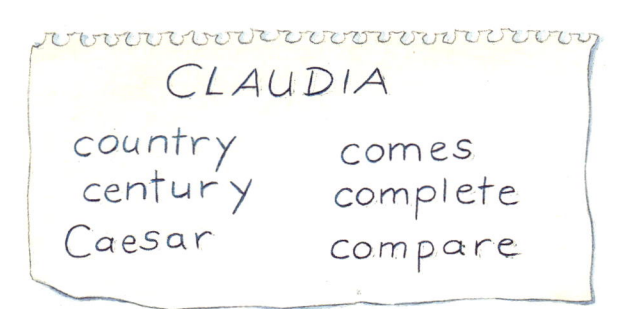

CLAUDIA
country   comes
century   complete
Caesar   compare

PRONUNCIATION

8 Practise saying this poem.

There's Dick and Diana
And Sally and Sam
And friends like Joanna
And Peter and Pam

There's Christopher, Cathy
And Mary and Mike
There's all of my family
And others I like

There's Mark and there's Mandy
And all of the rest
But only one Sandy
The one I like best!

9
Write down groups of four to five words or phrases from the book which have something in common in their pronunciation. The others guess what the 'something' is.

magazine 15

A do-it-yourself love song for EUROPE

Complete the song using the words below or using your own words.
Have fun writing your own song!

We first met …
in the London underground   at midnight.
at the Spanish supermarket   in November.
in a café in Paris   late one afternoon.
under the table in an Italian restaurant   on Christmas Day.

I can still remember …
your exotic eyes and the timetable in your hand.
the spicy sausage in your basket.
the romantic song on the radio and the rose.
the warm, windy weather.

You said …
Do you play chess?
I love winter because it's often foggy.
Thank goodness, the coffee is hot.
Excuse me, I'm never late for work.

I answered …
Yes, a little.
Let's go out for a drink.
Sorry, I don't speak English very well.
Let's go then.

You didn't …
like my Celtic cooking.
discuss Danish dances with me after work.
understand my jokes or my love letters.
put garlic in the seafood salad.

But I didn't care. We used to …
read books about bridges all night.
play bingo in the spring.
swim in the sea at sunset.
visit Czech churches on holiday.

But when we had … together,   **I knew …**
French fish   you would learn to spell my name.
Swedish soup   we would always speak English together.
Belgian bread   you would never listen to your friends again.
Polish potatoes   life would really be more interesting.

15 language checklist

Sie können jetzt:

Wendungen

benennen/definieren
… someone who (speaks seven languages).

berichten
He says (his name means …).

widersprechen
No, I don't think so.

zustimmen
I think you're right.

Gewißheit ausdrücken
That must be (a Spanish name).
I'm sure (that's Scottish).

Ungewißheit/Möglichkeit ausdrücken
Perhaps (it's Greek).
(That) could be (a man's name).
(That's) probably (a family name).
Are you sure?

Grammatik

- Bezügliche Fürwörter: *who, whose* → S. 152: IVd
- Unbestimmte Fürwörter: *someone, anyone* → S. 152: IVe
- Jahreszahlen: *twelve ten, seventy-four B.C.* → S. 154: VId
- Indirekte Rede: *he says …* → S. 158: IXc

sniff – beschnuppern
lampposts – Laternenpfähle

PREVIEW E

1 The bookworm game

Look at File 19.

one hundred and thirty-one 131

PREVIEW E

2 Course magazine

Look at File 34.

See you later, alligator.

FILES

File 1 (UNIT 1, Step 4C, p. 12)

Sie gehen mit Ihrer Partnerin/Ihrem Partner auf eine Party. Stellen Sie Ihre/n Partner/in anderen Gästen vor. Es wird etwas Musik gespielt. Jedesmal, wenn die Musik unterbrochen wird, wechseln Sie Ihre/n Partner/in.

File 2 (UNIT 1, Step 10, p. 17)

Schreiben Sie Wörter oder Wendungen für Begrüßungen und Verabschiedungen einzeln auf Karten. Mischen Sie die Karten und legen Sie sie verdeckt auf den Tisch. Der Reihe nach ziehen alle eine Karte und lesen sie vor. Der Tischnachbar/die Tischnachbarin muß entsprechend reagieren.

File 3 (UNIT 2, Step 1B, p. 19)

In diesem Spiel geht es darum, eine Zeichnung zu vervollständigen, indem man die Punkte in der richtigen Reihenfolge mit Strichen verbindet. Die Punkte sind durch Buchstaben gekennzeichnet. Damit Ihr/e Partner/in seine/ihre Zeichnung nachzeichnen kann, müssen Sie die Buchstabenreihenfolge „diktieren".
Damit Sie Ihre Zeichnung vervollständigen können, brauchen Sie die entsprechenden Informationen von Ihrer Partnerin/Ihrem Partner.
Sie fangen an zu diktieren:

z, g, e, s, p, a, m, y, f, l, r, x, j,
o, n, d, b, t, h, c, v, q, i, k, w, u

File 4 (UNIT 4, Step 4, p. 40)

a) In Ihrem Adreßbuch sind einige Lücken. Sie telefonieren mit Ihrem Partner/Ihrer Partnerin und fragen nach den fehlenden Informationen.

b) Jetzt ruft Ihr/e Partner/in Sie an, und Sie geben die gewünschten Informationen.

Name	Glasgow Tourist Board
Address	35/39 St. Vincent Place Glasgow
Post code	G1 2ER
Phone	041 204 4480

Name	S. and H. Jones
Address	135 Wilton Street Cambridge
Post code	CB2 2RU
Phone	

Name	Penny and Gareth Steel
Address	_____ London
Post code	_____
Phone	_____

Name	K. and R. Williams
Address	_____ Bristol
Post code	_____
Phone	0272 702906

c) Kontrollieren Sie Ihre Ergebnisse zusammen mit Ihrem Partner/Ihrer Partnerin.

F

File 5 (UNIT 2, Step 1B, p. 19)

In diesem Spiel geht es darum, eine Zeichnung zu vervollständigen, indem man die Punkte in der richtigen Reihenfolge mit Strichen verbindet. Die Punkte sind durch Buchstaben gekennzeichnet. Damit Ihr/e Partner/in seine/ihre Zeichnung nachzeichnen kann, müssen Sie die Buchstabenreihenfolge „diktieren":

l, t, j, o, e, y, i, a, n, s, c, g, m,
u, p, f, b, k, d, h, q, w, r, z, v, x

Damit Sie Ihre Zeichnung vervollständigen können, brauchen Sie die entsprechenden Informationen von Ihrer Partnerin/Ihrem Partner.
Ihr/e Partner/in fängt an zu diktieren.

File 6 (PREWIEW A, Step 1, p. 33)

Sie brauchen 20 kleine Karteikarten oder entsprechend zugeschnittenen Karton. Gespielt wird in Gruppen von 3 – 4 Personen. Auf die Karten zeichnen oder schreiben Sie etwas aus den ersten 3 Units, z.B. ein Hobby, eine Begrüßung etc. Die Karten werden gemischt und in einem Stapel verdeckt auf den Tisch gelegt.
Alle Spieler/innen ziehen der Reihe nach eine Karte und sagen etwas dazu: ein Wort, einen Satz, eine Erwiderung.
Sind die anderen einverstanden, darf man die Karte behalten.

File 7 (UNIT 4, Step 4, p. 40)

a) Ihr/e Partner/in ruft Sie an und bittet Sie um Informationen, um sein/ihr Adreßbuch zu vervollständigen.

b) Nun rufen Sie Ihre/n Partner/in an und erfragen die Ihnen fehlenden Angaben.

Name	Glasgow Tourist Board
Address	
	Glasgow
Post code	
Phone	

Name	S. and H. Jones
Address	
	Cambridge
Post Code	
Phone	0223 663553

Name	Penny and Gareth Steel
Address	5 Dartmouth Road
	London
Post code	SE10 8AX
Phone	081 6929744

Name	K. and R. Williams
Address	180 Gower Road
	Bristol
Post code	BS6 6HX
Phone	

c) Kontrollieren Sie Ihre Ergebnisse zusammen mit Ihrem Partner/Ihrer Partnerin.

File 8 (Unit 4, Step 5D, p. 41)

Bei diesem Spiel in der Runde geht es darum, einen angefangenen Satz weiterzuführen. Eine Person fängt an, indem sie das erste Wort vorgibt. Die nächste Person nennt ein zweites Wort, das den Satz weiterführt. Verloren hat, wer den Satz nicht mehr weiterführen kann.

File 9 (Unit 5, Step 5B, p. 49)

A Railway Station

WAY IN.
WAY OUT.
Where am I?
A railway station?
Travel?
But where to?
What for?
No, thank you.
Not today.
So the way out.
But where to?

L. L. Szkutnik

File 10 (Preview B, Step 1B, p. 62)

a) Sie haben die folgenden Informationen über ein Londoner Hotel. Beantworten Sie die Fragen Ihrer Partnerin/Ihres Partners.

OLD PARK HOTEL
192 Regent Street, London W1H 8DD
Telephone 071- 604 9233

- 18 single rooms (£ 85)
- 37 double rooms (£ 120 - 175)
- Breakfast 6.30 - 10 a.m.
- Full English or Continental breakfast
- Restaurant open 12.15 a.m.- 2 p.m. & 7 - 11.30 p.m.
- Colour TV in all rooms
- 5 minutes from Piccadilly Circus

b) Ihre Partnerin/Ihr Partner hat Informationen über ein anderes Hotel. Erfragen Sie folgendes:

- Name des Hotels
- Adresse
- Telefonnummer
- Preis für Doppelzimmer
- Öffnungszeiten des Restaurants
- Ruhige Lage?

File 11 (Unit 5, Step 9A, p. 52)

Sie sind in einem Reisebüro in Oslo und möchten am nächsten Freitagmorgen von Oslo nach Düsseldorf fliegen. Erfragen Sie die folgenden Informationen und machen Sie sich Notizen.

Flight leaves at _____
Flight arrives at _____

File 12 (Unit 5, Step 9B, p. 52)

Sie sind in Norwegen und möchten am Samstagabend von Oslo nach Hamburg fliegen. Rufen Sie in Oslo in einem Reisebüro an und erfragen Sie die folgenden Informationen.

Flight leaves at _____
Flight arrives at _____

File 13 (Preview C, Step 2, p. 86)

Ihre Kursleiterin/Ihr Kursleiter verteilt die Kartenspiele. Das Spiel wird in Gruppen von jeweils 3 – 4 Personen gespielt. Jede Gruppe braucht ein Kartenspiel. Die Karten liegen verdeckt auf dem Tisch.

Der Reihe nach ziehen alle die oberste Karte und schlagen zu diesem Bild mindestens einen passenden englischen Satz vor. Wer einen inhaltlich passenden und sprachlich richtigen Satz gebildet hat, bekommt einen Punkt und darf weitere Sätze versuchen. Ist der Satz nicht passend oder sprachlich nicht richtig, kann eine andere Person den Punkt bekommen, wenn sie einen richtigen Satz vorschlägt.

So wird der Reihe nach gespielt, bis alle Karten durchgenommen sind. Wer am Ende die meisten Punkte hat, hat gewonnen.

F

File 14   (Unit 5, Step 9A, p. 52)

Sie arbeiten in einem Osloer Reisebüro. Ein/e Tourist/in möchte Auskunft über Flugzeiten von Oslo nach Düsseldorf.

Oslo →	Düsseldorf	
Flights	Departure	Arrival
Mo-Fri	08.35	10.35
daily	15.30	18.15

File 15   (Preview B, Step 1B, p. 62)

a) Ihre Partnerin/Ihr Partner hat Informationen über ein Hotel in London. Erfragen Sie folgendes:

- Name des Hotels
- Adresse
- Telefonnummer
- Preis für ein Einzelzimmer
- Frühstückszeiten
- Zentrumsnahe Lage?

b) Nun beantworten Sie die Fragen Ihres Partners/Ihrer Partnerin.

NELSON HOTEL   N

18 Wigmore Street, London W1G 3JP
Telephone 071- 885 6061

- Single rooms £72 - 90
- Double rooms £145 -185
- Continental breakfast
- Restaurant 7.30 -11 p.m.
- 24-hour room service
- Very quiet
- Near Victoria Station

File 16   (Unit 9, Step 4D, p. 82)

Jemand aus der Gruppe denkt sich einen Beruf aus. Eine andere Person aus der Gruppe fängt an zu fragen. Bei *Yes* darf sie weiterfragen, bei *No* stellt die nächste Person eine Frage. Dies wird so lange fortgesetzt, bis der Beruf richtig geraten wurde.

File 17   (Unit 5, Step 9B, p. 52)

Sie arbeiten in einem Osloer Reisebüro. Ein/e Tourist/in ruft Sie an und möchte Auskunft über Flugzeiten von Oslo nach Hamburg.

Oslo →	Hamburg	
Flights	Departure	Arrival
Mo-Fri	09.55	11.50
daily	18.50	20.15

File 18   (Unit 12, Step 2, p. 102)

33 per cent do absolutely nothing for three hours a week.
43 per cent spend no time on exercise.
7 per cent watch television for 11 hours a day or more.
Only 12 per cent read for 10 hours a week or more.
More than eight million cats and dogs watch television.
50 per cent of British people could not live happily without a television, 66 per cent without radio.
More than two million make love in front of the television.

File 19   (Preview E, Step 1, p. 131)

Arbeiten Sie in Paaren. Es spielen jeweils 2 oder 3 Paare gegeneinander, die der Reihe nach würfeln. Wenn ein Paar z.B. eine 3 würfelt, rückt es zunächst 3 Felder vor und muß einen Dialog bilden, der in irgendeiner Verbindung zu dem Bild auf diesem Feld steht.

Wenn die Gegner mit dem Dialog einverstanden sind, bleibt das Paar dort, wenn nicht, dann muß es auf das Feld zurück, das es zuletzt besetzt hatte. Wenn in Ihrem Dialog eine Vergangenheitsform vorkommt, dürfen Sie um ein Feld vorrücken.

Gewonnen hat das Paar, das als erstes das Ziel erreicht.

F

File 20

(UNIT 8, Step 3, p. 73)

a) Auf Ihrem Stadtplan fehlen einige Angaben.
   Fragen Sie Ihre/n Partner/in nach:

   - DC Supermarket
   - Blue Moon Pub
   - LP Garage
   - Black Bridge Pub
   - newsagent's
   - post office
   - museum

   Vervollständigen Sie Ihren Stadtplan und vergleichen Sie ihn mit Ihrer Partnerin/Ihrem Partner.

b) Jetzt geben Sie Ihrer Partnerin/Ihrem Partner die gewünschten Informationen für ihren/seinen Stadtplan.

File 21   (UNIT 13, Step 9, p. 117)

In diesem Spiel geht es darum, 10 Aufgaben zum Thema Essen und Trinken zu lösen, die Ihnen Ihr/e Partner/in stellt.
Für jede Lösung können Sie maximal 3 Punkte erhalten.

Wechseln Sie sich mit dem Fragen ab. Sie beginnen.

1. What's your favourite restaurant, and why?
2. Name three vegetables.
3. What time do you usually have lunch?
4. When was the last time you went to a restaurant? What did you have?
5. Name three items of food you associate with Spain.
6. Name three items of food you associate with summer.
7. Name a dish you don't like, and say why.
8. What do you say before you start to eat?
9. You want to order food in a restaurant. What do you say to the waiter?
10. What are the three most important items of food in your kitchen?

F

File 22

(UNIT 8, Step 3, p. 73)

a) Geben Sie Ihrer Partnerin/Ihrem Partner die gewünschten Angaben zum Stadtplan.

b) Jetzt fragen Sie Ihre/n Partner/in nach den folgenden auf Ihrem Stadtplan fehlenden Angaben:

- AC Supermarket
- bookshop
- Good Food Café
- Midland Bank
- Victoria Hotel
- Welcome Inn Restaurant
- St. John's Church

Vervollständigen Sie Ihren Stadtplan und vergleichen Sie ihn mit Ihrer Partnerin/Ihrem Partner.

File 23   (UNIT 13, Step 9, p. 117)

In diesem Spiel geht es darum, 10 Aufgaben zum Thema Essen und Trinken zu lösen, die Ihnen Ihr/e Partner/in stellt.
Für jede Lösung können Sie maximal 3 Punkte erhalten.

Wechseln Sie sich mit dem Fragen ab. Ihr/e Partner/in beginnt.

1. Name three things that make a good restaurant.
2. Name three types of fruit.
3. What do you usually have for dinner?
4. When was the last time you went shopping for food? What did you buy?
5. Name three items of food or drink you associate with Italy.
6. Name three items of food you associate with winter.
7. What was your favourite food when you were a child?
8. You want to pay at the end of a meal. What do you say to the waiter?
9. You're in a pub with some friends. What do say when you want to buy the drinks?
10. Name three food items you always have in your fridge.

File 24

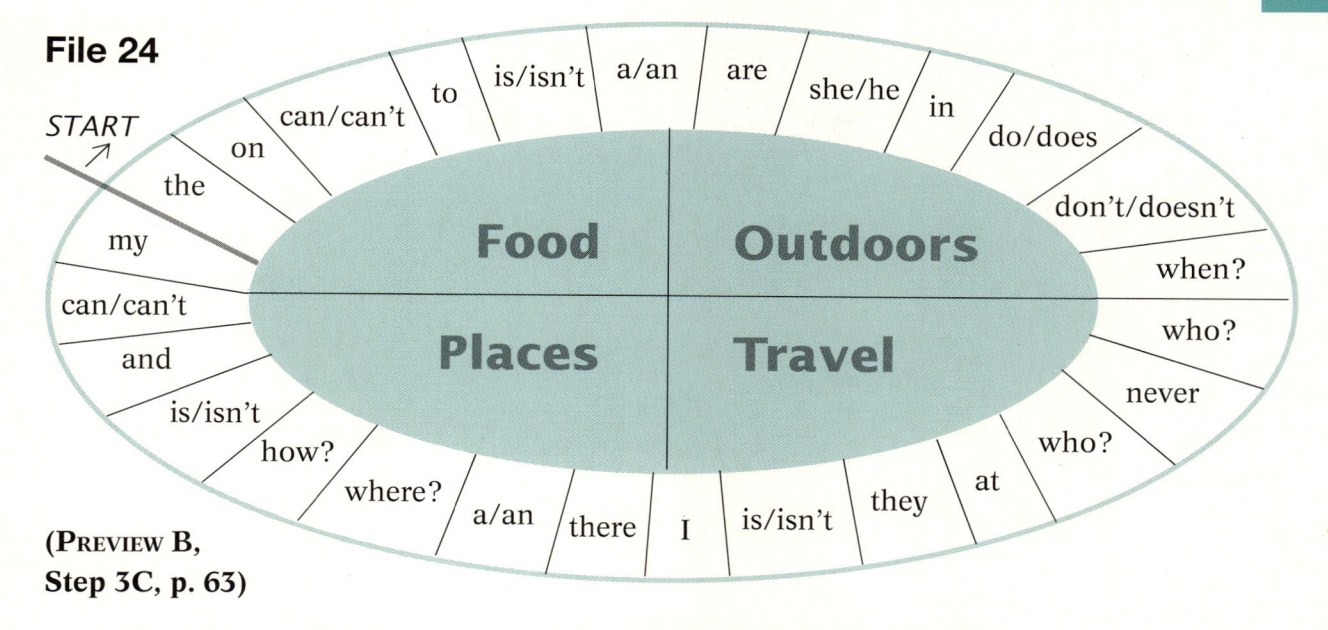

(PREVIEW B, Step 3C, p. 63)

Board (clockwise from START): the, on, can/can't, to, is/isn't, a/an, are, she/he, in, do/does, don't/doesn't, when?, who?, never, who?, at, they, is/isn't, I, there, a/an, where?, how?, is/isn't, and, can/can't, my

Centre quadrants: Food | Outdoors | Places | Travel

Gespielt wird in Dreiergruppen mit je einem Würfel und einer Spielfigur, z.B. einer Münze. Der Spielanfang ist oben links bei START.

Alle würfeln und ziehen der Reihe nach entsprechend der Punktzahl im Uhrzeigersinn um das Spielfeld. Nach jedem Wurf notieren die Spieler/innen die Wörter der Felder, auf denen sie gelandet sind.

Wenn alle sechsmal gewürfelt haben, versuchen alle einzeln aus den sechs aufgeschriebenen Wörtern einen oder zwei korrekte und sinnvolle Sätze zu bilden. Dabei kann man zusätzliche Wörter aus den in 3A erstellten Wortlisten dazunehmen. Hat man ein Wort, mit dem man nichts anfangen kann, darf man versuchen, mit einem/einer anderen Spieler/in zu tauschen. Jedes Wort kann auch zweimal benutzt werden.

Beispiel: I / to / isn't / a / the / can't
I can't go to the supermarket. There isn't a bus.

Gewonnen hat, wer keine Fehler gemacht und so wenig zusätzliche Wörter wie möglich benutzt hat.

File 25

(UNIT 15, Step 1B, p. 126)

Names	Country of origin	First name	Family name	Male	Female
1. Penelope	Greece	X			X
2. O'Brian	Ireland		X		
3. Llewellyn	Wales		X		
4. Lesley	England	X		X	X
5. Oquendo	Spain		X		
6. MacDonald	Scotland		X		
7. April	England	X			X
8. István	Hungary	X		X	

F

File 26 (UNIT 9, Step 6, p. 83)

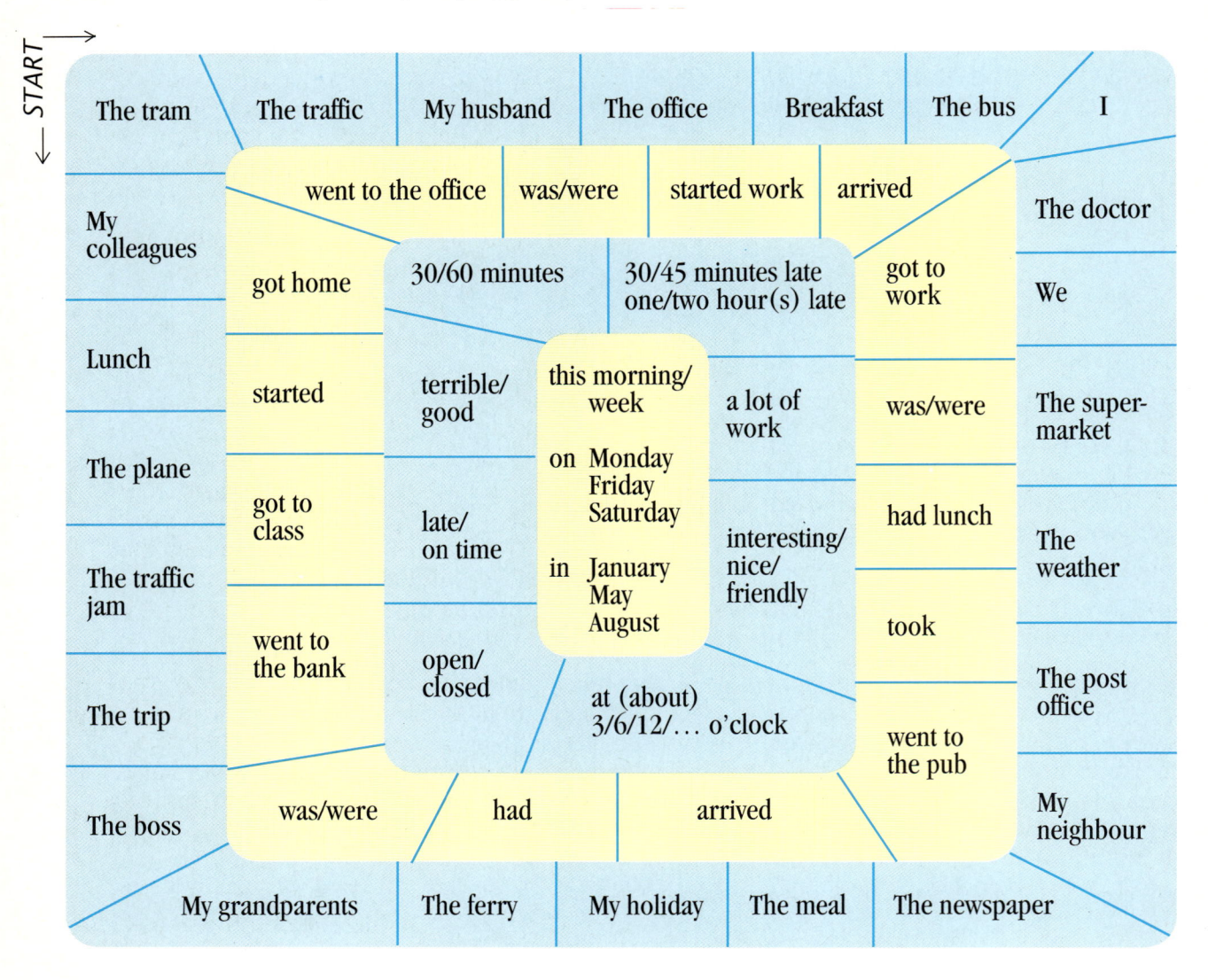

START →

Outer ring (clockwise from top-left): The tram | The traffic | My husband | The office | Breakfast | The bus | I | The doctor | We | The supermarket | The weather | The post office | My neighbour | The newspaper | The meal | My holiday | The ferry | My grandparents | The boss | The trip | The traffic jam | The plane | Lunch | My colleagues

Second ring (clockwise from top): went to the office | was/were | started work | arrived | got to work | was/were | had lunch | took | went to the pub | arrived | had | was/were | went to the bank | got to class | started | got home

Centre:
- 30/60 minutes
- 30/45 minutes late one/two hour(s) late
- a lot of work
- interesting/ nice/ friendly
- at (about) 3/6/12/… o'clock
- this morning/ week; on Monday Friday Saturday; in January May August
- open/ closed
- late/ on time
- terrible/ good

Für dieses Spiel zu zweit brauchen Sie einen Würfel sowie pro Person eine Münze zum Setzen. Fangen Sie bei START an.

Eine/r würfelt, und <u>beide</u> Spieler/innen ziehen gleichzeitig den äußeren Ring entlang *Around the Block*, wobei eine/r im Uhrzeigersinn, die/der andere gegen den Uhrzeigersinn setzt.

Die Aufgabe besteht darin, ausgehend von dem Wort auf dem Feld, auf dem Sie gelandet sind, maximal 3 sinnvolle Sätze zu bilden, wobei Sie das zweite Wort des Satzes aus dem zweiten Ring, das dritte Wort aus dem dritten Ring und das letzte Wort aus der Mitte des Spielfeldes nehmen. Dabei dürfen pro Würfelrunde die Wörter nur jeweils einmal benutzt werden.

Beispiel:

Sie stehen auf dem Feld „My neighbour".

My neighbour …

  … got home late on Friday.
  … had lunch at 12 o'clock on Monday.
  … had a lot of work this week.

Wenn beide ihre Sätze aufgeschrieben haben bzw. keinen Satz mehr finden können, wird erneut gewürfelt.

Nach 4mal Würfeln tauschen Sie zur Kontrolle Ihre Sätze mit Ihrer Mitspielerin/ Ihrem Mitspieler aus. Für jeden richtigen Satz gibt es einen Punkt. Für jeden falschen Satz gibt es einen Punkt Abzug. Gewonnen hat, wer am Schluß die meisten Punkte hat.

File 27 (PREVIEW C, Step 3, p. 86)

Bilden Sie Gruppen mit je 7 Personen. Jede Gruppe schreibt die folgenden 24 Buchstaben auf Blätter (ein Buchstabe pro Blatt):

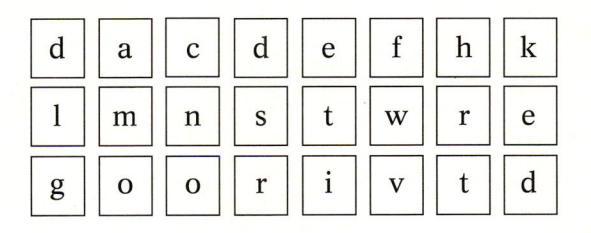

d	a	c	d	e	f	h	k
l	m	n	s	t	w	r	e
g	o	o	r	i	v	t	d

Die Blätter werden nun gleichmäßig auf alle Mitspieler/innen verteilt.

Aufgabe der Gruppe ist es, Vergangenheitsformen englischer Verben zu bilden, indem sich die Mitspieler/innen mit ihren jeweiligen Buchstaben so schnell wie möglich in die richtige Reihenfolge stellen.

Ihr/e Kursleiter/in wird Ihnen jetzt die Gegenwartsform eines englischen Verbs nennen. Alle, die keiner Gruppe angehören, sind Schiedsrichter. Sie müssen entscheiden, welche Gruppe die erste war und ob das Verb richtig buchstabiert wurde.

File 28 (PREVIEW D, Step 3, p. 110)

Arbeiten Sie in Gruppen. Schreiben Sie je 10 Eigenschaftswörter, Hauptwörter und Zeitwörter auf Karten, ein Wort pro Karte. Mischen Sie die Karten und legen Sie sie verdeckt auf den Tisch. Halten Sie dabei die 3 Stapel auseinander.

Ziehen Sie jetzt der Reihe nach jeweils ein Eigenschaftswort, ein Hauptwort und ein Zeitwort, bis Sie zum Schluß 10 Nonsenszeilen haben. Welche der Zeilen gefallen Ihnen am besten?

Stellen Sie aus den gelungensten Zeilen der verschiedenen Gruppen ein langes Gedicht zusammen.

File 29 (UNIT 12, Step 3B, p. 104)

Ireland, Wales and Scotland, share strong Celtic traditions, including a great love of music. This tradition includes singing, dancing and playing instruments such as the fiddle, the Uilleann pipes and the harp, which is the national symbol.

It's easy to find traces of this tradition in Ireland. Just look at the list of events in the Irish Times or the Evening Press under "music session" or "ceól", the Irish word for music.

There are concerts and music festivals but the most Irish of institutions is the fiddler in the pub. The Irish meet in pubs to drink and talk but also to sing and play music together. "Singing pubs" are more than just tourist attractions. People sing because they like singing and others in the pub don't just watch and listen, they sing along or play an Irish ballad.

And what kind of music is Irish folk music? Some ballads are happy, some are sad, some are very fast and others slow. There are love songs, drinking songs, songs about hard work and hard times and, of course, songs against the English.

File 30 (PREVIEW D, Step 1, p. 109)

Gespielt wird in Kleingruppen. Sie benötigen einen Würfel und einen Spielstein pro Person.

Würfeln und setzen Sie der Reihe nach. Landen Sie auf einem gelben Feld, dann stellen Sie eine Frage zu dem angegebenen Thema. Landen Sie auf einem blauen Feld, sagen Sie etwas zu dem Thema.

Wenn Ihr Satz oder Ihre Frage nicht richtig ist (das entscheiden die Mitspieler/innen), müssen Sie auf Ihre vorherige Position zurückgehen.

Gewonnen hat, wer zuerst im Ziel ist.

F

File 31 (PREVIEW C, Step 4, p. 86)

Gespielt wird in Kleingruppen. Schreiben Sie in Ihrer Gruppe 10 Wortpaare nach dem Muster von Seite 86 auf ein Blatt Papier. Schneiden Sie dann das Blatt durch und geben Sie die eine Hälfte der Wortpaare einer anderen Gruppe. Sie wiederum erhalten von dieser Gruppe eine Liste mit deren Wörtern. Bilden Sie nun Paare mit den erhaltenen Wörtern. Vergleichen Sie am Ende die Ergebnisse mit den Ausgangslisten.

File 32 (PREVIEW D, Step 2, p. 110)

Sammeln Sie aus den vorangehenden Units so viele Verben wie möglich und schreiben Sie sie an die Tafel. Die Verben werden verteilt, ein Verb pro Teilnehmer/in.

Jetzt wird eine Kettengeschichte erzählt. Alle tragen zur Geschichte bei, indem sie der Reihe nach einen Satz hinzufügen. Dieser Satz muß das zugeteilte Verb in der Vergangenheitsform (!) enthalten.
Ein Beispiel für einen Satzanfang finden Sie auf Seite 110.

File 33 (UNIT 13, Step 3C, p. 113)

a) Schreiben Sie zuerst zusammen eine englische Speisekarte.

b) Spielen Sie nun die folgende Szene: Sie sind mit einer Gruppe von Freunden in einem Restaurant. Eine/r von Ihnen ist die Kellnerin/der Kellner.

   1. Fragen Sie nach der Speisekarte.
   2. Wählen Sie aus, was Sie essen möchten, und sprechen Sie darüber.
   3. Bestellen Sie.
   4. Bitten Sie um die Rechnung.

File 34 (PREVIEW E, Step 2, p. 132)

Sicher haben Sie vieles in Ihrem Englischkurs mit BRIDGES gemacht, was Sie als Anregung oder vielleicht sogar als Material für die Kurszeitschrift übernehmen können, z.B. Texte, Zeichnungen, Wortbilder, Poster.

Vergessen Sie dabei nicht das Practice Book.

Wichtig ist es natürlich, Aufgaben zu verteilen: Es soll nicht jede/r alles machen. Es wäre schön, die Kurszeitschrift in einer Form herzustellen, die sich zum Fotokopieren eignet, damit alle ein eigenes Exemplar als Souvenir bekommen.

GRAMMAR

Einleitung

In diesem Anhang finden Sie eine Zusammenstellung der in BRIDGES 1 NEU enthaltenen Grammatik. Zur besseren Übersicht gibt es ein Inhaltsverzeichnis, mit dessen Hilfe die einzelnen Strukturen gefunden werden können.

Damit erhalten Sie sowohl einen Überblick über die grammatischen Inhalte des Lehrbuchs als auch eine Hilfe für das Lernen und das Wiederholen von Strukturen.

Inhalte

Zur Erleichterung des Umgangs mit dieser Grammatik-Übersicht möchten wir Ihnen vorab ein paar Hinweise zum Aufbau geben:

- Bei allen grammatischen Strukturen in dieser Zusammenstellung handelt es sich um aktive Lerninhalte aus den Units 1 – 15, das heißt Strukturen, die in dem Buch aktiv geübt und angewendet werden. Mit Hilfe der Querverweise lassen sich auch die Units feststellen, in denen die Strukturen erstmals vorkommen.

- Alle grammatischen Strukturen werden in Sätzen wiedergegeben, damit der jeweilige Zusammenhang deutlich wird. In Fällen, in denen es sinnvoll erscheint, auf den Kontrast zwischen der englischen Struktur und der deutschen Entsprechung hinzuweisen, wurde auch die deutsche Übersetzung hinzugefügt.

- In Fällen, bei denen auf wichtige Unterschiede gegenüber dem deutschen Gebrauch oder auf Besonderheiten bei der Anwendung der englischen Struktur zu achten ist, gibt es besondere Hinweise.

Empfehlungen zur Arbeitsweise

Diese Grammatik-Übersicht eignet sich für die Arbeit sowohl im Unterricht als auch zu Hause.

- *Im Unterricht,* wenn Sie mit Hilfe Ihrer/Ihres Kursleiterin/Kursleiters eine Übersicht über alle Einzelheiten einer bestimmten Struktur bekommen möchten.
- *Zu Hause,* wenn Sie als Wiederholung eine bestimmte Struktur nachschlagen möchten.

G

INDEX	INHALTSVERZEICHNIS

I The Verb — **Das Zeitwort**
- a Infinitives — Die Grundform des Zeitworts
- b Imperatives — Aufforderungssätze
- c Tenses — Zeitformen
  - Present — Gegenwart
  - Past — Vergangenheit
- d Modal Verbs — Modalverben
  - *can, could, must* — *can, could, must*
- e Short Forms — Kurzformen
- f Short Answers — Kurzantworten

II Nouns — **Hauptwörter**
- a Plural Forms — Bildung der Mehrzahlformen
- b 's Genitive — Genitiv mit 's

III Definite/Indefinite Article — **Bestimmter/Unbestimmter Artikel**

IV Pronouns — **Fürwörter**
- a Personal Pronouns — Persönliche Fürwörter
- b Possessive Pronouns — Besitzanzeigende Fürwörter
- c Demonstrative Pronouns — Hinweisende Fürwörter
- d Relative Pronouns — Bezügliche Fürwörter
- e Indefinite Pronouns — Unbestimmte Fürwörter

V Quantifiers — **Mengenangaben**

VI Numerals — **Zahlen**
- a Cardinal Numbers — Grundzahlen
- b Ordinal Numbers — Ordnungszahlen
- c Time of Day — Uhrzeit
- d Date — Datum
- e Telephone Numbers — Telefonnummern

VII Adjectives — **Eigenschaftswörter**
- Comparison — Steigerung

VIII Adverbs/Adverbial Phrases — **Umstandswörter/Umstandsbestimmungen**
- a Frequency — Häufigkeitsangaben
- b Time — Zeitangaben
- c Place — Ortsangaben
- d Sequence of Adverbs — Reihenfolge bei zwei Umstandsbestimmungen
- e Modifiers — Verstärkende oder abschwächende Umstandswörter

IX Sentence Patterns — **Satzmuster**
- a Statements — Aussagesätze
- b Questions — Fragesätze
- c Reported Speech — Indirekte Rede

G

I The Verb Das Zeitwort

Ia Infinitives Die Grundform des Zeitwortes [Units 5, 6, 15]

The children can **play** on the beach. That could **be** a French name.	Die Kinder können am Strand spielen. Das könnte ein französischer Name sein.
Hinweis:	In Verbindung mit einigen Zeitwörtern wird der Grundform *to* vorangesetzt, z.B. *I'd like **to go** to London.* Ich möchte nach London fahren.

Ib Imperatives Aufforderungssätze [Unit 8]

Go down Lord Street. **Just go** down Lord Street.	Gehen Sie Lord Street hinunter. Gehen Sie einfach Lord Street hinunter.
Hinweise:	• Die Form des Zeitworts in Aufforderungssätzen ist die Grundform. • Aufforderungen können durch das Wort *just* abgeschwächt werden.

Ic Tenses Zeitformen

Present Tense: Present Simple Gegenwartsform: Present Simple

The Verb *be* Das Zeitwort *be* [Units 1 – 4, 6]

Affirmative Form Bejahte Form	Question Form Frageform	Negative Form Verneinte Form
I'm/I am you're/you are he's/he is she's/she is it's/it is we're/we are you're/you are they're/they are	am I? are you? is he? is she? is it? are we? are you? are they?	I'm not you aren't/you're not he isn't/he's not she isn't/she's not it isn't/it's not we aren't/we're not you aren't/you're not they aren't/they're not

there is/there are [Units 6, 8]

	Affirmative Form Bejahte Form	Question Form Frageform	Negative Form Verneinte Form
Singular Einzahl	there is/there's	is there?	there isn't/there's no
Plural Mehrzahl	there are	are there?	there aren't/there are no

G

The Verbs *have / have got*   Die Zeitwörter *have / have got*   [Units 3, 7, 8]

Affirmative Form Bejahte Form	Question Form Frageform	Negative Form Verneinte Form
I have (got) you have (got) he has (got) she has (got) it has (got) we have (got) you have (got) they have (got)	do I have?/have I got? do you have?/have you got? does he have?/has he got? does she have?/has she got? does it have?/has it got? do we have?/have we got? do you have?/have you got? do they have?/have they got?	I don't have/I haven't got you don't have/you haven't got he doesn't have/he hasn't got she doesn't have/she hasn't got it doesn't have/it hasn't got we don't have/we haven't got you don't have/you haven't got they don't have/they haven't got

Regular Verbs   Regelmäßige Zeitwörter   [Units 1 – 5]

Affirmative Form Bejahte Form	Question Form Frageform	Negative Form Verneinte Form	Hinweis:
I work you work he works she works it works we work you work they work	do I work? do you work? does he work? does she work? does it work? do we work? do you work? do they work?	I don't work you don't work he doesn't work she doesn't work it doesn't work we don't work you don't work they don't work	Bei den Personen *he, she* und *it* wird normalerweise ein *-s* angehängt. (Besonderheiten: *do – does, go – goes; kiss – kisses, wish – wishes; try – tries*.)

Die *Present Simple*-Zeitform drückt aus:
1. daß es sich um eine Tatsache handelt, z.B.
   I live in a small flat. Ich wohne in einer kleinen Wohnung.
2. daß es sich um Gewohnheiten handelt, z.B.
   I normally have tea for breakfast. Ich trinke normalerweise Tee zum Frühstück.
3. daß es sich um einen Zeitplan für die Zukunft handelt, z.B.
   The flight leaves at 8.30. Der Flug geht um 8.30 Uhr.

Past Tense: Past Simple   Vergangenheitsform: Past Simple

The Verb *be*   Das Zeitwort *be*   [Units 9, 10]

Affirmative Form Bejahte Form	Question Form Frageform	Negative Form Verneinte Form
I was you were he was she was it was we were you were they were	was I? were you? was he? was she? was it? were we? were you? were they?	I wasn't you weren't he wasn't she wasn't it wasn't we weren't you weren't they weren't

Regular Verbs Regelmäßige Zeitwörter [Units 9 – 11]

Affirmative Form Bejahte Form	Question Form Frageform	Negative Form Verneinte Form
I worked you worked he worked she worked it worked we worked you worked they worked	did I work? did you work? did he work? did she work? did it work? did we work? did you work? did they work?	I didn't work you didn't work he didn't work she didn't work it didn't work we didn't work you didn't work they didn't work

Hinweise: 1. Die *Past Simple*-Form der regelmäßigen Zeitwörter wird durch Anhängen von **-ed** an die Grundform gebildet, z. B. *work**ed**, rain**ed**, stay**ed**, start**ed*** (Besonderheiten: *travel – travel**led**; try – tr**ied**; marry – marr**ied***).
2. Endet die Grundform des Zeitwortes auf **-e** wird nur **-d** angehängt, z.B. *lik**ed**, lov**ed**, arriv**ed**, liv**ed***.
3. Wie in der Tabelle oben dargestellt, bleibt die *Past Simple*-Form des Zeitworts in allen Personen – Einzahl wie Mehrzahl – gleich.

Die *Past Simple*-Zeitform drückt aus, daß die Handlung bereits vor dem jetzigen Augenblick abgeschlossen war. So ist diese Zeitform häufig zu finden bei Zeitangaben wie *last year, last month, last week, yesterday, (15 years) ago, in (1943)* usw., d.h. in Verbindung mit einem Zeitpunkt oder einem Zeitraum, der schon vorbei ist, z.B.

- *I went to Scotland **last year**.* Ich bin letztes Jahr nach Schottland gefahren.
- *I was born **in 1956**.* Ich bin/wurde 1956 geboren.
- ***At school** he didn't like maths.* In der Schule mochte er Mathe nicht.
- ***Last night** we went to a pub.* Gestern abend sind wir in eine Kneipe gegangen.

Irregular Verbs Unregelmäßige Zeitwörter [Units 9 – 11]

Infinitive Grundform	Past Simple *Past Simple*-Form	
be	was/were	sein
buy	bought	kaufen
can	could	können
choose	chose	wählen
come	came	kommen
cost	cost	kosten
do	did	tun, machen
draw	drew	malen, zeichnen
drink	drank	trinken
drive	drove	(Auto) fahren
eat	ate	essen
feel	felt	(sich) fühlen
find	found	finden, suchen
fight	fought	kämpfen
get	got	kommen, bekommen
go	went	gehen, fahren

G

grow up	grew up	aufwachsen
have (got)	had (got)	haben
hear	heard	hören
hold up	held up	hochhalten
know	knew	wissen, kennen
leave	left	abfahren, abfliegen
lie	lay	liegen
make	made	machen, anfertigen
mean	meant	bedeuten
meet	met	kennenlernen
put	put	legen
read	read	lesen
ride	rode	(rad)fahren
run	ran	laufen
say	said	sagen
see	saw	sehen
sell	sold	verkaufen
shine	shone	scheinen (die Sonne)
sing	sang	singen
sit	sat	sitzen
sleep	slept	schlafen
speak	spoke	sprechen
spend	spent	(Zeit) verbringen
swim	swam	schwimmen
take	took	nehmen, dauern
teach	taught	beibringen
tell	told	erzählen
think	thought	denken, glauben
understand	understood	verstehen
wake up	woke up	aufwachen
win	won	gewinnen
write	wrote	schreiben

Hinweis:

In Band 1 von BRIDGES sind die oben aufgeführten unregelmäßigen Zeitwörter enthalten.
Die *Past Simple*-Formen der unregelmäßigen Zeitwörter müssen – genau wie neue Vokabeln – einzeln gelernt werden.

used to [Unit 12]

Before there was TV, people **used to** listen to the radio more.	Bevor es Fernsehen gab, hörte man mehr Radio.
Hinweise: 1. Die *used to*-Form ist in allen Personen gleich. 2. Die *used to*-Form wird normalerweise nicht mit genauen Zeitangaben wie *in 1965* usw. verwendet.	

Die *used to*-Form drückt eine Gewohnheit in der Vergangenheit aus.

1d Modal Verbs Modalverben

The Verb *can* Das Zeitwort *can* [Unit 6]

| Affirmative Form
Bejahte Form | Question Form
Frageform | Negative Form
Verneinte Form | Hinweis:
Das Zeitwort *can* ist in allen Personen gleich. |
|---|---|---|---|
| I **can** go swimming. | **Can** I go swimming? | I **can't** go swimming. | |

The Verbs *could* and *must* Die Zeitwörter *could* und *must* [Unit 15]

| | | Hinweis:
Die Zeitwörter *could* und *must* sind in allen Personen gleich. |
|---|---|---|
| That **could** be a man's name. | Das könnte ein Männername sein. | |
| That **must** be a Spanish name. | Das muß (wohl) ein spanischer Name sein. | |

1e Short Forms Kurzformen [Units 1–4, 6–8, 10]

| | | | | Hinweis:
Die aufgelisteten Kurzformen sind in der gesprochenen Sprache geläufig. In der Schriftsprache dagegen werden die Langformen bevorzugt, es sei denn, es handelt sich um einen informellen Brief an eine/n Bekannte/n. |
|---|---|---|---|---|
| I'm | I am | I've | I have | |
| you're | you are | you've | you have | |
| he's | he is | he's | he has | |
| she's | she is | she's | she has | |
| it's | it is | it's | it has | |
| we're | we are | we've | we have | |
| they're | they are | they've | they have | |
| she isn't | she is not | he hasn't | he has not | |
| we aren't | we are not | they haven't | they have not | |
| it wasn't | it was not | there's | there is | |
| we weren't | we were not | | | |
| I didn't | I did not | I can't | I cannot | |
| I'd | I would | I couldn't | I could not | |

1f Short Answers Kurzantworten [Unit 9]

Are you a civil servant?	Yes, I am. / No, I'm not.
Have you got an interesting job?	Yes, I have. / No, I haven't.
Do you work in an office?	Yes, I do. / No, I don't.

| Hinweise: | 1. Auf Ja/Nein-Fragen können Kurzantworten der oben gezeigten Art gegeben werden. Die Form der Kurzantwort richtet sich nach dem Zeitwort in der Frage.
2. Solche Kurzantworten können etwas abrupt wirken. Es empfiehlt sich daher, eine zusätzliche Information hinzuzufügen, z.B.
Have you got an interesting job? Yes, (I have.) **I'm a teacher.**
Do you work in an office? No, (I don't.) **I'm a bus-driver.**
3. Die Kurzform des Zeitworts kann, wie in den beiden Beispielen gezeigt, auch weggelassen werden. |
|---|---|

G

II Nouns Hauptwörter

IIa Plural Forms Bildung der Mehrzahlformen [Units 3, 4, 7, 8]

Regular Plurals Regelmäßige Mehrzahlformen		Other Plural Forms Andere Mehrzahlformen	
shop	shop**s**	child	child**ren**
book	book**s**	man	men
flat	flat**s**	woman	women
pear	pear**s**	wife	wi**ves**
egg	egg**s**		
apple	apple**s**		
room	room**s**		
brother-in-law	brother**s**-in-law		
country	countr**ies**		
tomato	tomato**es**		
church	church**es**		
address	address**es**		

Hinweis:
Folgende Hauptwörter werden nur in der Einzahl verwendet:
information, furniture
sowie in der Regel
food, bread, butter, jam, milk, muesli, toast.

IIb 's-Genitive Genitiv mit 's [Units 7, 8, 12]

Linda**'s** husband Bruce**'s** birthday Linda**'s** husband**'s** birthday	Lindas Ehemann der Geburtstag von Bruce der Geburtstag von Lindas Ehemann
the newsagent**'s** the baker**'s** the chemist**'s** at O'Reilly**'s** St. Mary**'s** Church	der Zeitungsladen der Bäckerladen die Apotheke bei O'Reilly

Hinweis:
Bei *newsagent's, baker's* usw. ist das Wort *shop* mitzudenken.

III Definite/Indefinite Article Bestimmter/Unbestimmter Artikel [Units 4, 9]

Definite Article Der bestimmte Artikel	Indefinite Article Der unbestimmte Artikel
the flat **the** civil servant	**a** flat **a** civil servant
the old flat **the** engineer	**an** old flat **an** engineer

Hinweise:

1. Vor einem Wort, das mit einem Selbstlaut (a,e,i,o,u) beginnt, wird statt **a** der unbestimmte Artikel **an** verwendet.

2. Im großen und ganzen werden die bestimmten und unbestimmten Artikel ähnlich verwendet wie im Deutschen. Auf folgende Beispiele sollte allerdings geachtet werden:

   Der bestimmte Artikel wird verwendet
   - bei einigen Ländernamen, z.B. ***The** Netherlands*, ***The** United States*, ***The** United Kingdom*.

   Der unbestimmte Artikel wird verwendet
   - bei Berufsangaben: *He's **a** civil servant.* Er ist Beamter.
   - bei Häufigkeitsangaben: *Twice **a** day.* Zweimal am Tag.

   Kein Artikel wird verwendet
   - bei Straßennamen: *I live **in** Church Street.* Ich wohne in der Church Street.
   - bei Verkehrsmitteln: *I went **by** car.* Ich fuhr mit dem Auto.
   - in Sätzen wie: ***At** school he didn't like German.* In der Schule mochte er Deutsch nicht.

IV Pronouns Fürwörter

IVa Personal Pronouns Persönliche Fürwörter [Units 1 – 3, 8, 9, 11]

Subject Pronouns als Satzgegenstand		Object Pronouns als Satzergänzung	
I	ich	me	mich, mir
you	du, Sie	you	dich, dir, Sie, Ihnen
he	er	him	ihn, ihm
she	sie	her	sie, ihr
it	es	it	es, ihm
we	wir	us	uns
you	ihr, Sie	you	euch, Sie, Ihnen
they	sie	them	sie, ihnen

G

IVb Possessive Pronouns
Besitzanzeigende Fürwörter [Units 4, 7]

my	mein, meine
your	dein, deine, Ihr, Ihre
his	sein, seine
her	ihr, ihre
its	sein, seine
our	unser, unsere
your	euer, eure, Ihr, Ihre
their	ihr, ihre

IVc Demonstrative Pronouns
Hinweisende Fürwörter [Units 1, 4]

| **This** is Linda. | Dies (hier) ist Linda. |
| **That's** a nice place. | Das ist ein schöner Ort. |

IVd Relative Pronouns Bezügliche Fürwörter [Unit 15]

| Do you know anyone **who** speaks two languages? | Kennen Sie jemanden, der zwei Sprachen spricht? |
| Do you know anyone **whose** parents were born abroad? | Kennen Sie jemanden, dessen Eltern im Ausland geboren sind/wurden? |

IVe Indefinite Pronouns Unbestimmte Fürwörter

some/any [Unit 8]

We've got **some** good shops. We'd like **some** more shops.	Wir haben ein paar gute Läden. Wir möchten ein paar Läden mehr.
Have you got **any** children? Are there **any** cinemas near here?	Haben Sie Kinder? Gibt es Kinos in der Nähe?
We haven't got **any** good shops. There aren't **any** good shops.	Wir haben keine guten Läden. Es gibt keine guten Läden.
Hinweis:	*Some* wird in der Regel bei bejahten Aussagen verwendet, *any* dagegen bei verneinten Äußerungen und bei Fragen.

someone/anyone [Unit 15]

I know **someone** who speaks seven languages.	Ich kenne jemanden, der sieben Sprachen spricht.
Do you know **anyone** who was born outside Europe?	Kennen Sie jemanden, der außerhalb Europas geboren ist/wurde?
Christel doesn't know **anyone** whose parents were born abroad.	Christel kennt niemanden, dessen Eltern im Ausland geboren sind/wurden.
Hinweis:	Die Grundregel für *some* und *any* gilt auch für Zusammensetzungen wie *someone* und *anyone*.

everybody/nobody [Unit 12]

| **Everybody** (in our group) thinks … | Jeder (in unserer Gruppe) meint … |
| **Nobody** (in our group) thinks … | Keiner (in unserer Gruppe) meint … |

both [Unit 12]

| We **both** go jogging every day. | Wir gehen beide jeden Tag joggen. |
| Hinweis: | Das Wort **both** wird normalerweise vor das Zeitwort gesetzt. |

The Substitute Word *one* Das Ersatzwort *one* [Unit 11]

| I'd like to try the local restaurants. What's your favourite **one**? | Ich möchte die einheimischen Restaurants ausprobieren. Welches ist Ihr Lieblingsrestaurant? |
| Hinweis: | Zur Vermeidung einer unnötigen Wiederholung kann ein Hauptwort durch das Wort *one* ersetzt werden. |

V Quantifiers Mengenangaben

most/a lot of/some [Unit 8]

Most shops are open till 5.30.	Die meisten Läden haben bis 5.30 geöffnet.
A lot of pubs are open in the afternoon.	Viele Kneipen haben nachmittags geöffnet.
Some supermarkets open on Sunday.	Einige Supermärkte sind am Sonntag geöffnet.

VI Numerals Zahlen

VIa Cardinal Numbers Grundzahlen [Units 2 – 4, 11]

0	oh/zero	10	ten	20	twen**ty**
1	one	11	eleven	21	twen**ty**-one
2	two	12	twelve	30	thir**ty**
3	three	13	thir**teen**	40	for**ty**
4	four	14	four**teen**	50	fif**ty**
5	five	15	fif**teen**	60	six**ty**
6	six	16	six**teen**	70	seven**ty**
7	seven	17	seven**teen**	80	eigh**ty**
8	eight	18	eigh**teen**	90	nine**ty**
9	nine	19	nine**teen**	100	one hundred

G

	108	one hundred **and** eight
	421	four hundred **and** twenty-one
	999	nine hundred **and** ninety-nine
	1,000	one thousand
	1,019	one thousand **and** nineteen
	74,991	seventy-four thousand nine hundred **and** ninety-one
	100,000	one hundred thousand
	221,000	two hundred **and** twenty-one thousand
	1,000,000	one million
	1,659,400	one million six hundred **and** fifty-nine thousand four hundred

Hinweis:	Große Zahlen werden normalerweise auf- bzw. abgerundet mit ***about***, z.B. *5,908,647 – That's **about** 6 million.*

VIb Ordinal Numbers Ordnungszahlen [Units 4, 7]

1st	**first**	10th	**ten**th	20th	**twent**ieth
2nd	**second**	11th	**eleven**th	21st	twenty-**first**
3rd	**third**	12th	**twelf**th	22nd	twenty-**second**
4th	**four**th	13th	**thirteen**th		
5th	**fif**th	14th	**fourteen**th	30th	**thirt**ieth
6th	**six**th	15th	**fifteen**th	31st	thirty-**first**
7th	**seven**th	16th	**sixteen**th		
8th	**eigh**th	17th	**seventeen**th		
9th	**nin**th	18th	**eighteen**th		
		19th	**nineteen**th		

VIc Time of Day Uhrzeit [Units 3, 5]

8.00	eight **o'clock**	8.30	**half past** eight	8.30	**eight thirty**
8.05	five **past** eight	8.35	twenty-five **to** nine	10.50	**ten fifty**
8.10	ten **past** eight	8.40	twenty **to** nine	13.25	**thirteen twenty-five**
8.15	**quarter past** eight	8.45	**quarter to** nine	23.15	**twenty-three fifteen**
8.20	twenty **past** eight	8.50	ten **to** nine		
8.25	twenty-five **past** eight	8.55	five **to** nine		

VId Date Datum [Units 7, 15]

Christmas Day is **December the twenty-fifth**.	Der erste Weihnachtstag ist der 25. Dezember.
My birthday's **July the twenty-seventh**.	Ich habe am 27. Juli Geburtstag.
I was born **in about 74 B.C.**	Ich wurde ca. 74 vor Christi Geburt geboren.
in twelve ten	(im Jahre) 1210
nineteen seventy-eight	1978

VIe Telephone Numbers
Telefonnummern

[Unit 2]

| 02373 | oh - two - three - seven - three |
| 660289 | double six - oh - two - eight - nine |

VII Adjectives Eigenschaftswörter

Comparison Steigerung [Units 4, 8, 10, 11, 14]

Regular Forms Regelmäßige Formen	Adjective Grundform	Comparative Komparativ	Superlative Superlativ
einsilbig	small nice big	small**er** nice**r** big**ger**	small**est** nice**st** big**gest**
zweisilbig auf -*y*	easy happy	eas**ier** happ**ier**	eas**iest** happ**iest**
zweisilbig	modern	**more** modern	**most** modern
drei- oder mehrsilbig	expensive interesting	**more** expensive **more** interesting	**most** expensive **most** interesting
Irregular Forms Unregelmäßige Formen	good bad many	**better** **worse** **more**	**best** **worst** **most**

Hinweise: Werden Sachen miteinander verglichen, verwendet man das Wort **than**, z.B.
- *Toronto is bigger **than** Stuttgart.* Toronto ist größer als Stuttgart.
- *Flats are more expensive in Germany **than** in Scotland.* Wohnungen sind in Deutschland teurer als in Schottland.

VIII Adverbs/Adverbial Phrases Umstandswörter/Umstandsbestimmungen

VIIIa Frequency Häufigkeitsangaben [Units 3, 12]

			Hinweis:
I	**always** **normally** **usually** **often** **sometimes** **never**	have coffee for breakfast.	Häufigkeitsangaben werden meistens vor das Zeitwort gesetzt, wenn es sich nur um ein Wort handelt, z.B. *I **normally** get to the office at 8.30.* Ich komme normalerweise um 8.30 Uhr ins Büro.
I I We	watch TV have a lie in go dancing	**every day.** **once or twice a week.** **three or four times a year.**	Sind es dagegen Ausdrücke von mehr als einem Wort, werden sie an das Ende des Satzes gesetzt, z.B. *I watch TV **every day**.* Ich sehe jeden Tag fern.

G

VIIIb Time Zeitangaben [Units 3, 8]

The banks open
  at nine o'clock.
	Die Banken öffnen
	  um 9 Uhr.

The banks are open
  on Saturday morning.
  in the afternoon.
  at lunchtime.
  from nine thirty **to** four thirty.
  till 8 in the evening.
  on weekdays.
	Die Banken sind geöffnet
	  am Samstagvormittag.
	  am Nachmittag.
	  um die Mittagszeit.
	  von 9.30 Uhr bis 16.30 Uhr.
	  bis 20 Uhr.
	  an Werktagen.

The banks are closed
  at the weekend.
  in the evening.
	Die Banken sind geschlossen
	  am Wochenende.
	  am Abend.

Hinweis: Zeitangaben werden meistens an das Ende des Satzes gesetzt.	

VIIIc Place Ortsangaben [Units 8, 14]

at **at** **at** **in**	the newsagent's the chemist's a bank a restaurant	beim Zeitungshändler beim Apotheker auf einer Bank in einem Restaurant
opposite **next to** **on** **on** **in** **near**	the railway station the hotel the corner the left/right Station Road the railway station	gegenüber dem Bahnhof neben dem Hotel an der Ecke auf der linken/rechten Seite in der Station Road in der Nähe des Bahnhofs
in front of **behind** **between** **on**	the window the television the sofa and the armchair the coffee table	vor dem Fenster hinter dem Fernseher zwischen dem Sofa und dem Sessel auf dem Couchtisch
Hinweis: Ortsangaben werden meistens an das Ende des Satzes gesetzt.		

VIIId Sequence of Adverbs Reihenfolge bei zwei Umstandsbestimmungen [Units 5, 9, 12]

Martin gets I usually get Let's stay	**here** **to work** **at home**	**by bus.** **at about 8.30.** **this weekend.**	Martin kommt mit dem Bus hierher. Normalerweise komme ich gegen 8.30 Uhr zur Arbeit. Laß uns dieses Wochenende zu Hause bleiben.
Hinweis: Sind zwei verschiedene Umstandsbestimmungen in einem Satz, kommen die Ortsangaben normalerweise zuerst.			

G

VIIIe Modifiers Verstärkende oder abschwächende Umstandswörter [Unit 11, 13]

The town is	**very**	interesting.	Die Stadt ist sehr interessant.
The area is	**quite**	pleasant.	Die Gegend ist recht schön.
This food is	**especially**	healthy.	Dieses Essen ist besonders gesund.
Which items are	**not so**	healthy?	Welche Dinge sind weniger gesund?

Hinweis:	Durch die Verwendung von *Modifiers* können Eigenschaftswörter in ihrer Bedeutung verstärkt bzw. abgeschwächt werden.

IX Sentence Patterns Satzmuster

IXa Statements Aussagesätze [Units 6, 10]

Main Clause Hauptsatz	Conjunction Bindewort	Main Clause Hauptsatz
There's a disco next door Nebenan ist eine Disco,	**so** so daß	we can't sleep. wir nicht schlafen können.
At school he didn't like music, In der Schule mochte er Musik nicht,	**but** aber	he does now. jetzt ja.

Main Clause Hauptsatz	Conjunction Bindewort	Subordinate Clause Nebensatz
I hate winter Ich hasse den Winter,	**because** weil	it's cold. es (dann) kalt ist.
He liked rock music Er mochte Rockmusik,	**when** als	he was 15. er 15 war.

IXb Questions Fragesätze

The Verb *be:* Yes/No Questions
Das Zeitwort *be:* Ja/Nein-Fragen [Units 9, 11]

Are	you	an engineer?	Sind Sie Ingenieur?
Is	it	a country?	Ist es ein Land?

Other Verbs: Yes/No Questions
Andere Verben: Ja/Nein-Fragen [Units 4, 7, 11]

Can	you	help me?	Können Sie mir helfen?
Has	she	got any children?	Hat sie Kinder?
Did	you	go abroad?	Sind Sie ins Ausland gefahren?

G

Questions with Question Words Fragen mit Fragewörtern   [Units 5 – 7]

Question Word Fragewort	Auxiliary Hilfszeitwort	Subject Satzgegenstand	Infinitive Grundform des Zeitworts
How How much How long How often How many When	do does does does have does	you the ticket the train the ferry you the flight	get to work? cost? take? go? got? arrive?
What Where Where	's does does	the weather the ferry the ferry	like? leave from? go to?
Hinweis:	\multicolumn{3}{l	}{Gehört zum Fragewort ein Verhältniswort (z.B. **like, from, to**), wird das Verhältniswort ans Ende des Fragesatzes gesetzt.}

IXc Reported Speech Indirekte Rede   [Unit 15]

"My name means …" **He says his** name means …	„Mein Name bedeutet …" Er sagt, sein Name bedeutet …
"I don't like my family name." **He says he doesn't** like his family name.	„Ich mag meinen Familiennamen nicht." Er sagt, er mag seinen Familiennamen nicht.

VOCABULARY

Phonetic alphabet Lautschrift

[ː] bedeutet, daß der vorangehende Laut lang ist
[ˈ] bedeutet, daß die folgende Silbe eine Hauptbetonung erhält
[ˌ] bedeutet, daß die folgende Silbe eine Nebenbetonung erhält

[iː]	meet [miːt]	[eɪ]	name [neɪm]	[f]	fine [faɪn]
[ɑː]	father [ˈfɑːðə]	[aɪ]	my [maɪ]	[v]	very [ˈverɪ]
[ɔː]	morning [ˈmɔːnɪŋ]	[ɔɪ]	boiled [bɔɪld]	[θ]	thanks [θæŋks]
[uː]	blue [bluː]	[əʊ]	phone [fəʊn]	[ð]	this [ðɪs]
[ɜː]	Germany [ˈdʒɜːmənɪ]	[aʊ]	now [naʊ]	[s]	son [sʌn]
		[ɪə]	beer [bɪə]	[z]	is [ɪz]
[ɔ̃ː]	restaurant [ˈrestərɔ̃ːŋ]	[eə]	where [weə]	[ʃ]	she [ʃiː]
		[ʊə]	tourist [ˈtʊərɪst]	[ʒ]	television [ˈtelɪˌvɪʒn]
[ɪ]	in [ɪn]			[h]	he [hiː]
[e]	yes [jes]	[p]	pub [pʌb]	[m]	my [maɪ]
[æ]	thanks [θæŋks]	[b]	bye [baɪ]	[n]	now [naʊ]
[ʌ]	much [mʌtʃ]	[t]	town [taʊn]	[ŋ]	evening [ˈiːvnɪŋ]
[ɒ]	what [wɒt]	[d]	drink [drɪŋk]	[l]	like [laɪk]
[ʊ]	good [gʊd]	[k]	coffee [ˈkɒfɪ]	[r]	room [ruːm]
[ə]	number [ˈnʌmbə]	[g]	good [gʊd]	[w]	we [wiː]
		[tʃ]	church [tʃɜːtʃ]	[j]	yes [jes]
		[dʒ]	job [dʒɒb]		

Unit Vocabulary Kapitel-Wörterverzeichnis

In diesem Wörterverzeichnis finden Sie Wörter und Wendungen, die zum Verständnis und zur Durchführung der Aufgaben in BRIDGES 1 NEU benötigt werden, in der Reihenfolge ihres Auftretens unter der Kapitel- und Schrittnummer.

Aller relevante Wortschatz wird beim ersten Auftreten aufgenommen. Wörter und Wendungen, die mehr als eine Bedeutung haben bzw. die zunächst nur verstanden und erst später gelernt werden sollen, werden nochmals an den entsprechenden Stellen aufgeführt.

Die Arbeitsanweisungen sind kursiv gedruckt und werden, wenn nötig, im Ganzen übersetzt. Alle Einträge mit Ausnahme der Arbeitsanweisungen werden auch in Lautschrift angegeben. Die deutschen Übersetzungen beziehen sich immer auf den jeweiligen Kontext im Buch.

Die wichtigsten Einzelwörter aus den Arbeitsanweisungen und aus den Wendungen werden anschließend auch einzeln aufgeführt.

Weitere Listen:

Unregelmäßige Verben, siehe Seite 147
Zahlen, siehe 153

one hundred and fifty-nine

V

UNIT 1

Nice to meet you. [naɪs tə 'miːt jʊ] — Nett, dich/Sie kennenzulernen.
Hello, I'm Alexander Alligator. [he'ləʊ aɪm͜ ælɪk'sɑːndə 'ælɪgeɪtə] — Hallo, ich heiße Alexander Alligator.
Do we kiss them or just shake hands? [duː wiː kɪs ðem͜ ɔː dʒʌst ʃeɪk hændz] — Sollen wir sie küssen oder geben wir ihnen nur die Hand?
airport ['eəpɔːt] — Flughafen
arrivals [ə'raɪvəlz] — Ankunft
See you later, alligator. [siː juː 'leɪtər͜ 'ælɪgeɪtə] — Bis später, Alligator. *(Liedtitel)*

1

hello [he'ləʊ] — hallo, guten Tag
I'm Bruce [aɪm 'bruːs] — Ich heiße Bruce
I [aɪ] — ich
and this is Linda. [ən ðɪs͜ ɪz 'lɪndə] — und das ist Linda.
and [ænd] — und
this [ðɪs] — dies
is [ɪz] — ist
hi [haɪ] — hallo

2

I'm from England. [aɪm frəm͜ 'ɪŋglənd] — Ich komme aus England.
Bavaria [bə'veərɪə] — Bayern
Nuremberg ['njʊərəmbɜːg] — Nürnberg
America [ə'merɪkə] — (Vereinigte Staaten von) Amerika
I'm from Texas, too. [aɪm frəm 'teksəs tuː] — Ich komme auch aus Texas.
too [tuː] — auch
And you? [ənd͜ 'juː] — Und du/Sie?
you [juː] — du, Sie
memo pad ['meməʊ pæd] — Notizblock
Germany ['dʒɜːmənɪ] — Deutschland

3A

She's from Amarillo. [ʃiːz frəm͜ æmə'rɪləʊ] — Sie kommt aus Amarillo.
she [ʃiː] — sie
he [hiː] — er

3B

Write sentences. — Schreiben Sie Sätze.
write [raɪt] — schreiben
sentence ['sentəns] — Satz

4A

Write the dialogue in the correct order. — Schreiben Sie den Dialog in der richtigen Reihenfolge.
the [ðə] — der, die, das
dialogue ['daɪəlɒg] — Dialog
in [ɪn] — in
correct order [kə'rekt͜ 'ɔːdə] — richtige Reihenfolge
Nice to meet you. [naɪs tə 'miːt jʊ] — Nett, dich/Sie kennenzulernen.
I'm fine. [aɪm 'faɪn] — Es geht mir gut.
by the way [baɪ ðə 'weɪ] — übrigens
How are you? [haʊ ə juː] — Wie geht es dir/Ihnen?
how [haʊ] — wie
thanks [θæŋks] — danke
And you? [ənd͜ 'juː] — Und dir/Ihnen?

4B

Listen and check. — Hören Sie zu und überprüfen Sie.
listen ['lɪsn] — zuhören
check [tʃek] — überprüfen
Read the dialogue aloud in groups. — Lesen Sie den Dialog in Gruppen laut vor.
read aloud [riːd͜ ə'laʊd] — laut lesen
group [gruːp] — Gruppe

4C

Look at File 1. — Sehen Sie sich File 1 an.
look at ['lʊk͜ ət] — ansehen
file [faɪl] — *hier:* Informationskarte

5A

Read and complete. — Lesen (Sie) und vervollständigen Sie.
read [riːd] — lesen
complete [kəm'pliːt] — vervollständigen
I am [aɪ͜ 'æm] — ich bin
you are [juː͜ 'ɑː] — du bist
because [bɪ'kɒz] — weil
without [wɪ'ðaʊt] — ohne
meaningless ['miːnɪŋlɪs] — bedeutungslos, sinnlos

6A

good morning [gʊd 'mɔːnɪŋ] — guten Morgen

UNIT 1

good [gʊd]	gut
morning ['mɔ:nɪŋ]	Morgen
afternoon [ɑ:ftə'nu:n]	Nachmittag
evening ['i:vnɪŋ]	Abend
Mrs (Irving) ['mɪsɪz]	Frau (Irving)
Welcome to Berlin. ['welkəm tə bɜ:'lɪn]	Willkommen in Berlin.
welcome to ['welkəm tu:]	willkommen in
Mr (Adler) ['mɪstə]	Herr (Adler)

7 A

Match the songs and the pictures. — Ordnen Sie die Lieder den Bildern zu.

match [mætʃ]	zuordnen
song [sɒŋ]	Lied
picture ['pɪktʃə]	Bild
goodnight [gʊd'naɪt]	gute Nacht
lady, ladies [leɪdɪ, leɪdɪz]	Dame, Damen
goodbye [gʊd'baɪ]	auf Wiedersehen
bye bye [baɪ baɪ]	auf Wiedersehen, tschüs
love [lʌv]	Liebe

7 B

Write one of these expressions on a card. — Schreiben Sie einen dieser Ausdrücke auf eine Karte.

one of these [wʌn əv 'ði:z]	eine (-r, -s) dieser
expression [ɪk'spreʃn]	Ausdruck
on [ɒn]	auf
a [ə]	ein (-e, -er)
card [kɑ:d]	Karte

Hold it up when you hear your expression. — Halten Sie sie hoch, wenn Sie Ihren Ausdruck hören.

when [wen]	*hier:* wenn
hear [hɪə]	hören

7 C

Say goodbye. — Verabschieden Sie sich.

say [seɪ]	sagen
bye [baɪ]	(auf) Wiedersehen, tschüs

See you next week. [si: jʊ neks 'wi:k] — Bis nächste Woche.

8 A

What's the English for Lesen? [wɒts ði: 'ɪŋglɪʃ fə] — Was heißt ‚Lesen' auf englisch?

what [wɒt]	was
English ['ɪŋglɪʃ]	Englisch
reading ['ri:dɪŋ]	Lesen
flower ['flaʊə]	Blume
I like beer. [aɪ laɪk 'bɪə]	Ich mag Bier.
like [laɪk]	(gerne) mögen
beer [bɪə]	Bier
She likes singing. [ʃi: laɪks 'sɪŋɪŋ]	Sie singt gern.
singing ['sɪŋɪŋ]	Singen
gardening ['gɑ:dnɪŋ]	Gartenarbeit
I like your tie. [aɪ laɪk jə 'taɪ]	Mir gefällt deine/Ihre Krawatte.

9 A

Where are they from? [weər ə ðeɪ 'frɒm] — Woher kommen sie?

where from [weə frɒm]	woher
they [ðeɪ]	sie
What do they like? [wɒt dʊ ðeɪ 'laɪk]	Was mögen sie?
jazz [dʒæz]	Jazz
skiing ['ski:ɪŋ]	Skifahren
travelling ['trævlɪŋ]	Reisen
camping ['kæmpɪŋ]	Camping, Zelten

9 B

Listen and fill in. — Hören Sie zu und füllen Sie aus.

fill in [fɪl ɪn]	ausfüllen
wine [waɪn]	Wein
music ['mju:zɪk]	Musik

10

I hate long goodbyes. [aɪ 'heɪt lɒŋ gʊd'baɪz] — Ich mag langes Abschiednehmen nicht.

11

pronunciation [prənʌnsɪ'eɪʃn]	Aussprache

Write these words in the correct boxes. — Schreiben Sie diese Wörter in die richtigen Kästen.

word [wɜ:d]	Wort
box [bɒks]	Kasten

V

UNIT 2

Names and numbers ['neɪmz ən 'nʌmbəz]	Namen und Zahlen
A to Z [eɪ tə 'zed]	A bis Z
Europe ['jʊərəp]	Europa

1A

The alphabet [ðiː 'ælfəbet]	Das Alphabet
an alphabet rhyme [ən 'ælfəbet raɪm]	ein Buchstabenreim
Listen and practise.	Hören Sie zu und üben Sie.
practise ['præktɪs]	üben
How do you spell ...? [haʊ dʊ jʊ 'spel]	Wie buchstabiert man ...?
yes and no [jes ən 'nəʊ]	ja und nein
here we are [hɪə wiː 'ɑː]	*etwa:* Da wären wir nun.
rhymes with sex [raɪms wɪð 'seks]	reimt sich auf Sex

1B

student ['stjuːdnt]	Student/in, *hier:* Kursteilnehmer/in

2

European neighbours [jʊərə'piːən 'neɪbəz]	europäische Nachbarn
European [jʊərə'piːən]	europäisch
neighbour ['neɪbə]	Nachbar/in

2A

Which country is it?	Welches Land ist das?
which [wɪtʃ]	welche (-r, -s)
country ['kʌntrɪ]	Land
France [frɑːns]	Frankreich
Luxembourg ['lʌksəmbɜːg]	Luxemburg
Belgium ['beldʒəm]	Belgien
Great Britain [greɪt 'brɪtn]	Großbritannien
Ireland ['aɪələnd]	Irland
The Netherlands [ðə 'neðələndz]	Niederlande
Denmark ['denmɑːk]	Dänemark
Poland ['pəʊlənd]	Polen
The Czech Republic [ðə ˌtʃek rɪ'pʌblɪk]	Tschechische Republik
Austria ['ɒstrɪə]	Österreich
Switzerland ['swɪtsələnd]	Schweiz

we think [wiː θɪŋk]	wir glauben
we [wiː]	wir
think [θɪŋk]	*hier:* glauben
How do you say that? [haʊ dʊ jʊ 'seɪ ðæt]	Wie sagt man das?
that [ðæt]	das

2B

Match these languages and the countries in A.	Ordnen Sie diesen Sprachen die Länder aus A zu.
language ['læŋgwɪdʒ]	Sprache
is spoken in [ɪs spəʊkn ɪn]	wird gesprochen in
Czech [tʃek]	Tschechisch
Danish ['deɪnɪʃ]	Dänisch
Dutch [dʌtʃ]	Niederländisch
Flemish ['flemɪʃ]	Flämisch
French [frentʃ]	Französisch
German ['dʒɜːmən]	Deutsch
Italian [ɪ'tæljən]	Italienisch
Polish ['pəʊlɪʃ]	Polnisch
knowledge of foreign languages in European countries ['nɒlɪdʒ əv 'fɒrɪn 'læŋgwɪdʒɪz ɪn jʊərə'piːən 'kʌntrɪz]	Fremdsprachenkenntnisse in europäischen Ländern
no foreign languages [nəʊ 'fɒrɪn 'læŋgwɪdʒɪz]	keine Fremdsprachen (kenntnisse)
two or more [tuː ɔː 'mɔː]	zwei oder mehr

3B

Report.	Berichten Sie.
one [wʌn]	eins
two [tuː]	zwei
three [θriː]	drei
four [fɔː]	vier
five [faɪv]	fünf
six [sɪks]	sechs
seven ['sevn]	sieben
eight [eɪt]	acht
nine [naɪn]	neun
ten [ten]	zehn
number ['nʌmbə]	*hier:* Nummer
no idea [nəʊ aɪ'dɪə]	keine Ahnung

4A

Italy ['ɪtəlɪ]	Italien
food [fuːd]	Essen
speak [spiːk]	sprechen

Unit 2

I don't like swimming. [aɪ dəʊnt laɪk 'swɪmɪŋ] — Ich schwimme nicht gern.
swimming ['swɪmɪŋ] — Schwimmen
understand [ʌndə'stænd] — verstehen

4B

Write four or five sentences about yourself on a card. — Schreiben Sie vier oder fünf Sätze über sich auf eine Karte.
about yourself [ə'baʊt jə'self] — *hier:* über dich/sich (selbst)
Put the card in the hat. (No name!) — Legen Sie die Karte in den Hut. (Ohne Namen!)
put [pʊt] — *hier:* legen
hat [hæt] — Hut

4C

Take a card. — Nehmen Sie eine Karte.
take [teɪk] — nehmen
Who is it? — Wer ist das?
who [huː] — wer
it's ... [ɪts] — das ist ...
Sorry, I don't know. [sɒrɪ aɪ dəʊnt 'nəʊ] — Es tut mir leid, das weiß ich nicht.
sorry [sɒrɪ] — es tut mir leid
know [nəʊ] — wissen

5A

What's your phone number? [wɒts jə 'fəʊn ˌnʌmbə] — Wie ist deine/Ihre Telefonnummer?
your [jɔː] — dein(-e)/Ihr(-e)
phone number ['fəʊn ˌnʌmbə] — Telefonnummer
phone/telephone [fəʊn/'telɪfəʊn] — Telefon
double (two) ['dʌbl] — (Für doppelte Ziffern in Telefonnummern wird im Englischen *double* + *Zahl* verwendet.)
oh [əʊ] — *hier:* null
etc [ɪt 'setərə] — usw.

5B

Make a phone call. — Führen Sie ein Telefongespräch.
phone call ['fəʊn kɔːl] — Telefongespräch

6A

the seven days of the week [ðə 'sevn deɪz əv ðə 'wiːk] — die sieben Tage der Woche
day [deɪ] — Tag
Ask and fill in. — Fragen Sie und füllen Sie aus.
ask [ɑːsk] — fragen
Monday ['mʌndɪ] — Montag
Tuesday ['tjuːzdɪ] — Dienstag
Wednesday ['wenzdɪ] — Mittwoch
Thursday ['θɜːzdɪ] — Donnerstag
Friday ['fraɪdɪ] — Freitag
Saturday ['sætədɪ] — Samstag
Sunday ['sʌndɪ] — Sonntag
How do you spell that? [haʊ də jʊ 'spel ðæt] — Wie buchstabiert man das?
spell [spel] — buchstabieren

6B

Listen and write down the days. — Hören Sie zu und schreiben Sie die Tage auf.
write down [raɪt 'daʊn] — aufschreiben
Is today Sunday? [ɪz tədeɪ 'sʌndɪ] — Ist heute Sonntag?
today [tə'deɪ] — heute
That's funny. [ðæts 'fʌnɪ] — Das ist komisch.
It feels like Sunday to me. [ɪt fiːlz laɪk 'sʌndɪ tə 'miː] — Mir kommt es wie Sonntag vor.

7

spelling ['spelɪŋ] — Buchstabieren
Think of a word and ask your partner how to spell it. — Denken Sie sich ein Wort aus und fragen Sie Ihren Partner/Ihre Partnerin, wie es buchstabiert wird.
think of ['θɪŋk əv] — *hier:* ausdenken
partner ['pɑːtnə] — Partner/in
Take turns. — Wechseln Sie sich ab.
That's wrong. [ðæts 'rɒŋ] — Das ist falsch./Das stimmt nicht.
wrong [rɒŋ] — falsch
That's right. [ðæts 'raɪt] — Das ist richtig./Das stimmt.
right [raɪt] — richtig

8

booking a room ['bʊkɪŋ ə 'rʊm] — ein Zimmer reservieren
book [bʊk] — *hier:* reservieren
room [rʊm] — Zimmer

V

UNIT 2

8A

hotel [həʊˈtel]	Hotel
Thank you very much. [θæŋk jʊ ˈveri ˈmʌtʃ]	Vielen Dank.
Thank you. [θæŋk juː]	Danke.
see you on Friday [siː jʊ ɒn ˈfraɪdɪ]	bis Freitag
Yes, of course. [jes ˌəv ˈkɔːs]	Ja, natürlich.
What's your name, please? [wɒts jə ˈneɪm pliːz]	Wie ist Ihr Name, bitte?
name [neɪm]	Name
please [pliːz]	bitte
OK [əʊˈkeɪ]	*hier etwa:* gut
I'd like a double room for Friday evening. [aɪd laɪk ˌə ˈdʌbl rʊm fə ˈfraɪdɪ ˈiːvnɪŋ]	Ich hätte gerne ein Doppelzimmer für Freitag(abend).
I'd like [aɪd ˈlaɪk]	ich hätte gerne
a [ə]	ein (-e, -er)
double room [ˈdʌbl rʊm]	Doppelzimmer
for [fɔː]	*hier:* für
Pardon? [ˈpɑːdn]	Wie bitte?

8C

Act out the dialogue. — Spielen Sie den Dialog nach.

act out [ækt ˌaʊt]	nachspielen
Use your own names and choose different days.	Verwenden Sie Ihren eigenen Namen und wählen Sie andere Tage.
use [juːz]	*hier:* verwenden
your own name [jər ˌəʊn neɪm]	Ihr eigener Name
own [əʊn]	eigene (-r, -s)
choose [tʃuːz]	(aus)wählen
different days [ˈdɪfrənt deɪz]	andere Tage
different [ˈdɪfrənt]	anders
guest [gest]	Gast

9

Find rhymes and compare results. — Suchen Sie Reime und vergleichen Sie Ihre Ergebnisse.

find [faɪnd]	*hier:* suchen
compare [kəmˈpeə]	vergleichen
result [rɪˈzʌlt]	Ergebnis

UNIT 3

Breakfast time [ˈbrekfəst taɪm]	Frückstückszeit
around the clock [əˈraʊnd ðə ˈklɒk]	(rund) um die Uhr
What do cows eat for breakfast? [wɒt dʊ kaʊz ˌiːt fə ˈbrekfəst]	Was fressen Kühe zum Frühstück?
answer: mooseli.	Antwort: Muhsli.

1A

Practise with your teacher. — Üben Sie mit Ihrer Kursleiterin/Ihrem Kursleiter.

with [wɪð]	mit
teacher [ˈtiːtʃə]	*hier:* Kursleiter/in
What's the time? [wɒts ðə ˈtaɪm]	Wie spät ist es?
time [taɪm]	(Uhr)Zeit
It's about nine o'clock. [ɪts ˌəˈbaʊt naɪn ˌəˈklɒk]	Es es ungefähr neun Uhr.
about [əˈbaʊt]	ungefähr
o'clock [əˈklɒk]	Uhr
a.m. [ˌeɪ ˈem]	vor 12.00 mittags
p.m. [ˌpiː ˈem]	nach 12.00 mittags
eleven [ɪˈlevn]	elf
twelve [twelv]	zwölf
in the morning [ɪn ðə ˈmɔːnɪŋ]	morgens
in the afternoon [ɪn ðɪ ˌɑːftəˈnuːn]	nachmittags
in the evening [ɪn ðɪ ˌˈiːvnɪŋ]	abends

1B

Now practise these times. — Üben Sie jetzt diese Zeiten.

now [naʊ]	jetzt
quarter past [ˈkwɔːtə pɑːst]	viertel nach
half past 8 [hɑːf pɑːst]	halb neun
quarter to [ˈkwɔːtə tuː]	viertel vor
twenty past [ˈtwenti pɑːst]	zwanzig nach
twenty-five to [ˈtwenti ˈfaɪv tuː]	fünf nach halb

1C

Make four cards. — Fertigen Sie vier Karten an.

make [meɪk]	*hier:* anfertigen

UNIT 3

2A
breakfast ['brekfəst] — Frühstück
lunch [lʌntʃ] — Mittagessen
dinner ['dɪnə] — Abendessen
from ... to [frɒm ... tu:] — *hier:* von ... bis
at [æt] — *hier:* um

2B
have breakfast [hæv 'brekfəst] — frühstücken
have lunch/dinner [hæv lʌntʃ/'dɪnə] — zu Mittag/Abend essen
normally [nɔ:məli] — normalerweise

3
Listen and number the clocks. — Hören Sie zu und numerieren Sie die Uhren.
number ['nʌmbə] — numerieren
clock [klɒk] — Uhr

4A
menu ['menju:] — Speisekarte
full English breakfast [fʊl 'ɪŋglɪʃ 'brekfəst] — (traditionelles) englisches Frühstück
full [fʊl] — *hier:* komplett
fruit juice ['fru:t dʒu:s] — Fruchtsaft
fruit [fru:t] — Obst
or [ɔ:] — oder
cornflakes ['kɔ:nfleɪks] — Cornflakes
fried/boiled eggs [fraɪd/bɒɪld egz] — Spiegeleier/gekochte Eier
egg [eg] — Ei
bacon ['beɪkn] — Frühstücksspeck
sausage ['sɒsɪdʒ] — (Brat)Würstchen
tomato [tə'mɑ:təʊ] — Tomate
toast [təʊst] — Toastbrot
marmalade ['mɑ:məleɪd] — Marmelade *(aus Zitrusfrüchten)*
tea [ti:] — Tee
coffee ['kɒfi] — Kaffee
continental breakfast [ˌkɒntɪ'nentl 'brekfəst] — (kleines) Frühstück
continental [ˌkɒntɪ'nentl] — *hier:* wie auf dem europäischen Kontinent
roll [rəʊl] — Brötchen
butter ['bʌtə] — Butter
jam [dʒæm] — Marmelade
yoghurt ['jɒgət] — Joghurt

4B
Now write a breakfast menu in your language. — Schreiben Sie jetzt eine Frühstückskarte in Ihrer Sprache.
Translate it for your English-speaking guests. — Übersetzen Sie sie für Ihre englischsprachigen Gäste.
translate [træns'leɪt] — übersetzen

4D
he has ... for breakfast [hi: hæz ... fə 'brekfəst] — er ißt/trinkt ... zum Frühstück
they have ... for breakfast [ðeɪ hæv ... fə 'brekfəst] — sie essen/trinken ... zum Frühstück

5A
I don't have coffee for breakfast. [aɪ 'dəʊnt həv 'kɒfi fə 'brekfəst] — Ich trinke keinen Kaffee zum Frühstück.

5B
What about your breakfast? [wɒt ə'baʊt 'jɔ: brekfəst] — Was ist mit deinem/Ihrem Frühstück?
what about [wɒt ə'baʊt] — was ist mit
he doesn't have [hi: 'dʌznt hæv] — *hier:* er ißt/trinkt kein (-e, -en)

6
What about breakfast in other countries? — Was ist mit dem Frühstück in anderen Ländern?
other countries ['ʌðə 'kʌntrɪz] — andere Länder
bread [bred] — Brot
cheese [tʃi:z] — Käse

7A
apple ['æpl] — Apfel
grapefruit ['greɪpfru:t] — Grapefruit, Pampelmuse
cake [keɪk] — Kuchen
sugar ['ʃʊgə] — Zucker
milk [mɪlk] — Milch
orange ['ɒrɪndʒ] — Orange, Apfelsine
pear [peə] — Birne
muesli ['mju:zli] — Müsli

7B
How many words are the same or similar in your language? — Wie viele Wörter sind in Ihrer Sprache gleich oder ähnlich?
how many [haʊ 'meni] — wie viele
same [seɪm] — gleich

V

similar ['sɪmɪlə] — ähnlich
Underline them. — Unterstreichen Sie sie.
underline ['ʌndəlaɪn] — unterstreichen

7C
supermarket ['su:pə,mɑ:kɪt] — Supermarkt
Tick the words you hear on the list above. — Kreuzen Sie auf der Liste oben die Wörter an, die Sie (auf der Cassette) hören.
tick [tɪk] — ankreuzen
list [lɪst] — Liste
above [ə'bʌv] — oben

8A
never ['nevə] — nie
sometimes ['sʌmtaɪmz] — manchmal
often ['ɒfn, 'ɒftn] — oft
always ['ɔ:lweɪz] — immer
eat [i:t] — essen
fresh fruit [freʃ 'fru:t] — frisches Obst
fresh [freʃ] — frisch
drink [drɪŋk] — trinken

8B
Find something you have in common. — Suchen Sie etwas, was sie miteinander gemein haben.
have something in common [hæv 'sʌmθɪŋ ɪn 'kɒmən] — etwas miteinander gemein haben
something ['sʌmθɪŋ] — etwas

9A
Read and listen to the poem. — Lesen Sie das Gedicht und hören Sie es an.
listen to ['lɪsn tu:] — anhören
poem ['pəʊɪm] — Gedicht
pronoun ['prəʊnaʊn] — Pronomen, Fürwort
love [lʌv] — Liebe
rock and folk songs [rɒk ən 'fəʊk sɒŋz] — Rock und Folk
rock [rɒk] — Rock(musik)
folk [fəʊk] — Volksmusik, Folk
great [greɪt] — *hier:* großartig
May the first [meɪ ðə fɜ:st] — der erste Mai
my birthday [maɪ 'bɜ:θdeɪ] — mein Geburtstag
date [deɪt] — Datum

10
syllable ['sɪləbl] — Silbe
Which is the stressed syllable? — Welche Silbe wird betont?

Preview A

2A
hidden dialogue — Versteckter Dialog

3B
Write ten more cards. — Schreiben Sie zehn weitere Karten.

3C
Now make sentences with all the cards. How many different sentences can you make and write down in ten minutes? — Bilden Sie jetzt Sätze mit den Karten. Wie viele verschiedene Sätze können Sie in zehn Minuten bilden und aufschreiben?

4
Learning words — Wörter lernen
Do exercise 5 in Preview A of the Practice Book. Discuss. — Machen Sie Übung 5 der Preview A im Practice Book. Diskutieren Sie.

5A
A lot of English words are like German words. How many can you find in the first three units? Can you group them? — Viele englische und deutsche Wörter sind gleich oder ähnlich. Wie viele können Sie in den ersten drei Kapiteln finden? Können Sie sie in Gruppen einteilen?

5B
These words are in Units 4 to 6. What are they in German? Can you guess? — Diese Wörter kommen in den Kapiteln 4 bis 6 vor. Wie heißen sie auf deutsch? Können Sie es erraten?

UNIT 4

Where do you live? — Wo wohnen Sie?
[weə du ju 'lɪv]

1A

Fill in the missing numbers. — Tragen Sie die fehlenden Zahlen ein.

missing	['mɪsɪŋ]	fehlende (-r, -s)
thirteen	[ˌθɜː'tiːn]	dreizehn
fourteen	[ˌfɔː'tiːn]	vierzehn
fifteen	[ˌfɪf'tiːn]	fünfzehn
sixteen	[ˌsɪks'tiːn]	sechzehn
seventeen	[ˌsevn'tiːn]	siebzehn
eighteen	[ˌeɪ'tiːn]	achtzehn
nineteen	[ˌnaɪn'tiːn]	neunzehn
twenty-one	[ˌtwentɪ 'wʌn]	einundzwanzig
twenty-two	[ˌtwentɪ 'tuː]	zweiundzwanzig
thirty	['θɜːtɪ]	dreißig
forty	['fɔːtɪ]	vierzig
fifty	['fɪftɪ]	fünfzig
sixty	['sɪkstɪ]	sechzig
seventy	['sevntɪ]	siebzig
eighty	['eɪtɪ]	achtzig
ninety	['naɪntɪ]	neunzig
one hundred	[wʌn 'hʌndrəd]	hundert

1B

Which number is it? — Welche Zahl ist das?

1C

bingo ['bɪŋgəʊ] — Bingo (*Name eines in England weitverbreiteten Glücksspiels*)

2

Ask questions and make notes. — Stellen Sie Fragen und machen Sie sich Notizen.

question	['kwestʃən]	Frage
make notes	[meɪk 'nəʊts]	sich Notizen machen
note	[nəʊt]	Notiz
first name	[fɜːst neɪm]	Vorname
surname	['sɜːneɪm]	Familienname, Nachname
address	[ə'dres]	Adresse
our	['aʊə]	unser (-e)
number of letters	['nʌmbər əv 'letəz]	Anzahl der Buchstaben
number	['nʌmbə]	*hier:* Anzahl
letter	['letə]	*hier:* Buchstabe
longest	['lɒŋgɪst]	längste (-r, -s)
shortest	['ʃɔːtɪst]	kürzeste (-r, -s)
street	[striːt]	Straße
house number	['haʊs nʌmbə]	Hausnummer
house	[haʊs]	Haus
biggest	['bɪgɪst]	größte (-r, -s)
smallest	['smɔːlɪst]	kleinste (-r, -s)

You know, most people's favourite number is 7, but mine is … — Wissen Sie, die Lieblingszahl der meisten Leute ist 7, aber meine ist …
[ju nəʊ məʊst 'piːplz 'feɪvrɪt 'nʌmbər ɪz 'sevn bət maɪn ɪz]

3A

post code ['pəʊst kəʊd] — Postleitzahl

3B

Can you help me, please? — Kannst du mir bitte helfen?
[kən ju 'help mi pliːz]

can	[kæn]	können
help	[help]	helfen
me	[miː]	mir, mich

What's their new address? [wɒts ðeə njuː ə'dres] — Wie lautet ihre neue Adresse?

their	[ðeə]	ihr (-e)
new	[njuː]	neu

Sorry, can you repeat that, please? ['sɒri kən ju rɪ'piːt ðæt pliːz] — Verzeihung, können Sie / kannst du das bitte wiederholen?

repeat [rɪ'piːt] — wiederholen

You're welcome. [juə 'welkəm] — Gern geschehen.

3C

Now listen again and check. — Hören Sie noch einmal zu und überprüfen Sie.

again [ə'gen] — wieder, noch einmal

5A

church	[tʃɜːtʃ]	Kirche
flat	[flæt]	Wohnung
park	[pɑːk]	Park
pub	[pʌb]	Kneipe
shop	[ʃɒp]	Geschäft, Laden
station	['steɪʃn]	Bahnhof

V

UNIT 4

Add these words and compare results. — Fügen Sie diese Worte hinzu und vergleichen Sie Ihre Ergebnisse.

add [æd]	*hier:* hinzufügen
old [əʊld]	alt
modern ['mɒdn]	modern, neu
big [bɪg]	groß
small [smɔːl]	klein
quiet ['kwaɪət]	ruhig
noisy ['nɔɪzi]	laut

5B

Where do they live? [weə dʊ ðeɪ 'lɪv]	Wo wohnen sie?
live [lɪv]	*hier:* wohnen
but my flat's quiet [bət maɪ 'flæts 'kwaɪət]	aber meine Wohnung ist ruhig
but [bʌt]	aber
garden ['gɑːdn]	Garten
town [taʊn]	Stadt
near [nɪə]	in der Nähe von
railway station ['reɪlweɪ ˌsteɪʃn]	Bahnhof
railway ['reɪlweɪ]	Eisenbahn
woods [wʊdz]	Wald

5C

people ['piːpl]	Leute
the first person [ðə fɜːst 'pɜːsn]	die erste Person
person ['pɜːsn]	Person
first [fɜːst]	erste (-r, -s)
second ['sekənd]	zweite (-r, -s)
third [θɜːd]	dritte (-r, -s)

6A

Answer the questions. — Beantworten Sie die Fragen.

answer ['ɑːnsə]	(be)antworten
Do you live in a house or a flat? [dʊ jʊ lɪv ɪn ə 'haʊs ɔːr ə 'flæt]	Wohnen Sie in einem Haus oder in einer Wohnung?
Do you live near here? [dʊ jʊ 'lɪv nɪə hɪə]	Wohnen Sie hier in der Nähe?
no [nəʊ]	nein
here [hɪə]	hier

6B

Find someone with similar answers. — Suchen Sie jemanden mit ähnlichen Antworten.

someone ['sʌmwʌn]	jemand
answer ['ɑːnsə]	Antwort

7A

long [lɒŋ]	lang
newest ['njuːɪst]	neueste (-r, -s)
nicest ['naɪsɪst]	schönste, netteste (-r, -s)
nice [naɪs]	schön, nett
noisiest ['nɔɪziɪst]	lauteste (-r, -s)
oldest ['əʊldɪst]	älteste (-r, -s)
quietest ['kwaɪətɪst]	ruhigste (-r, -s)
short [ʃɔːt]	kurz
post office ['pəʊst ˌɒfɪs]	Postamt
Britain ['brɪtn]	Großbritannien

7B

Make four pairs of opposites from the words in A. — Bilden Sie vier Gegensatzpaare mit den Wörtern in A.

pair [peə]	Paar
opposite ['ɒpəzɪt]	Gegensatz, Gegenteil
Which word is left?	Welches Wort bleibt übrig?
left [left]	*hier:* übrig

8

record ['rekɔːd]	Rekord
youngest ['jʌŋgɪst]	jüngste (-r, -s)
Belgian ['beldʒən]	belgisch
phone book ['fəʊn bʊk]	Telefonbuch
3,300 years old ['θriː 'θaʊznd 'θriː 'hʌndrəd jɪəz ˌəʊld]	3.300 Jahre alt
thousand ['θaʊznd]	tausend
year [jɪə]	Jahr
the biggest bookshop in the world [ðə 'bɪgɪst 'bʊkʃɒp ɪn ðə 'wɜːld]	die größte Buchhandlung der Welt
bookshop ['bʊkʃɒp]	Buchhandlung
world [wɜːld]	Welt
kilometre ['kɪləʊˌmiːtə]	Kilometer
book [bʊk]	Buch
2.13 × 1.37 metres ['tuː pɔɪnt wʌn 'θriː baɪ 'wʌn pɔɪnt 'θriː 'sevn 'miːtəz]	2,13 mal 1,37 Meter
× (= by) [baɪ]	*hier:* mal
run [rʌn]	(ver)laufen
border ['bɔːdə]	Grenze

9A

Make six questions and write them down. — Bilden Sie sechs Fragen und schreiben Sie sie auf.

write down [raɪt daʊn]	aufschreiben

Unit 4

9B
Ask other people in the class and report.

class [klɑːs]

Fragen Sie andere Leute in der Klasse und berichten Sie.

Klasse, Kurs

10A
place [pleɪs]
I can't even remember [aɪ ˈkɑːnt_iːvn rɪˈmembə]
remember [rɪˈmembə]

Platz, Ort
ich kann mich nicht einmal daran erinnern
sich erinnern

10B
Now write a poem like this.

Schreiben Sie jetzt ein Gedicht wie dieses.

12
Listen and mark the stressed word(s).

mark [mɑːk]

Hören Sie zu und markieren Sie das/die betonte/n Wort/Wörter.

markieren

Unit 5

travel [ˈtrævl]   Reisen

1A
train [treɪn]   Zug
plane [pleɪn]   Flugzeug
ferry [ˈferɪ]   Fähre
coach [kəʊtʃ]   Reisebus
car [kɑː]   Auto

2A
getting information [ˈgetɪŋ_ˌɪnfəˈmeɪʃn]
information [ˌɪnfəˈmeɪʃn]
ads (= advertisements) [ædz (ədˈvɜːtɪsmənts)]
by train [baɪ ˈtreɪn]
by [baɪ]

Information bekommen
Information
Werbeanzeigen
mit dem Zug
hier: mit

2B
When does flight number BA 5843 arrive in Glasgow? [wen dəz ˈflaɪt ˈnʌmbə biː eɪ faɪv eɪt fɔː θriː əˈraɪv_ɪn ˈglɑːzgəʊ]

Wann kommt der Flug (mit der) Nummer BA 5843 in Glasgow an?

Glasgow [ˈglɑːzgəʊ]
when [wen]
flight number [ˈflaɪt ˈnʌmbə]
flight [flaɪt]
arrive [əˈraɪv]
how much [haʊ mʌtʃ]
cost [kɒst]
standard return [ˈstændəd rɪˈtɜːn]
£ (= pound) [paʊnd]
how long [haʊ lɒŋ]
take [teɪk]
from Gatwick to Victoria [frɒm ˈgætwɪk tə vɪkˈtɔːrɪə]

(Stadt in Schottland)
hier: wann
Flugnummer

Flug
ankommen
wieviel
kosten
etwa: Rückfahrkarte 2. Klasse
(englisches) Pfund
wie lange
hier: dauern
von Gatwick *(Londoner Flughafen)* nach Victoria *(Londoner Bahnhof)*

from … to … [frɒm … tuː]
minute [ˈmɪnɪt]
how often [haʊ ˈɒfn, haʊ ˈɒftn]
car ferry [ˈkɑː ˌferɪ]
go to Greece [gəʊ tə ˈgriːs]
every day [ˈevrɪ ˈdeɪ]
every [ˈevrɪ]
hour [aʊə]
where from [weə frɒm]
leave [liːv]

hier: von … nach …

Minute
wie oft

Autofähre
nach Griechenland fahren
jeden Tag
jede (-r, -s)
Stunde
von wo
hier: abfahren

3A
timetable [ˈtaɪmˌteɪbl]
flight no. [ˈflaɪt ˈnʌmbə]
no. (= number) [ˈnʌmbə]
departure [dɪˈpɑːtʃə]
arrival [əˈraɪvl]
price [praɪs]

hier: Flugplan
Flugnr.
Nr.

Abflug, Abfahrt
Ankunft
Preis

4A
trip [trɪp]
travel agent's [ˈtrævl ˈeɪdʒənts]
want to go [wɒnt_tə gəʊ]

Reise
Reisebüro

fahren wollen

5
return ticket [rɪˈtɜːn ˈtɪkɪt]
ticket [ˈtɪkɪt]
where to [weə tuː]

Rückfahrkarte

hier: Fahrkarte
wohin

V

UNIT 5

5A
Make a poem from these lines. — Machen Sie aus diesen Zeilen ein Gedicht.
way in [weɪ ˈɪn] — Eingang
what for? [wɒt ˈfɔː] — wofür? wozu?
where am I? [weə ˈæm aɪ] — wo bin ich?
not today [nɒt təˈdeɪ] — heute nicht
way out [weɪ ˈaʊt] — Ausgang

5B
original [əˈrɪgɪnl] — Original-
this way [ðɪs ˈweɪ] — *hier:* hier entlang

6A
How do you get here? [haʊ dʊ jʊ ˈget hɪə] — Wie kommen Sie / kommst du hierher?
get here [get hɪə] — hierherkommen
underground [ˈʌndəgraʊnd] — U-Bahn
bike (= bicycle) [baɪk (ˈbaɪsɪkl)] — Fahrrad
tram [træm] — Straßenbahn
bus [bʌs] — Bus
motorbike [ˈməʊtəbaɪk] — Motorrad

6B
Interview two people. — Befragen Sie zwei Personen.
interview [ˈɪntəvjuː] — befragen
get to work [get tə ˈwɜːk] — zur Arbeit kommen
walk [wɔːk] — zu Fuß gehen
I work at home [aɪ ˈwɜːk ət ˈhəʊm] — ich arbeite zu Hause
work [wɜːk] — arbeiten
at home [ət ˈhəʊm] — zu Hause

6C
Report the results and make a class survey. — Berichten Sie die Ergebnisse und erstellen Sie eine Klassenübersicht.
public transport [ˈpʌblɪk ˈtrænspɔːt] — öffentliche Verkehrsmittel

7A
night train [ˈnaɪt treɪn] — Nachtzug
oh [əʊ] — *hier:* ach so
madam [ˈmædəm] — (gebräuchliche höfliche Anrede) etwa: meine Dame
British Rail [ˈbrɪtɪʃ ˈreɪl] — Britische Eisenbahngesellschaft *(Name)*
Glasgow Central [ˈglɑːzgəʊ ˈsentrəl] — Glasgow Hauptbahnhof

8A
British Airways [ˈbrɪtɪʃ ˈeəweɪz] — Britische Fluggesellschaft *(Name)*
sir [sɜː] — (gebräuchliche höfliche Anrede) etwa: mein Herr
Sorry? [ˈsɒrɪ] — *hier:* Wie bitte?
When would you like to go? [wen wʊd jʊ laɪk tə ˈgəʊ] — Wann möchten Sie fahren?
would like [wʊd laɪk] — mögen

9
role play [ˈrəʊl pleɪ] — Rollenspiel

10
Draw your own word map of this unit. — Zeichnen Sie Ihr eigenes Wörternetz von diesem Kapitel.
draw [drɔː] — zeichnen
word map [ˈwɜːd mæp] — Wörternetz
unit [juːnɪt] — Kapitel

11
Listen to the 'r' sound and practise. — Hören Sie auf den r-Laut und üben Sie.
sound [saʊnd] — Laut, Ton

UNIT 6

outdoors [ˌaʊtˈdɔːz] — draußen, im Freien

1A
colour [ˈkʌlə] — Farbe
balloon [bəˈluːn] — Ballon
blue [bluː] — blau
yellow [ˈjeləʊ] — gelb
red [red] — rot
orange [ˈɒrɪndʒ] — orange
dark green [dɑːk griːn] — dunkelgrün
dark [dɑːk] — dunkel-
green [griːn] — grün
light [laɪt] — hell-
brown [braʊn] — braun
white [waɪt] — weiß
black [blæk] — schwarz
pink [pɪŋk] — rosa
purple [ˈpɜːpl] — lila

UNIT 6

1 B

all [ɔːl]	alle
submarine [ˌsʌbməˈriːn]	Unterseeboot
I'll touch [aɪl tʌtʃ]	ich werde berühren
grass [grɑːs]	Gras
rain [reɪn]	Regen
I'm dreaming of [aɪm ˈdriːmɪŋ ɒv]	ich träume von
dream [driːm]	träumen
Christmas [ˈkrɪsməs]	Weihnachten
moon [muːn]	Mond
She's the black sheep of the family. [ʃiːz ðə ˈblæk ʃiːp ɒv ðə ˈfæməlɪ]	Sie ist das schwarze Schaf der Familie.

1 C

What do you think of when you see this colour?	Woran denken Sie, wenn Sie diese Farbe sehen?
think of [θɪŋk ɒv]	denken an

2

weather [ˈweðə]	Wetter

2 A

What do the colours mean?	Was bedeuten die Farben?
mean [miːn]	bedeuten
very cold [ˈverɪ kəʊld]	sehr kalt
cold [kəʊld]	kalt
cool [kuːl]	kühl
warm [wɔːm]	warm
hot [hɒt]	heiß

2 B

Match the words and the symbols.	Ordnen Sie die Wörter den Symbolen zu.
symbol [ˈsɪmbl]	Symbol
foggy [ˈfɒgɪ]	neblig
windy [ˈwɪndɪ]	windig
sunny [ˈsʌnɪ]	sonnig
cloudy [ˈklaʊdɪ]	bewölkt
rainy [ˈreɪnɪ]	regnerisch
word association test [wɜːd əˌsəʊsɪˈeɪʃn test]	Wortassoziationstest
Guinness [ˈgɪnɪs]	*(irisches dunkles Bier)*
snow [snəʊ]	Schnee
pure genius [pjʊə ˈdʒiːnjəs]	*etwa:* einfach genial

2 C

weather map [ˈweðə mæp]	Wetterkarte
map [mæp]	Landkarte
Scotland [ˈskɒtlənd]	Schottland
Norway [ˈnɔːweɪ]	Norwegen
Sweden [ˈswiːdn]	Schweden
Spain [speɪn]	Spanien
Majorca [məˈdʒɔːkə]	Mallorca
Corsica [ˈkɔːsɪkə]	Korsika
Sardinia [sɑːˈdɪnjə]	Sardinien
What's the weather like? [wɒts ðə ˈweðə laɪk]	Wie ist das Wetter?
What's … like? [wɒts … laɪk]	Wie ist …?
southern [ˈsʌðən]	südlich (-e, -er, -es)
eastern [ˈiːstən]	östlich (-e, -er, -es)
northern [ˈnɔːðən]	nördlich (-e, -er, -es)
western [ˈwestən]	westlich (-e, -er, -es)

3

One of you chooses a country on the map. The others can ask three questions to find out which country it is. You can only answer with 'yes' or 'no'.	Jemand von Ihnen wählt ein Land auf der Karte aus. Die anderen stellen drei Fragen um herauszufinden, um welches Land es sich handelt. Sie dürfen nur mit ‚ja' oder ‚nein' antworten.
answer [ˈɑːnsə]	antworten
the others [ðɪ ˈʌðəz]	die anderen
find out [faɪnd aʊt]	herausfinden
only [ˈəʊnlɪ]	nur
area [ˈeərɪə]	Bereich

4 A

It is May. You are on holiday on the French Riviera.	Es ist Mai. Sie machen Urlaub an der französischen Riviera.
on holiday [ɒn ˈhɒlədeɪ]	in Urlaub/Ferien
holiday [ˈhɒlədeɪ]	Urlaub, Ferien
What would you like to do?	Was möchten Sie gerne machen?
do [duː]	machen, tun
Mediterranean holiday [ˈmedɪtəˈreɪnjən ˈhɒlədeɪ]	Urlaub am Mittelmeer
newspaper [ˈnjuːsˌpeɪpə]	Zeitung
go jogging [gəʊ ˈdʒɒgɪŋ]	joggen gehen
go [gəʊ]	gehen
play cards [pleɪ kɑːdz]	Karten spielen
play [pleɪ]	spielen

V

UNIT 6

card [kɑ:d] — Karte
postcard ['pəʊstkɑ:d] — Postkarte
some [sʌm] — einige
lie on the beach [laɪ ɒn ðə 'bi:tʃ] — am Strand liegen
lie [laɪ] — liegen
beach [bi:tʃ] — Strand
go for a walk [gəʊ fɔ:r ə 'wɔ:k] — einen Spaziergang machen
walk [wɔ:k] — Spaziergang
museum [mju:'zɪəm] — Museum
go for a meal [gəʊ fɔ:r ə 'mi:l] — Essen gehen
meal [mi:l] — Essen, Mahlzeit
tennis ['tenɪs] — Tennis
shopping ['ʃɒpɪŋ] — Einkaufen
café ['kæfeɪ] — Café
hire a bike ['haɪər ə 'baɪk] — ein Fahrrad mieten
hire ['haɪə] — mieten

4B
weather report ['weðə rɪ'pɔ:t] — Wetterbericht
report [rɪ'pɔ:t] — Bericht
plan [plæn] — Plan
I'd still like to [aɪd 'stɪl laɪk tə] — Ich möchte immer noch
still [stɪl] — (immer) noch

5A
positive ['pɒzətɪv] — positiv
negative ['negətɪv] — negativ
with a great view of the sea [wɪð ə 'greɪt vju: əv ðə 'si:] — mit großartigem Blick auf das Meer
view [vju:] — Blick
sea [si:] — Meer
so [səʊ] — *hier:* so daß
we can't [wi: kɑ:nt] — wir können nicht
restaurant ['restərɔ̃:ŋ] — Restaurant
expensive [ɪk'spensɪv] — teuer
terrible ['terəbl] — schrecklich, furchtbar
there's [ðeəz] — es gibt
disco ['dɪskəʊ] — Diskothek
next door [neks 'dɔ:] — nebenan
sleep [sli:p] — schlafen
child, children [tʃaɪld, 'tʃɪldrən] — Kind, Kinder
all day [ɔ:l deɪ] — den ganzen Tag
cheap [tʃi:p] — billig
beautiful ['bju:təfʊl] — schön

5B
Dear Susan, [dɪə 'su:zn] — Liebe Susan,
dear [dɪə] — liebe (-r)
well [wel] — *etwa:* also, tja
here we are [hɪə wɪ 'ɑ:] — hier sind wir (nun)
Wish you were here. [wɪʃ ju wə 'hɪə] — *etwa:* Schade, daß Du nicht hier bist.
love [lʌv] — *etwa:* Liebe Grüße (informelle Schlußformel in Brief/Postkarte)
Back home next week. [bæk həʊm neks 'wi:k] — *etwa:* Nächste Woche sind wir wieder zu Haus.
Thank goodness! [θæŋk 'gʊdnɪs] — Zum Glück! Gott sei Dank!

6
countryside ['kʌntrɪsaɪd] — *hier:* Landschaft

6A
sky [skaɪ] — Himmel
forest ['fɒrɪst] — Wald
field [fi:ld] — Feld
tree [tri:] — Baum
mountain ['maʊntɪn] — Berg
cloud [klaʊd] — Wolke
river ['rɪvə] — Fluß

6B
Which group can find the most differences between the two pictures? — Welche Gruppe kann die meisten Unterschiede zwischen den beiden Bildern finden?
difference ['dɪfrəns] — Unterschied
between [bɪ'twi:n] — zwischen
There are no flowers in picture 2. [ðər ɑ: nəʊ 'flaʊəz ɪn 'pɪktʃə tu:] — Auf Bild 2 gibt es keine Blumen.
There's no [ðeəz nəʊ] — Es gibt kein (-e, -en)
There are [ðeər ɑ:] — Es gibt

7A
The months of the year [ðə mʌnθs əv ðə 'jɪə] — Die Monate (eines Jahres)
January ['dʒænjʊərɪ] — Januar
February ['febrʊərɪ] — Februar
March [mɑ:tʃ] — März
April ['eɪprəl] — April
May [meɪ] — Mai

UNIT 6

June [dʒu:n]	Juni
July [dʒu:'laɪ]	Juli
August ['ɔ:gəst]	August
September [sep'tembə]	September
October [ɒk'təʊbə]	Oktober
November [nəʊ'vembə]	November
December [dɪ'sembə]	Dezember
All the rest have thirty one, except [ɔ:l ðə rest‿əv 'θɜ:tɪ wʌn ɪk'sept]	Alle anderen haben 31 (Tage), außer
have [hæv]	haben
except [ɪk'sept]	außer, bis auf
leaf, leaves [li:f, li:vz]	Blatt, Blätter
bird [bɜ:d]	Vogel

8

season ['si:zn]	Jahreszeit
spring [sprɪŋ]	Frühling
summer ['sʌmə]	Sommer
autumn ['ɔ:təm]	Herbst
winter ['wɪntə]	Winter

9B

Make a class poster of the seasons. Write sentences or draw a picture for each season.	Fertigen Sie ein Klassenposter von den Jahreszeiten an. Schreiben Sie Sätze oder malen Sie ein Bild für jede Jahreszeit.
class poster ['klɑ:s ˌpəʊstə]	Klassenposter
poster ['pəʊstə]	Poster, Plakat
each [i:tʃ]	jede (-r, -s)
love [lʌv]	mögen, lieben
hate [heɪt]	nicht mögen, hassen

PREVIEW B

1

planning a class trip ['plænɪŋ‿ə 'klɑ:s trɪp]	eine Klassenreise planen
plan [plæn]	planen
tariff ['tærɪf]	Preise, Preisliste
standard room ['stændəd rʊm]	Zimmer mit Standardausstattung
single [sɪŋgl]	Einzelzimmer
per person per day [pɜ: 'pɜ:sn pɜ: 'deɪ]	pro Person pro Tag
include VAT [ɪnklu:d vi: eɪ ti:]	inklusive Mehrwertsteuer
VAT (= Value Added Tax) [vi: eɪ ti: ('vælju: ˌ'ædɪd tæks)]	Mehrwertsteuer
colour TV ['kʌlʌ ti: vi:]	Farbfernseher
teamaker ['ti:meɪkə]	Teemaschine

2B

Make a negative sentence ending with one of the following words and phrases.	Bilden Sie einen verneinten Satz, der mit einem der folgenden Wörter oder Wendungen endet.

2C

Can the others guess the beginning of your sentence?	Können die anderen Ihren Satzanfang erraten?

3A

grammar game ['græmə geɪm]	Grammatikspiel
topic ['tɒpɪk]	Thema

4

word pictures ['wɜ:d ˌpɪktʃəz]	Wortbilder
the following ['fɒləʊɪŋ]	der/die/das folgende
rain [reɪn]	Regen
umbrella [ʌm'brelə]	Regenschirm
Take one of the words from Units 1 to 6 and try to make a word picture.	Nehmen Sie eines der Wörter aus den Kapiteln 1 bis 6 und versuchen Sie, ein Wortbild daraus zu machen.

5

Can you guess what units the following words are in?	Können Sie erraten, in welchen Kapiteln die folgenden Wörter vorkommen?

one hundred and seventy-three 173

UNIT 7

family ['fæməlɪ]	Familie		

1

Faith Desai needs a visa for a visit to the United States. This is her form:	Faith Desai braucht ein Visum für einen Besuch in den Vereinigten Staaten. Dies ist ihr Formular:
need [niːd]	brauchen
visa ['viːzə]	Visum
visit ['vɪzɪt]	Besuch
United States [juːˈnaɪtɪd ˈsteɪts]	Vereinigte Staaten (von Amerika)
visa application form ['viːzə ˌæplɪˈkeɪʃn fɔːm]	Visumsantrag
family name ['fæməlɪ neɪm]	Nachname, Familienname
middle name ['mɪdl neɪm]	zweiter (Vor)Name
middle ['mɪdl]	Mitte, Mittel-
date of birth [deɪt əv ˈbɜːθ]	Geburtsdatum
date [deɪt]	Datum
birth [bɜːθ]	Geburt
year [jɪə]	Jahr
place of birth [pleɪs əv ˈbɜːθ]	Geburtsort
city ['sɪtɪ]	Stadt
nationality [ˌnæʃəˈnælətɪ]	Staatsangehörigkeit
passport ['pɑːspɔːt]	Paß
home address [həʊm əˈdres]	Heimatanschrift
business telephone number ['bɪznɪs ˈtelɪfəʊn ˈnʌmbə]	Geschäftstelefonnummer
business ['bɪznɪs]	Firma
sex [seks]	Geschlecht
male [meɪl]	männlich
female ['fiːmeɪl]	weiblich
marital status ['mærɪtl ˈsteɪtəs]	Familienstand
married ['mærɪd]	verheiratet
single ['sɪŋgl]	alleinstehend
divorced [dɪˈvɔːst]	geschieden
widowed ['wɪdəʊd]	verwitwet
separated ['sepəreɪtɪd]	getrennt
child, children [tʃaɪld, ˈtʃɪldrən]	Kind, Kinder
purpose ['pɜːpəs]	Zweck
U.S.A. [ˌjuːesˈeɪ]	United States of America, USA
date of application [deɪt əv ˌæplɪˈkeɪʃn]	Antragsdatum
signature ['sɪgnətʃə]	Unterschrift
she was born [ʃiː wəz ˈbɔːn]	sie ist geboren
she has got [ʃiː həz gɒt]	sie hat
daughter ['dɔːtə]	Tochter
son [sʌn]	Sohn
friend [frend]	Freund/in

2A

on the way [ɒn ðə ˈweɪ]	auf dem Weg
age [eɪdʒ]	Alter
How many children has Faith got? [haʊ menɪ ˈtʃɪldrən həz feɪθ gɒt]	Wie viele Kinder hat Faith?
how many [haʊ ˈmenɪ]	wie viele
She's got two children. [ʃiːs gɒt ˈtuː ˈtʃɪldrən]	Sie hat zwei Kinder.

3A

Read the text. Which picture is it?	Lesen Sie den Text. Um welches Bild handelt es sich?
text [tekst]	Text
Irish ['aɪrɪʃ]	*hier:* Irin
they've got [ðeɪv gɒt]	sie haben
called Jean [kɔːld ʒɑ̃]	namens Jean

3C

Can they guess which picture it is?	Können sie raten, um welches Bild es sich handelt?
guess [ges]	raten

4A

husband ['hʌzbənd]	Ehemann
wife [waɪf]	Ehefrau
mother ['mʌðə]	Mutter
father ['fɑːðə]	Vater
her [hɜː]	ihr (-e)
his [hɪz]	sein (-e)

5A

family tree ['fæməlɪ triː]	Stammbaum
grandson ['grænsʌn]	Enkel(sohn)
sister ['sɪstə]	Schwester
brother ['brʌðə]	Bruder

UNIT 7

parents [ˈpeərənts]	Eltern	thirtieth [ˈθɜːtɪəθ]	dreißigster
grandparents [ˈgrænˌpeərənts]	Großeltern	thirty-first [ˌθɜːtɪ ˈfɜːst]	einunddreißigster
grandchildren [ˈgrænˌtʃɪldrən]	Enkelkinder		
brother-in-law [ˈbrʌðərɪnlɔː]	Schwager		

5B

Show photos of your family and introduce the people to your group. — Zeigen Sie Fotos Ihrer Familie und stellen Sie die Personen Ihrer Gruppe vor.

show [ʃəʊ] — zeigen
photo [ˈfəʊtəʊ] — Foto
introduce [ˌɪntrəˈdjuːs] — vorstellen

7A

holiday [ˈhɒlədeɪ] — Ferien, Urlaub
special day [ˈspeʃl deɪ] — Feiertag
special [ˈspeʃl] — besonders
Boxing Day [ˈbɒksɪŋdeɪ] — zweiter Weihnachtsfeiertag
New Year's Eve [ˌnjuː jɪəz ˈiːv] — Sylvester
Christmas Day [ˈkrɪsməs ˈdeɪ] — erster Weihnachtsfeiertag
New Year's Day [ˌnjuː jɪəz ˈdeɪ] — Neujahr, 1. Januar
Christmas Eve [ˈkrɪsməs ˈiːv] — 24. Dezember, Heiligabend
fourth [fɔːθ] — vierter
fifth [fɪfθ] — fünfter
sixth [sɪksθ] — sechster
seventh [ˈsevnθ] — siebter
eighth [eɪtθ] — achter
ninth [naɪnθ] — neunter
tenth [tenθ] — zehnter
eleventh [ɪˈlevnθ] — elfter
twelfth [twelfθ] — zwölfter
thirteenth [ˌθɜːˈtiːnθ] — dreizehnter
fourteenth [ˌfɔːˈtiːnθ] — vierzehnter
fifteenth [ˌfɪfˈtiːnθ] — fünfzehnter
sixteenth [ˌsɪksˈtiːnθ] — sechzehnter
seventeenth [ˌsevnˈtiːnθ] — siebzehnter
eighteenth [ˌeɪˈtiːnθ] — achtzehnter
nineteenth [ˌnaɪnˈtiːnθ] — neunzehnter
twentieth [ˈtwentɪəθ] — zwanzigster
twenty-first [ˌtwentɪ ˈfɜːst] — einundzwanzigster
twenty-second [ˌtwentɪ ˈsekənd] — zweiundzwanzigster
twenty-third [ˌtwentɪ ˈθɜːd] — dreiundzwanzigster

8A

happy birthday [ˈhæpɪ ˈbɜːθdeɪ] — herzlichen Glückwunsch zum Geburtstag
happy [ˈhæpɪ] — glücklich
birthday [ˈbɜːθdeɪ] — Geburtstag
today [təˈdeɪ] — heute
man [mæn] — Mann
why [waɪ] — warum

8B

calendar [ˈkælɪndə] — Kalender

8C

Are there any birthdays on the same day? — Gibt es Geburtstage, die auf demselben Tag liegen?

any [ˈenɪ] — irgendein (-e), irgendwelche
my [maɪ] — mein (-e, -er)
aunt [ɑːnt] — Tante
uncle [ˈʌŋkl] — Onkel

9A

Have you got any children? [hæv jʊ gɒt enɪ ˈtʃɪldrən] — Hast du / Haben Sie Kinder?
relative [ˈrelətɪv] — Verwandte (-r)
another [əˈnʌðə] — ein anderes (Land)

10

In each group one word has a different vowel sound. Which one is it? — In jeder Gruppe gibt es ein Wort mit einem anderen Vokallaut. Welches Wort ist es?

vowel [ˈvaʊəl] — Vokal, Selbstlaut

11

Look through this unit and find examples of words with these stress patterns. — Gehen Sie dieses Kapitel durch und suchen Sie Beispiele von Wörtern mit diesen Betonungsmustern.

example [ɪgˈzɑːmpl] — Beispiel

12

Say these lines with a steady rhythm. — Sprechen Sie diese Zeilen mit gleichmäßigem Rhythmus.

V

UNIT 8

In town [ɪn taʊn] — In der Stadt

1A
buy [baɪ] — kaufen
thing [θɪŋ] — Ding, Sache
get petrol [get 'petrəl] — tanken
petrol ['petrəl] — Benzin
petrol station ['petrəl ˌsteɪʃn] — Tankstelle
garage ['gæra:dʒ] — Autoreparaturwerkstatt
cash cheques [ˌkæʃ 'tʃeks] — Schecks einlösen
cheque [tʃeks] — Scheck
bank [bæŋk] — Bank
sell [sel] — verkaufen
household goods ['haʊshəʊld 'gʊdz] — Haushaltswaren
goods [gʊdz] — Waren
newsagent's ['nju:zˌeɪdʒənts] — Zeitungshändler/in
aspirin ['æsprɪn] — Aspirin
chemist's ['kemɪsts] — Apotheke
have a drink [hæv ə 'drɪŋk] — etwas trinken
drink [drɪŋk] — trinken
a cup of coffee [ə ˌkʌp əv 'kɒfɪ] — eine Tasse Kaffee
cup [kʌp] — Tasse
post office ['pəʊst ˌɒfɪs] — Post(amt)
stamp [stæmp] — Briefmarke
tourist information centre ['tʊərɪst ˌɪnfə'meɪʃn 'sentə] — Touristeninformationsbüro

1B
How many of the things above are near your school? — Wie viele der obigen Dinge befinden sich in der Nähe Ihrer (Volkshoch)Schule?

There's a post office in Königstraße. [ðeəz ə 'pəʊst ˌɒfɪs ɪn] — In der Königstraße gibt es ein Postamt.

The station's near here. [ðə 'steɪʃns nɪə hɪə] — Der Bahnhof ist hier in der Nähe.
near [nɪə] — in der Nähe

2A
Station Road ['steɪʃn 'rəʊd] — Bahnhofstraße
road [rəʊd] — Straße

opposite ['ɒpəzɪt] — gegenüber
next to ['neks tu:] — neben
go down [gəʊ 'daʊn] — hinunter-/entlanggehen
on the left [ɒn ðə 'left] — auf der linken Seite
on the right [ɒn ðə 'raɪt] — auf der rechten Seite
on the corner [ɒn ðə 'kɔ:nə] — an der Ecke
corner ['kɔ:nə] — Ecke

2B
What can you say about these places? — Was können Sie über diese Orte sagen?
say about [seɪ ə'baʊt] — sagen über

4A
asking for directions [ˌɑ:skɪŋ fə dɪ'rekʃnz] — nach dem Weg fragen
ask for [ɑ:sk fɔ:] — fragen nach
directions [dɪ'rekʃnz] — Richtungen, *hier:* Weg
thanks a lot [ˌθæŋks ə 'lɒt] — vielen Dank
just go down [dʒʌst gəʊ daʊn] — gehen Sie einfach hinunter
just [dʒʌst] — *hier:* einfach
far [fɑ:] — weit
excuse me [ɪk'skju:z mɪ] — Verzeihung
not at all [ˌnɒt ət 'ɔ:l] — *hier:* keine Ursache, gern geschehen
Can I help you? [kən aɪ 'help jʊ] — Kann ich Ihnen helfen?
over there ['əʊvə 'ðeə] — dort drüben
over ['əʊvə] — *hier:* drüben
That's very kind of you. [ðæts 'verɪ 'kaɪnd əv jʊ] — Das ist sehr nett von Ihnen.
kind [kaɪnd] — nett, freundlich

4D
record shop ['rekɔ:d ʃɒp] — Schallplattengeschäft
record ['rekɔ:d] — Schallplatte
Where's the nearest bank, please? [weəz ðə 'nɪərɪst 'bæŋk pli:z] — Wo ist bitte die nächste Bank?

5A
When are shops, banks and pubs open and closed in your area? — Wann haben Geschäfte, Banken und Kneipen in Ihrer Gegend geöffnet und geschlossen?

open ['əʊpən] — offen, geöffnet

Unit 8

closed [kləʊzd]	geschlossen
gone to lunch [gɒn tə'lʌntʃ]	*etwa:* Mittagspause
most shops are open [ˌməʊst ʃɒps ə'rəʊpən]	die meisten Geschäfte haben geöffnet
most [məʊst]	*hier:* die meisten

5B

(Great) Britain [greɪt 'brɪtn]	Großbritannien
on weekdays [ɒn 'wiːkdeɪz]	an Wochentagen
weekday ['wiːkdeɪ]	Wochentag
most banks open at 9.30 [ˌməʊst bæŋks 'əʊpən ət 'naɪn 'θɜːtɪ]	die meisten Banken öffnen um 9.30
some banks are open on Saturday morning [ˌsʌm bæŋks 'əʊpən ɒn 'sætədɪ 'mɔːnɪŋ]	manche Banken haben am Samstagvormittag geöffnet
some [sʌm]	manche (-r, -s)
on Saturday morning [ɒn 'sætədɪ 'mɔːnɪŋ]	(am) Samstagmorgen
at the weekend [æt ðə ˌwiːk'end]	am Wochenende
weekend [ˌwiːk'end]	Wochenende
a lot of [ə 'lɒt əv]	viele
till 8 o'clock [tɪl 'eɪt ə'klɒk]	bis 8 Uhr
till [tɪl]	bis
on Thursday [ɒn 'θɜːzdɪ]	(am) Donnerstag
including [ɪn'kluːdɪŋ]	einschließlich
usually ['juːʒwəlɪ]	normalerweise, für gewöhnlich
serve meals [sɜːv miːlz]	Mahlzeiten anbieten
at lunchtime [ət 'lʌntʃtaɪm]	mittags, zur Mittagszeit

5C

Collect time phrases from B and write them in the correct boxes.	Sammeln Sie Zeitangaben aus B und schreiben Sie sie in den richtigen Kasten.

5D

Make a poster with useful information for visitors to your town or area.	Fertigen Sie ein Poster mit nützlichen Informationen für Besucher Ihrer Stadt oder Gegend an.

useful ['juːsfʊl]	nützlich
visitor ['vɪzɪtə]	Besucher

6

baker's ['beɪkəz]	Bäcker
butcher's ['bʊtʃəz]	Metzger, Fleischer
clothes shop ['kləʊðz ʃɒp]	Bekleidungsgeschäft
clothes [kləʊðz]	Kleidung
department store [dɪ'pɑːtmənt ˌstɔː]	Kaufhaus
greengrocer's ['griːnˌgrəʊsəz]	Gemüsehändler
shoe shop ['ʃuː ʃɒp]	Schuhgeschäft
shoe [ʃuː]	Schuh

7A

Listen to these people talking about the villages they live in. Tick the things they say they have got.	Hören Sie, was diese Leute über ihr Dorf berichten. Kreuzen Sie an, was sie haben.
talk about [tɔːk ə'baʊt]	sprechen über
village ['vɪlɪdʒ]	Dorf
woman, women ['wʊmən, 'wɪmɪn]	Frau, Frauen
man, men [mæn, men]	Mann, Männer
school [skuːl]	Schule
bus service ['bʌs ˌsɜːvɪs]	Busverkehr
service ['sɜːvɪs]	*hier:* Verkehr, Verbindung

7B

we've got some [wiːv gɒt sʌm]	wir haben einige
we haven't got any [wiː 'hævnt gɒt 'enɪ]	wir haben keine
there aren't any [ðeər 'ɑːnt 'enɪ]	es gibt keine
there isn't a [ðeər 'ɪznt ə]	es gibt kein (-e, -en)
some more [sʌm 'mɔː]	ein paar mehr

8A

Which is the best pub in your town or village? Discuss.	Welches ist die beste Kneipe in Ihrer Stadt oder in Ihrem Dorf? Diskutieren Sie.
which [wɪtʃ]	welche (-r, -s)
discuss [dɪ'skʌs]	diskutieren
best [best]	beste (-r, -s)
cheapest ['tʃiːpɪst]	billigste (-r, -s)

one hundred and seventy-seven 177

most interesting [ˌməʊst ˈɪntrəstɪŋ]	interessanteste (-r, -s)	a safe job [ə ˈseɪf ˈdʒɒb]	hier: ein sicherer Arbeitsplatz
interesting [ˈɪntrəstɪŋ]	interessant	safe [seɪf]	sicher

9A

How many words can you find in this unit which begin with 'B'?	Wieviele Wörter mit dem Anfangsbuchstaben ‚B' können Sie in diesem Kapitel finden?		

10

First listen and say the words. Then listen and say the sentences.	Hören Sie zunächst zu und sagen Sie die Wörter. Hören Sie dann zu und sagen Sie die Sätze.		
first [fɜːst]	zuerst, zunächst		
then [ðen]	dann		

2

reason [ˈriːzn]	Grund
secretary [ˈsekrətrɪ]	Sekretär/in
footballer [ˈfʊtbɔːlə]	Fußballspieler/in
flight attendant [ˈflaɪt əˈtendənt]	Flugbegleiter/in, Steward/ess
teacher [ˈtiːtʃə]	Lehrer/in
artist [ˈɑːtɪst]	Künstler/in

3A

doctor [ˈdɒktə]	Arzt, Ärztin

3B

Tick the words and phrases that describe it.	Kreuzen Sie die Wörter und Wendungen an, die ihn (den Beruf) beschreiben.
phrase [freɪz]	Ausdruck
describe [dɪˈskraɪb]	beschreiben
work with other people [ˌwɜːk wɪð ˈʌðə ˈpiːpl]	mit anderen Menschen arbeiten
work with [ˌwɜːk wɪð]	arbeiten mit
alone [əˈləʊn]	allein
building [ˈbɪldɪŋ]	Gebäude
make things [ˈmeɪk θɪŋz]	Dinge herstellen
do shiftwork [duː ˈʃɪftwɜːk]	Schichtarbeit machen
my own boss [maɪ ˈəʊn ˈbɒs]	mein eigener Chef, meine eigene Chefin
travel [ˈtrævl]	reisen
much [mʌtʃ]	viel

11

Which word do you hear first, the German one or the English one? Tick the 'G' for German or the 'E' for English.	Welches Wort hören Sie zuerst, das deutsche oder das englische? Kreuzen Sie ‚G' für Deutsch oder ‚E' für Englisch an.
the German one [ðə ˈdʒɜːmən wʌn]	das deutsche (Wort)
German [ˈdʒɜːmən]	deutsch

UNIT 9

at work [ət ˈwɜːk]	bei der Arbeit
40 hour week [ˈfɔːtɪ ˈaʊə ˈwiːk]	40-Stunden-Woche

1

important [ɪmˈpɔːtnt]	wichtig
job [dʒɒb]	(Arbeits)Stelle
Choose three points that are important to you.	Wählen Sie drei Punkte, die wichtig für Sie sind.
point [pɔɪnt]	Punkt
flexible [ˈfleksəbl]	flexibel
regular [ˈregjʊlə]	regelmäßig
friendly [ˈfrendlɪ]	freundlich
pay [peɪ]	Bezahlung
working hours [ˈwɜːkɪŋ ˌaʊəz]	Arbeitszeit
colleague [ˈkɒliːg]	Kollege, Kollegin
office [ˈɒfɪs]	Büro
boss [bɒs]	Chef/in

3C

bus driver [ˈbʌs ˈdraɪvə]	Busfahrer/in
engineer [ˌendʒɪˈnɪə]	Ingenieur/in

4A

policewoman [pəˈliːsˈwʊmən]	Polizistin
shop assistant [ˈʃɒp əˈsɪstənt]	Verkäufer/in
dentist [ˈdentɪst]	Zahnarzt, Zahnärztin
housewife [ˈhaʊswaɪf]	Hausfrau
travel agent [ˈtrævl ˈeɪdʒənt]	Reisebüroangestellte/r
writer [ˈraɪtə]	Schriftsteller/in
waiter [ˈweɪtə]	Kellner/in
nurse [nɜːs]	Krankenschwester, Krankenpfleger

UNIT 9

4B
Try to guess what jobs other people in the class have. Collect questions.
try [traɪ]
collect [kəˈlekt]

Versuchen Sie zu erraten, welche Berufe andere Leute in der Klasse haben. Sammeln Sie Fragen.
versuchen
sammeln

4D
Yes, I do. [ˈjes aɪ ˈduː]

Ja.

5A
the big jam [ðə ˌbɪg ˈdʒæm]
start work [stɑːt wɜːk]

on time [ɒn ˈtaɪm]
I'm never late for work. [aɪm ˈnevə leɪt fə ˈwɜːk]
traffic jam [ˈtræfɪk ˌdʒæm]

der große (Verkehrs) Stau
mit der Arbeit beginnen
pünktlich
Ich komme nie zu spät zur Arbeit.

Verkehrsstau

5B
In the evening the same people talk about the traffic jam.
same [seɪm]
were [wɜː]
the last people [ðə ˈlɑːst ˈpiːpl]
the last [ðə ˈlɑːst]
had [hæd]

got to [gɒt tə]

The tram was fifteen minutes late. [ðə ˈtræm wəz ˈfɪftiːn ˈmɪnɪts ˈleɪt]
was [wɒz]
late [leɪt]
took [tʊk]

as usual [æs ˈjuːʒwl]

went [went]

arrived [əˈraɪvd]

started [ˈstɑːtɪd]

Am Abend sprechen dieselben Leute über den Verkehrsstau.
hier: dieselben
Verg.-Form v. *be:* sein
die letzten (Leute)

der/die/das Letzte
Verg.-Form v. *have:* haben
Verg.-Form v. *get to:* ankommen
Die Straßenbahn hatte 15 Minuten Verspätung.

Verg.-Form v. *be:* sein
spät
Verg.-Form v. *take:* nehmen
wie immer, wie gewöhnlich
Verg.-Form v. *go:* gehen
Verg.-Form v. *arrive:* ankommen
Verg.-Form v. *start:* beginnen

6
round the block [ˌraʊnd ðə ˈblɒk]

um den Block

7A
Read this 50-word story and choose a title.
story [ˈstɔːrɪ]
title [ˈtaɪtl]
saw [sɔː]

her [hɜː]
wanted [ˈwɒntɪd]

speak to [spiːk tʊ]
decided [dɪˈsaɪdɪd]

wasn't there [ˈwɒznt ˈðeə]
wasn't [ˈwɒznt]
that's life [ðæts ˈlaɪf]

life, lives [laɪf, laɪvz]

Lesen sie diese Geschichte mit 50 Wörtern und wählen Sie einen Titel.
Geschichte
Titel
Verg.-Form v. *see:* sehen
sie, ihr
Verg.-Form v. *want:* wollen
hier: ansprechen
Verg.-Form v. *decide:* entscheiden
war nicht da

war nicht
etwa: so spielt das Leben
Leben

9A
Listen to the sentences on the cassette and mark the places where you hear the same weak vowel as in 'husband', 'autumn' and 'modern'.

Hören Sie die Sätze auf der Cassette an und kennzeichnen Sie die Stellen, an denen Sie denselben schwachen Vokal wie in ‚husband', ‚autumn' und ‚modern' hören.

PREVIEW C

1A
Look quickly at the three texts.
dictionary [ˈdɪkʃənrɪ]

Sehen Sie sich kurz die drei Texte an.
Wörterbuch

1B
Read the texts again quickly and match them to the topics.

Lesen Sie die Texte noch einmal kurz durch und ordnen Sie sie den Themen zu.

V

PREVIEW C

1D

family planning ['fæməlɪ 'plænɪŋ]	Familienplanung
half way between rain and snow [ˌhɑːlf 'weɪ bɪ'twiːn 'reɪn ən 'snəʊ]	*etwa:* eine Mischung aus Regen und Schnee
a long way away from reality [ə 'lɒŋ weɪ ə'weɪ frɒm rɪ'æləti]	*etwa:* weit entfernt von der Realität
I heard your voice [aɪ hɜːd jə 'vɔɪs]	hörte ich deine Stimme
Piccadilly Circus [ˌpɪkə'dɪli 'sɜːkəs]	*(große Kreuzung im Zentrum Londons)*
I told you. [aɪ 'təʊld jʊ]	*hier:* Ich sagte es dir.
you said [jʊ sed]	du sagtest
I wonder. [aɪ 'wʌndə]	*hier:* Frage ich mich.
Friendship International ['frenʃɪp ˌɪntə'næʃnl]	*(Firmenname)*
hard [hɑːd]	hart
Frank received lots of letters [fræŋk rɪ'siːvd 'lɒts ɒv 'letəz]	Frank erhielt viele Briefe
FSI products [efesaɪ 'prɒdʌkts]	*(Eigenname eines Produkts)*
strange [streɪndʒ]	*hier:* seltsam
from all over the world [frɒm 'ɔːl 'əʊvə ðə 'wɜːld]	aus der ganzen Welt
"Yes", replied Frank [jes rɪ'plaɪd]	„Ja", antwortete Frank

3

Be a verb! — Sei ein Verb!

5

These are the topics of the next 3 units: Memories (Unit 10), Living in Europe (Unit 11) and Leisure (Unit 12). — Dieses sind die Themen der nächsten 3 Kapitel: Erinnerungen (Unit 10), In Europa leben (Unit 11) und Freizeit (Unit 12).

UNIT 10

memories ['meməriz]	Erinnerungen
report [rɪ'pɔːt]	*hier:* Zeugnis
subject ['sʌbdʒɪkt]	*hier:* Schulfach
grade [greɪd]	Zensur, Note
Wait a minute! This is my history shirt! [ˌweɪt ə 'mɪnɪt ðɪs ɪz maɪ 'hɪstəri ʃɜːt]	Moment mal! Das ist (ja) mein Geschichte-Hemd!

1A

maths (= mathematics) [mæθs, ˌmæθ'mætɪks]	Mathematik
history ['hɪstəri]	Geschichte
geography [dʒɪ'ɒgrəfi]	Geographie, Erdkunde
science ['saɪəns]	Naturwissenschaften
biology [baɪ'ɒlədʒɪ]	Biologie
chemistry ['kemɪstri]	Chemie
physics ['fɪzɪks]	Physik
art [ɑːt]	Kunst
PE (Physical Education) [piː 'iː]	Sport
education [ˌedʒʊ'keɪʃn]	(Aus)Bildung, Erziehung

2A

at school [ət 'skuːl]	in der Schule
favourite ['feɪvrɪt]	Lieblings-
boring ['bɔːrɪŋ]	langweilig
What were you good at? ['wɒt wɜː jʊ 'gʊd ət]	Worin warst du / waren Sie gut?
good at [gʊd æt]	gut in
bad at [bæd æt]	schlecht in
drink [drɪŋk]	Getränk
RE (Religious Education) [ɑːr iː, rɪ'lɪdʒəs ˌedʒʊ'keɪʃn]	Religion(sunterricht)

2D

I spoke to Christine. [aɪ spəʊk tə krɪs'tiːn]	Ich habe mit Christine gesprochen.
spoke [spəʊk]	Verg.-Form v. *speak:* sprechen

3A

Listen to the song from 1 again and tick the correct statement. — Hören Sie das Lied aus 1 noch einmal an und kreuzen Sie die richtige Aussage an.

singer ['sɪŋə]	Sänger/in
the singer is in love with a girl who loves him [ðə 'sɪŋər ɪz ɪn 'lʌv wɪð ə 'gɜːl huː 'lʌvz hɪm]	der Sänger ist in ein Mädchen verliebt, das ihn liebt
in love with [ɪn lʌv wɪð]	verliebt sein in
girl [gɜːl]	Mädchen
him [hɪm]	*hier:* ihn
if the singer wins the girl [ɪf ðə 'sɪŋə wɪnz ðə 'gɜːl]	wenn der Sänger das Mädchen (für sich) gewinnt
win [wɪn]	gewinnen

UNIT 10

the world will be wonderful [ðə 'wɜːld wɪl biː 'wʌndəfʊl]	wird die Welt wunderbar sein
be [biː]	sein
wonderful ['wʌndəfʊl]	wunderbar
easy ['iːzɪ]	leicht
good marks [gʊd mɑːks]	gute Noten
mark [mɑːk]	*hier:* Note
because of [bɪ'kɒz əv]	wegen

4A

then and now [ðen ənd naʊ]	damals und heute
then [ðen]	*hier:* damals
when he was 15 [wen hiː wɒz ˌfɪf'tiːn]	als er 15 (Jahre alt) war
when [wen]	als
chips [tʃɪps]	Pommes Frites

4B

Match the beginnings of the sentences and the ends.	Ordnen Sie die Satzanfänge den Satzenden zu.
he didn't like [hiː 'dɪdnt ˌlaɪk]	er mochte nicht
classical music ['klæsɪkl 'mjuːzɪk]	klassische Musik
classical ['klæsɪkl]	klassisch
thought [θɔːt]	Verg.-Form v. *think:* denken
couldn't ['kʊdnt]	Verg.-Form v. *can:* können
sing [sɪŋ]	singen
ate [et, eɪt]	Verg.-Form v. *eat:* essen
a day [ə 'deɪ]	am Tag
started ['stɑːtɪd]	Verg.-Form v. *start:* beginnen
so many ['səʊ ˌmenɪ]	so viele
he's very interested in it [hiːs 'verɪ 'ɪntrəstɪd ɪn ɪt]	er interessiert sich sehr dafür
be interested in [biː 'ɪntrəstɪd ɪn]	sich für etwas interessieren

5

What they remember [wɒt ðeɪ rɪ'membə]	Woran sie sich erinnern

5A

Here are some memories of school, jobs, learning experiences and holidays.	Hier sind einige Erinnerungen an die Schulzeit, die Arbeit, Lernerfahrungen und Ferien.
learning experience ['lɜːnɪŋ ɪk'spɪərɪəns]	Lernerfahrung

5B

theatre group [θɪ'ətə gruːp]	Theatergruppe
exciting [ɪk'saɪtɪŋ]	aufregend, spannend
I spent most of my time [aɪ spent 'məʊst əv maɪ 'taɪm]	Ich verbrachte die meiste Zeit mit …
spent [spent]	Verg.-Form v. *spend:* verbringen
most of my time ['məʊst əv maɪ 'taɪm]	die meiste Zeit
hockey ['hɒkɪ]	*hier:* Eishockey
baseball ['beɪsbɔːl]	Baseball *(amerikanisches Ballspiel)*
moved [muːvd]	Verg.-Form v. *move:* umziehen
several times ['sevrəl ˌtaɪmz]	einige Male
several ['sevrəl]	einige
a bit difficult [ə ˌbɪt 'dɪfɪkəlt]	ein bißchen schwierig
difficult ['dɪfɪkəlt]	schwierig
worst [wɜːst]	schlimmste (-s, -r)
move [muːv]	Umzug
prison ['prɪzn]	Gefängnis
learned [lɜːnd]	Verg.-Form v. *learn:* lernen
in the outside world [ɪn ðɪ 'aʊtsaɪd 'wɜːld]	*etwa:* draußen
wash dishes [wɒʃ 'dɪʃɪz]	Geschirr spülen, abwaschen
proud of [praʊd əv]	stolz auf
impossible [ɪm'pɒsəbl]	unmöglich
swim [swɪm]	schwimmen
quite late [kwaɪt 'leɪt]	recht spät
quite [kwaɪt]	recht, ganz (schön)
running dive ['rʌnɪŋ 'daɪv]	Kopfsprung mit Anlauf
I remember holidays best [aɪ rɪ'membə 'hɒlədeɪz best]	Ich erinnere mich am besten an die Ferien.
grandmother ['græn,mʌðə]	Großmutter
fantastic [fæn'tæstɪk]	fantastisch
panoramic [ˌpænə'ræmɪk]	Panorama-
gardener ['gɑːdnə]	Gärtner/in
those [ðəʊz]	*hier:* das
really ['rɪəlɪ]	wirklich
happy times ['hæpɪ ˌtaɪmz]	glückliche Zeiten
time [taɪm]	Zeit

V

UNIT 10

rained [reɪnd]	Verg.-Form v. *rain*: regnen	chess [tʃes]	Schach
		doctorate [ˈdɒktərət]	Doktor(titel)
5 C		Greek [griːk]	griechisch
Read the texts again. What belongs together?	Lesen Sie die Texte noch einmal. Was gehört zusammen?	count [kaʊnt]	zählen
		also [ˈɔːlsəʊ]	auch
belong together [bɪˈlɒŋ təˈgeðə]	zusammengehören	don't worry [ˌdəʊnt ˈwʌrɪ]	keine Sorge!
		worry [ˈwʌrɪ]	sich Sorgen machen
5 D		over 60 [ˈəʊvə ˈsɪkstɪ]	über 60 (Jahre alt)
Find ten past tense forms in the texts, five regular and five irregular.	Suchen Sie in den Texten zehn Vergangenheitsformen, fünf regelmäßige und fünf unregelmäßige.	over [ˈəʊvə]	über
		business [ˈbɪznɪs]	Firma
		American painter [əˈmerɪkən ˈpeɪntə]	amerikanische Malerin
past tense form [pɑːst tens fɔːm]	Vergangenheitsform	American [əˈmerɪkən]	amerikanisch
irregular [ɪˈregjʊlə]	unregelmäßig	painter [ˈpeɪntə]	Maler/in
		paint [peɪnt]	malen
5 E			
liked [laɪkd]	Verg.-Form v. *like*: mögen	**7 B**	
		drive [draɪv]	(Auto) fahren
That's true. [ðæts ˈtruː]	Das ist wahr.	use a computer [juːz ə kəmˈpjuːtə]	einen Computer benutzen
true [truː]	wahr		
false [fɔːls]	falsch	computer [kəmˈpjuːtə]	Computer
		use [juːz]	benutzen
7		ride a bike [raɪd ə ˈbaɪk]	radfahren
brilliant children [ˈbrɪljənt ˈtʃɪldrən]	*etwa:* Wunderkinder	**8**	
brilliant [ˈbrɪljənt]	brilliant	nonsense [ˈnɒnsəns]	Nonsens
		Illustrate something from the poems.	Zeichnen Sie etwas aus den Gedichten.
7 A			
Complete the following text. Fill in the verbs.	Vervollständigen Sie den folgenden Text. Setzen Sie die Zeitwörter ein.	city [ˈsɪtɪ]	Stadt
		The moon lay thick upon the ground [ðə ˈmuːn leɪ ˈθɪk əˈpɒn ðə ˌgraʊnd]	Der Mond lag hoch auf der Erde
following [ˈfɒləʊɪŋ]	folgende (-r, -s)		
verb [vɜːb]	Zeitwort	lay [leɪ]	Verg.-Form v. *lie:* liegen
could [kʊd]	Verg.-Form v. *can*: können	ground [graʊnd]	Erde, Boden
		The snow shone in the sky [ðə ˈsnəʊ ʃɒn ɪn ðə ˈskaɪ]	Der Schnee schien am Himmel
wrote [rəʊt]	Verg.-Form v. *write*: schreiben		
write music [ˌraɪt ˈmjuːzɪk]	komponieren	shone [ʃɒn]	Verg.-Form von *shine:* scheinen
won [wʌn]	Verg.-Form von *win*: gewinnen	The flowers were singing sweetly [ðə ˈflaʊəz wɜː ˌsɪŋɪŋ ˈswiːtlɪ]	Die Blumen sangen süß
study mathematics [ˈstʌdɪ ˌmæθəˈmætɪks]	Mathematik studieren	The birds were in full bloom [ðə ˈbɜːdz wɜːr ɪn fʊl ˈbluːm]	Die Vögel standen in voller Blüte
study [ˈstʌdɪ]	studieren	cellar [ˈselə]	Keller
mathematician [ˌmæθəˈtɪʃn]	Mathematiker	clean [kliːn]	sauber
		an upstairs room [ænˈʌpsteəz ˈrʊm]	eines der oberen Zimmer
British [ˈbrɪtɪʃ]	britisch		
chess player [ˈtʃes ˈpleɪə]	Schachspieler/in	said [sed]	Verg.-Form v. *say*: sagen

UNIT 10

kissed [kɪst]	Verg.-Form v. *kiss*: küssen
eye [aɪ]	Auge
worst luck [wɜːst lʌk]	*etwa:* so ein Pech
missed [mɪst]	Verg.-Form v. *miss*: daneben treffen, verfehlen

9

as quickly as [əs ˈkwɪklɪ æs]	so schnell wie
as ... as [æs ... æs]	so ... wie
quick [kwɪk]	schnell
an 'A student' [æn ˈeɪ ˌstjuːdnt]	*etwa:* Musterschüler

UNIT 11

Living in Europe [lɪvɪŋ ɪn ˈjʊərəp]	In Europa leben
Europe [ˈjʊərəp]	Europa

1

population [ˌpɒpjʊˈleɪʃn]	Bevölkerung
fairly [ˈfeəlɪ]	ziemlich
industrial [ɪnˈdʌstrɪəl]	industrialisiert, Industrie-
land [lænd]	Land, Boden
wages [ˈweɪdʒɪz]	Löhne
low [ləʊ]	niedrig
large [lɑːdʒ]	groß
company [ˈkʌmpənɪ]	Firma
factory [ˈfæktərɪ]	Fabrik
industry [ˈɪndəstrɪ]	Industrie
tourism [ˈtʊərɪsm]	Tourismus
offer [ˈɒfə]	(an)bieten
attractive [əˈtræktɪv]	attraktiv
tourist [ˈtʊərɪst]	Tourist/in
historical [hɪˈstɒrɪkl]	historisch
old parts of the towns [ˈəʊld pɑːts əv ðə ˈtaʊnz]	Altstädte
part [pɑːt]	Teil
clean [kliːn]	sauber
pleasant [ˈpleznt]	angenehm
local people [ˈləʊkl ˈpiːpl]	Einheimische
local [ˈləʊkl]	ortsansässig, lokal
healthy [ˈhelθɪ]	gesund
climate [ˈklaɪmɪt]	Klima
dry [draɪ]	trocken

2A

I know what it means. [aɪ ˈnəʊ wɒt ɪt ˈmiːnz]	Ich weiß, was es bedeutet.
I'm not sure. [aɪm nɒt ˈʃɔː]	Ich bin mir nicht sicher.
dirty [ˈdɜːtɪ]	schmutzig

3B

Listen again and write down the first two or three words at the beginning of the sentences. — Hören Sie noch einmal zu und schreiben Sie die ersten zwei oder drei Wörter am Anfang der Sätze auf.

4A

quite [kwaɪt]	ganz, ziemlich

4B

I'm afraid I don't agree. [aɪm əˈfreɪd aɪ dəʊnt əˈgriː]	*etwa:* Das finde ich nicht. / Ich fürchte, ich stimme nicht mit dir/Ihnen überein.
I'm afraid [aɪm əˈfreɪd]	ich fürchte
agree [əˈgriː]	übereinstimmen, zustimmen
It depends. [ɪt dɪˈpendz]	Es kommt darauf an.
I agree with that. [aɪ əˈgriː wɪð ðæt]	Ich stimme dem zu. / Das finde ich auch.
agree with [əˈgriː wɪð]	übereinstimmen mit

5

abroad [əˈbrɔːd]	im Ausland
bad weather [ˌbæd ˈweðə]	schlechtes Wetter
stay [steɪ]	*hier:* sein, sich aufhalten
at home [ət ˈhəʊm]	zu Hause
visit [ˈvɪzɪt]	besuchen
English-speaking [ˈɪŋglɪʃ ˈspiːkɪŋ]	englischsprachig
city [ˈsɪtɪ]	(Groß)Stadt
island [ˈaɪlənd]	Insel

6

twin town [twɪn taʊn]	Partnerstadt
probably more than any other town [ˈprɒbəblɪ ˈmɔː ðən ˈenɪ ˈʌðə taʊn]	wahrscheinlich mehr als jede andere Stadt
probably [ˈprɒbəblɪ]	wahrscheinlich
more than [ˈmɔː ðæn]	mehr als
following [ˈfɒləʊɪŋ]	*hier:* das folgende

V

UNIT 11

interview ['ɪntəvju:]	Interview	as you know [æs ju 'nəʊ]	wie Sie wissen
International Relations Officer [ˌɪntə'næʃənl rɪ'leɪʃnz 'ɒfɪsə]	*etwa:* Beauftragte für Auslandsbeziehungen	plan [plæn]	planen, vorhaben
contact ['kɒntækt]	Kontakt	stay a week [steɪ ə 'wi:k]	eine Woche bleiben
		enjoy [ɪn'dʒɔɪ]	etwas gerne tun

6A

Listen to the interview again and tick the towns and countries she mentions. — Hören Sie das Interview noch einmal an und kreuzen Sie die Städte und Länder an, die sie erwähnt.

mention ['menʃn]	erwähnen	walk around [wɔ:k ə'raʊnd]	umhergehen
		lots of [lɒts əv]	viele
		try [traɪ]	ausprobieren, versuchen

6B

Listen again and match each place and the reasons she gives. — Hören Sie noch einmal zu und ordnen Sie jedem Ort die Gründe zu, die sie angibt.

give [gɪv]	geben	that's probably enough questions already [ðæts 'prɒbəblɪ ɪ'nʌf 'kwestʃənz ɔ:l'redɪ]	das sind wahrscheinlich schon genug Fragen
language learning contacts ['læŋgwɪdʒ ˌlɜ:nɪŋ 'kɒntækts]	Sprachlernkontakte	enough [ɪ'nʌf]	genug
language learning ['læŋgwɪdʒ ˌlɜ:nɪŋ]	Sprachlern-	already [ɔ:l'redɪ]	schon
sporting contacts ['spɔ:tɪŋ 'kɒntækts]	Sportkontakte	invitation [ˌɪnvɪ'teɪʃn]	Einladung
political [pə'lɪtɪkl]	politisch	I'm really looking forward to the visit. [aɪm 'rɪəlɪ lʊkɪŋ 'fɔ:wəd tʊ ðə 'vɪzɪt]	Ich freue mich sehr auf den Besuch.
		look forward to [lʊk 'fɔ:wəd tʊ]	sich freuen auf
		Yours sincerely [jɔ:s sɪn'sɪəlɪ]	Mit freundlichen Grüßen

7

How many twin towns has your town or area got? — Wie viele Partnerstädte hat Ihre Stadt oder Gegend?

how far [haʊ fɑ:]	wie weit		
detail ['di:teɪl]	Detail, Angabe		

8A

A group of people from Britain plan to visit your town or area. Read this letter to one of the host families. — Eine Gruppe (von Leuten) aus Großbritannien plant einen Besuch in Ihrer Stadt oder Gegend. Lesen Sie den Brief an eine der Gastfamilien.

8B

host family ['həʊst ˌfæməlɪ]	Gastfamilie	Ms [mɪz]	Frau (*Anrede; auch für unverheiratete Frauen*)
thank you very much for your letter [θæŋk jʊ 'verɪ mʌtʃ fə jə 'letə]	vielen Dank für Ihren Brief	a little information [ə 'lɪtl ˌɪnfə'meɪʃn]	einige Informationen
letter ['letə]	Brief	in and around ['ɪn ənd ə'raʊnd]	in und um
I'd love to [aɪd 'lʌv tʊ]	ich würde gerne	you never know! [jʊ 'nevə nəʊ]	man kann nie wissen
stay with [steɪ wɪð]	wohnen bei		
come [kʌm]	kommen		

9A

fair city [feə 'sɪtɪ]	*hier:* schöne Stadt
pretty ['prɪtɪ]	hübsch
set eyes on [set 'aɪz ɒn]	ein Auge werfen auf
sweet [swi:t]	süß
bring [brɪŋ]	bringen
tulip ['tju:lɪp]	Tulpe
springtime ['sprɪŋtaɪm]	Frühling(szeit)
drizzle ['drɪzl]	nieseln
sizzle ['sɪzl]	brutzeln
what's the matter with ['wɒts ðə 'mætə wɪð]	was ist (los) mit
go round and round [gəʊ raʊnd ənd raʊnd]	sich im Kreis drehen
fall down [fɔ:l daʊn]	einstürzen

Unit 11

10A
Surprising statistics [sə'praɪzɪŋ stə'tɪstɪks] — Überraschende Statistiken
statistic [stə'tɪstɪk] — Statistik, statistischer Wert
all the names in the book ['ɔ:l ðə 'neɪmz ɪn ðə 'bʊk] — hier: alle dieser Namen
dog [dɒg] — Hund
register ['redʒɪstə] — registrieren
high [haɪ] — hoch
waterfall ['wɔ:təfɔ:l] — Wasserfall
wine barrel [waɪn 'bærəl] — Weinfaß
hold [həʊld] — (ent)halten
litre ['li:tə] — Liter
Cyprus ['saɪprəs] — Zypern
smoke [sməʊk] — rauchen
more cigarettes than any other people ['mɔ: ˌsɪgə'rets ðən 'enɪ ˌʌðə 'pi:pl] — mehr Zigaretten als jedes andere Volk
cigarette [ˌsɪgə'ret] — Zigarette
per person [pə 'pɜ:sn] — pro Person
per [pɜ:] — pro
on a good day [ɒn ə 'gʊd deɪ] — *etwa:* wenn er gut in Form ist

11B
Round off the following numbers. — Runden Sie die folgenden Zahlen ab/auf.
hundred ['hʌndrəd] — hundert
thousand ['θaʊznd] — tausend
million ['mɪljən] — Million
that's about [ðæts ə'baʊt] — das sind ungefähr

12A
Listen to the words on the cassette and mark 'f' or 'v' according to the sound in the word. — Hören Sie die Wörter auf der Cassette an und keuzen Sie entsprechend dem im Wort vorkommenden Laut ‚f' oder ‚v' an.

Unit 12

1
leisure activities ['leʒər æk'tɪvətɪz] — Freizeitbeschäftigungen

1A
Tick the things you do regularly in your free time. — Kreuzen Sie die Dinge an, die Sie regelmäßig in Ihrer Freizeit tun.
free time [fri: taɪm] — Freizeit
go dancing [gəʊ 'dɑ:nsɪŋ] — tanzen gehen
dance [dɑ:ns] — tanzen
have a lie-in [hæv ə 'laɪ ɪn] — ausschlafen, lange schlafen
play the piano [pleɪ ðə pɪ'ænəʊ] — Klavier spielen
piano [pɪ'ænəʊ] — Klavier
watch TV [wɒtʃ ˌti:'vi:] — fernsehen
watch [wɒtʃ] — ansehen
TV (= television) [ˌti:'vi:, telɪ'vɪʒn] — Fernsehen
get some exercise [get səm 'eksəsaɪz] — sich fit halten, sich Bewegung verschaffen
exercise ['eksəsaɪz] — Übung, Bewegung, auch: Gymnastik
relax at home [rɪ'læks ət 'həʊm] — sich zu Hause entspannen/ausruhen
relax [rɪ'læks] — sich entspannen/ausruhen
book [bʊk] — Buch

1B
once a week ['wʌns ə 'wi:k] — einmal in der Woche
twice a month ['twaɪs ə 'mʌnθ] — zweimal im Monat
three times a year ['θri: taɪmz ə 'jɪə] — dreimal im Jahr

1C
Report. What do you both do? — Berichten Sie. Was tun Sie beide?
both [bəʊθ] — beide

2
Here are some results from a survey about leisure activities in Britain. — Hier sind einige Ergebnisse einer Umfrage über Freizeitbeschäftigungen in Großbritannien.
per cent [pə 'sent] — Prozent

V

UNIT 12

do absolutely nothing [duː ˈæbsəluːtlɪ ˈnʌθɪŋ]	überhaupt nichts tun	Celtic [ˈkeltɪk]	keltisch
absolutely [ˈæbsəluːtlɪ]	überhaupt	tradition [trəˈdɪʃn]	Tradition
nothing [ˈnʌθɪŋ]	nichts	love of music [lʌv əv ˈmjuːzɪk]	Liebe zur Musik
three hours a week [ˈθriː ˈaʊəz ə ˈwiːk]	drei Stunden in der Woche / pro Woche	instrument [ˈɪnstrʊmənt]	(Musik)Instrument
cat [kæt]	Katze	fiddle [ˈfɪdl]	Fiedel, Geige
radio [ˈreɪdɪəʊ]	Radio	Uilleann pipes [ˈɪlən paɪps]	(irischer Dudelsack)
make love [meɪk ˈlʌv]	sich lieben, miteinander schlafen	harp [hɑːp]	Harfe
in front of [ɪn ˈfrʌnt əv]	vor	national symbol [ˈnæʃənl ˈsɪmbl]	Nationalsymbol, Wahrzeichen
		national [ˈnæʃənl]	national
3		list of events [ˌlɪst əv ɪˈvents]	Veranstaltungsprogramm
Céad míle fáilte (*Irish:* a hundred thousand welcomes) [ˈkɪad ˈmiːlɪ ˈfɑːlhɪ (ˈaɪrɪʃ ə ˈhʌndrəd ˈθaʊznd ˈwelkəmz)]	*Irisch:* Herzlich willkommen!	event [ɪˈvent]	Ereignis, Veranstaltung
		press [pres]	Presse, *hier:* Zeitung
		céol (*Irish:* music) [keɪl (ˈaɪrɪʃ ˈmjuːzɪk)]	*Irisch:* Musik
telling jokes [ˈtelɪŋ dʒəʊks]	Witze erzählen	concert [ˈkɒnsət]	Konzert
news [njuːz]	Neuigkeiten	festival [ˈfestəvl]	Festival
pass the time away [ˌpɑːs ðə ˈtaɪm əˈweɪ]	die Zeit vertreiben	institution [ˌɪnstɪˈtjuːʃn]	Institution
we watched the Galway salmon run [wɪ wɒtʃt ðə ˈɡɔːlweɪ ˈsæmən rʌn]	wir sahen den Galway-Lachs ziehen	talk [tɔːk]	reden, sich unterhalten
		play music [pleɪ ˈmjuːzɪk]	Musik machen
Galway [ˈɡɒlweɪ]	(Grafschaft in Irland)	together [təˈɡeðə]	zusammen
silver [ˈsɪlvə]	Silber	tourist attraction [ˈtʊərɪst əˈtrækʃn]	Touristenattraktion
darting [ˈdɑːtɪŋ]	*hier:* durchs Wasser schießen	sing along [sɪŋ əˈlɒŋ]	mitsingen
		ballad [ˈbæləd]	Ballade
sun [sʌn]	Sonne	kind of [kaɪnd əv]	Art von
shore [ʃɔː]	Ufer, Küste	sad [sæd]	traurig
sunset [ˈsʌnset]	Sonnenuntergang	fast [fɑːst]	schnell
stood [stʊd]	Verg.-Form v. *stand:* stehen	slow [sləʊ]	langsam
		hard work [hɑːd wɜːk]	harte Arbeit
Atlantic sea [ətˈlæntɪk ˈsiː]	Atlantik	hard times [hɑːd taɪmz]	harte Zeiten
		against [əˈɡenst]	gegen
fiddler [ˈfɪdlə]	Geigenspieler/in		
bow [bəʊ]	Bogen	**3B**	
reel [riːl]	Reel *(irischer Tanz)*	*Read the whole text.*	Lesen Sie den ganzen Text.
grand and gay [ˈɡrænd ənd ˈɡeɪ]	großartig und fröhlich		
cast [kɑːst]	die Angel auswerfen	**4A**	
wild foam [waɪld fəʊm]	wilde Gischt	Let's go out tonight. [lets ɡəʊ ˈaʊt təˈnaɪt]	Laß uns heute abend ausgehen.
bass [bæss]	Barsch	let's [lets]	laß uns
		go out [ɡəʊ ˈaʊt]	ausgehen
3A		tonight [təˈnaɪt]	heute abend
strong Celtic traditions [ˌstrɒŋ ˈkeltɪk trəˈdɪʃnz]	ausgeprägte keltische Traditionen	cinema [ˈsɪnəmə]	Kino
strong [strɒŋ]	stark, ausgeprägt	That's a good idea. [ðæts ə ˈɡʊd aɪˈdɪə]	Das ist eine gute Idee.

UNIT 12

idea [aɪˈdɪə]	Idee
Shall we [ʃæl wiː]	Sollen wir
I'd rather [aɪd ˈrɑːðə]	Ich würde lieber
so noisy [ˌsəʊ ˈnɔɪzi]	so laut
so [səʊ]	*hier:* so
noisy [ˈnɔɪzi]	laut

4C

I don't mind. [aɪ dəʊnt maɪnd]	Das ist mir egal.

4D

Great! [greɪt]	Toll!
What about you? [ˌwɒt əˈbaʊt ˈjuː]	Was meinst du?

4E

pick [pɪk]	*hier:* aussuchen
Mexican [ˈmeksɪkən]	mexikanisch
spicy [ˈspaɪsi]	gewürzt, scharf
heavy [ˈhevi]	schwer
Chinese [ˌtʃaɪˈniːz]	chinesisch
rich [rɪtʃ]	*etwa:* liegt schwer im Magen
exotic [ɪgˈzɒtɪk]	exotisch
headache [ˈhedeɪk]	Kopfschmerzen
I give up [aɪ gɪv ʌp]	Ich gebe (es) auf.
give up [gɪv ʌp]	aufgeben
told [təʊld]	Verg.-Form v. *tell:* erzählen

5A

What's on [wɒts ɒn]	Was läuft/gibt's
theatre [ˈθɪətə]	Theater

5B

You are on a class trip to Dublin.	Sie sind auf Kursreise in Dublin.

5C

Discuss a programme for an evening out with one or two other people.	Besprechen Sie ein Programm für einen Abend in der Stadt mit ein oder zwei anderen Leuten.
evening out [ˈiːvnɪŋ ˈaʊt]	Ausgehabend

6

You are now on the plane back home. Tell the others what you did on your last evening in Dublin.	Sie sind jetzt auf dem Rückflug. Erzählen Sie den anderen, was Sie an Ihrem letzten Abend in Dublin gemacht haben.
did [dɪd]	Verg.-Form v. *do:* machen, tun
yesterday [ˈjestədi]	gestern

7A

leisure facilities [ˈleʒə fəˈsɪlətiz]	Freizeiteinrichtungen
art gallery [ˈɑːt ˈgæləri]	Kunstgalerie
video rental shop [ˈvɪdɪəʊ ˈrentl ʃɒp]	Videoverleih
swimming pool [ˈswɪmɪŋ puːl]	Schwimmbad
youth club [ˈjuːθ klʌb]	Jugendklub
club [klʌb]	Klub, Verein
fitness club [ˈfɪtnɪs klʌb]	Fitnessklub
tennis court [ˈtenɪs kɔːt]	Tennisplatz
cycle path [ˈsaɪkl pɑːθ]	Fahrradweg
playground [ˈpleɪgraʊnd]	Spielplatz
too many [ˈtuː ˈmeni]	zu viele
enough [ɪˈnʌf]	genug

7B

nobody [ˈnəʊbədi]	niemand
everybody [ˈevrɪˌbɒdi]	jeder, alle

9A

What did people do before there was TV?	Was haben die Menschen gemacht, bevor es das Fernsehen gab?
before [bɪˈfɔː]	(be)vor
used to [ˈjuːs tə]	pflegen (Verg.-Form für frühere Gewohnheiten)

11

Practise these dialogues in pairs. Be careful about the intonation.	Üben Sie diese Dialoge in Partnerarbeit. Achten Sie auf die Intonation.

PREVIEW D

1

Ask and tell	Fragen und erzählen Sie

2

Chain story	Kettengeschichte

PREVIEW D

4
The topics of the next three units are: Eating out (13), Lifestyle (14) and Europeans (15).
Listen and decide which unit each extract is from.

Die Themen der nächsten drei Kapitel sind ‚Essen gehen' (13), ‚Lebensstil' (14) und ‚Europäer/innen' (15).
Hören Sie zu und entscheiden Sie, aus welchem Kapitel jeder Auszug kommt.

UNIT 13

Eating out ['iːtɪŋ‿'aʊt]   Essen gehen

1A
What makes a good restaurant for you?
Was zeichnet für Sie ein gutes Restaurant aus?

Write the items in order of importance.
Schreiben Sie die Punkte in der Reihenfolge ihrer Wichtigkeit auf.

item ['aɪtəm]	Punkt, Stichwort
atmosphere ['ætməˌsfɪə]	Atmosphäre
quality ['kwɒlətɪ]	Qualität
quantity ['kwɒntətɪ]	Quantität
service ['sɜːvɪs]	Bedienung
cleanliness ['klenlɪnɪs]	Sauberkeit
least important ['liːst ɪm'pɔːtnt]	am unwichtigsten
least [liːst]	am wenigsten

2A

carrot ['kærət]	Karotte, Möhre
ham [hæm]	Schinken
fried [fraɪd]	gebraten
pie [paɪ]	Pastete, Torte
soup [suːp]	Suppe
soup of the day ['suːp‿əv ðə 'deɪ]	Tagessuppe
steak [steɪk]	Steak
roast [rəʊst]	gebraten, Brat-
starter ['stɑːtə]	Vorspeise
egg mayonnaise [eg ˌmeɪə'neɪz]	Eiersalat
main dish [meɪn dɪʃ]	Hauptgericht
main [meɪn]	Haupt-
dish [dɪʃ]	Gericht, Speise
fillet ['fɪlɪt]	Filet
chicken ['tʃɪkɪn]	Hähnchen
steak and kidney pie [steɪk‿ən 'kɪdnɪ 'paɪ]	(Pastete mit einer Füllung aus Steak und Nieren)
kidney ['kɪdnɪ]	Niere
plaice [pleɪs]	Scholle
omelette ['ɒmlɪt]	Omelette
vegetable ['vedʒtəbl]	Gemüse
potato [pə'teɪtəʊ]	Kartoffel
pea [piː]	Erbse
side salad ['saɪd ˌsæləd]	Beilagensalat
green salad ['griːn ˌsæləd]	grüner Salat
dessert [dɪ'zɜːt]	Nachtisch, Dessert
ice cream [ˌaɪs 'kriːm]	Eis(krem)

2B
Now listen to an announcement in a department store.
Hören Sie jetzt eine Ansage in einem Kaufhaus an.

announcement [ə'naʊnsmənt]   Ansage

3A

there you are [ðeə juː‿ɑː]	bitte sehr
to start with [tə 'stɑːt wɪð]	als Vorspeise
Can we have …? [kən wiː hæv]	Können wir … haben?
I'll have [aɪl hæv]	Ich nehme
What shall we have? [ˌwɒt ʃəl wiː 'hæv]	Was sollen wir essen?
Oh, I'm sorry. [əʊ aɪm 'sɒrɪ]	Oh, das tut mir leid.
Let's see [lets siː]	Mal sehen
Are you ready to order yet? [ɑː juː 'redɪ tə 'ɔːdə jet]	Haben Sie schon gewählt?
bill [bɪl]	Rechnung
certainly ['sɜːtnlɪ]	natürlich, sicher
one moment [ˌwʌn 'məʊmənt]	einen Moment
moment ['məʊmənt]	Moment, Augenblick

4A

meat [miːt]	Fleisch
fish [fɪʃ]	Fisch
lamb chop [læm tʃɒp]	Lammkotelett
lamb [læm]	Lamm

4B
Make a group survey.   Führen Sie eine Gruppenumfrage durch.

UNIT 13

5

chef's special [ʃefs ˈspeʃl]	Spezialität des Küchenchefs
in the end [ɪn ðɪ ˈend]	schließlich
mixture [ˈmɪkstʃə]	Mischung
everything [ˈevrɪθɪŋ]	alles
found [faʊnd]	Verg.-Form v. *find*: finden
kitchen [ˈkɪtʃɪn]	Küche
finish [ˈfɪnɪʃ]	*hier:* aufessen
better [ˈbetə]	besser
inside [ˌɪnˈsaɪd]	drinnen
nobody else [ˈnəʊbədɪ ˌels]	niemand sonst
sat down [sæt ˈdaʊn]	Verg.-Form v. *sit down*: sich hinsetzen
sit [sɪt]	sitzen
study [ˈstʌdɪ]	*hier:* genau durchlesen
exotic [ɪgˈzɒtɪk]	exotisch
a few [ə fjuː]	einige
came [keɪm]	Verg.-Form v. *come*: kommen
table [ˈteɪbl]	Tisch
it's off [ɪts ˈɒf]	*etwa:* das ist aus
on the way home [ɒn ðə weɪ ˈhəʊm]	auf dem Weg nach Haus
hungry [ˈhʌŋgrɪ]	hungrig
stop [stɒp]	anhalten
night [naɪt]	Nacht
a few years ago [ə fjuː jɪəz əˈgəʊ]	vor einigen Jahren
ago [əˈgəʊ]	vor
a friend of mine [ə ˈfrend əv maɪn]	ein Freund/eine Freundin von mir
of mine [əv maɪn]	von mir
full [fʊl]	voll
a long way [ə lɒŋ ˈweɪ]	ein weiter Weg, weit

6A

disappointing [ˌdɪsəˈpɔɪntɪŋ]	enttäuschend

6C

Can you remember any good or bad experiences in restaurants?	Können Sie sich an irgendwelche guten oder schlechten Erlebnisse in einem Restaurant erinnern?
experience [ɪkˈspɪərɪəns]	Erfahrung, Erlebnis

7A

appetite [ˈæpɪtaɪt]	Appetit
It's my round. [ɪts ˈmaɪ raʊnd]	Das ist meine Runde.
It's my turn. [ɪts ˈmaɪ tɜːn]	Ich bin dran.
round [raʊnd]	Runde
thirsty [ˈθɜːstɪ]	durstig
Let me buy you a drink. [let mɪ baɪ juː ə ˈdrɪŋk]	Laß mich dir einen ausgeben.
let [let]	lassen
Dig in! [dɪg ˈɪn]	Haut rein!

8A

bean [biːn]	Bohne
red meat [red miːt]	(Fleisch von dunkelroter Färbung, z.B. Rind, Lamm)
garlic [ˈgɑːlɪk]	Knoblauch
seafood [ˈsiːfuːd]	Meeresfrüchte
lemon [ˈlemən]	Zitrone
rice [raɪs]	Reis
pasta [ˈpæstə]	Teigwaren
olive oil [ˈɒlɪv ɔɪl]	Olivenöl

8B

Which of these foods are more typical of northern Europe, and which of southern Europe?	Welche dieser Nahrungsmittel sind eher typisch für Nordeuropa, welche für Südeuropa?
typical of [ˈtɪpɪkl əv]	typisch für
north [nɔːθ]	Norden
south [saʊθ]	Süden

8C

Which of these items are especially healthy, and which are not so healthy?	Welche dieser Dinge sind besonders gesund, welche sind nicht so gesund?
especially healthy [ɪˈspeʃəlɪ ˈhelθɪ]	besonders gesund
healthy [ˈhelθɪ]	gesund

8D

diet [ˈdaɪət]	Ernährungs(weise), Diät
expert [ˈekspɜːt]	Experte/Expertin
traditional [trəˈdɪʃənl]	traditionell
low-fat [ˈləʊˌfæt]	fettarm
Spaniard [ˈspænjəd]	Spanier/in
dairy product [ˈdeərɪ ˈprɒdʌkt]	Milchproduckt
product [ˈprɒdʌkt]	Produckt

full-fat milk ['fʊl ˌfæt mɪlk]	Vollmilch
full-fat ['fʊl ˌfæt]	Vollfett-

10

sixpence ['sɪkspəns]	(alte englische Geldmünze)
a pocket full of rye [ə ˈpɒkɪt fʊl əv 'raɪ]	eine Tasche voll Roggen
blackbird ['blækbɜːd]	Amsel
began [bɪˈgæn]	Verg.-Form v. *begin*: beginnen, anfangen
bake [beɪk]	backen
a dainty dish [ə ˈdeɪntɪ dɪʃ]	ein feines Essen
to set before a king [tə set bɪˈfɔːr ə ˈkɪŋ]	*etwa:* für einen König

11

Listen to the dialogues and mark the main stress on the underlined sections.	Hören Sie die Dialoge an und kennzeichnen Sie die Hauptbetonung in den unterstrichenen Passagen.

12A

The past tense form of regular verbs ends in '-d' or '-ed'.	Die Vergangenheitsform der regelmäßigen Zeitwörter endet auf ‚-d' oder ‚-ed'.
This can be pronounced in three different ways.	Das kann auf drei verschiedene Arten ausgesprochen werden.
pronounce [prəˈnaʊns]	aussprechen
way [weɪ]	*hier:* Art
Listen to these examples and notice the differences.	Hören Sie diese Beispiele an und achten Sie auf den Unterschied.
notice ['nəʊtɪs]	achten auf

UNIT 14

lifestyle ['laɪfˌstaɪl]	Lebensstil

1A

furniture ['fɜːnɪtʃə]	Möbel
Write in the names of the rooms.	Tragen Sie die Bezeichnungen der Räume ein.
write in [raɪt ɪn]	eintragen, hineinschreiben
living room ['lɪvɪŋ ˌruːm]	Wohnzimmer
bedroom ['bedrʊm]	Schlafzimmer
kitchen ['kɪtʃɪn]	Küche
hall [hɔːl]	Flur
bathroom ['bɑːθrʊm]	Bad
toilet ['tɔɪlɪt]	Toilette

1C

clock [klɒk]	Uhr
dining area ['daɪnɪŋ ˌeərɪə]	Eßecke

2A

armchair ['ɑːmˌtʃeə]	Sessel
bed [bed]	Bett
chair [tʃeə]	Stuhl
coffee table ['kɒfɪ ˌteɪbl]	Couchtisch
cooker ['kʊkə]	Herd
cupboard ['kʌbəd]	(Küchen/Geschirr) Schrank
fridge [frɪdʒ]	Kühlschrank
lamp [læmp]	Lampe
sofa ['səʊfə]	Sofa
chest of drawers [tʃest əv 'drɔːəz]	Kommode
wardrobe ['wɔːdrəʊb]	Kleiderschrank
washing machine ['wɒʃɪŋ məˈʃiːn]	Waschmaschine
machine [məˈʃiːn]	Maschine
plant [plɑːnt]	Pflanze

2B

Listen to the conversation. Which piece of furniture goes where?	Hören Sie das Gespräch an. Welches Möbelstück soll wohin?
piece [piːs]	Stück
conversation [ˌkɒnvəˈseɪʃn]	Gespräch

3

in front of [ɪn ˈfrʌnt əv]	vor
behind [bɪˈhaɪnd]	hinter
between [bɪˈtwiːn]	zwischen
on [ɒn]	auf
window ['wɪndəʊ]	Fenster
door [dɔː]	Tür

4

home sweet home [həʊm swiːt həʊm]	*etwa:* trautes Heim
Now talk about this cartoon.	Sprechen Sie jetzt über diesen Cartoon.

Unit 14

Dammit, Teresa – not again! ['dæmɪt təˈriːzə nɒt ə'gen]	Verdammt, Teresa – nicht schon wieder!

5 A
series ['sɪəriːz]	Serie
foreigner ['fɒrənə]	Ausländer/in
come from [kʌm frɒm]	stammen, kommen aus

5 B
How do you think these two people compare their lives in Stuttgart to their home towns? Make comparisons for both John and Moira.

Wie vergleichen Ihrer Meinung nach diese beiden Personen ihr Leben in Stuttgart mit ihren Heimatstädten? Stellen Sie Vergleiche für John und Moira an.

home town [həʊm taʊn]	Heimatstadt
comparison [kəmˈpærɪsn]	Vergleich
more exciting [mɔːr ɪkˈsaɪtɪŋ]	aufregender
cheaper ['tʃiːpə]	billiger

5 C
How many of your guesses were correct?

Wie viele Ihrer Vermutungen waren richtig?

change [tʃeɪndʒ]	Veränderung
opera ['ɒpərə]	Oper
just [dʒʌst]	*hier:* nur
club [klʌb]	(Nacht)Klub
at first [ət ˈfɜːst]	zuerst
easier ['iːzɪə]	einfacher
I was lucky [aɪ wɒz ˈlʌki]	ich hatte Glück
villa ['vɪlə]	Villa
floor [flɔː]	*hier:* Stockwerk
apartment building [əˈpɑːtmənt ˈbɪldɪŋ]	Wohnblock/haus
city centre [ˈsɪti ˈsentə]	Stadtzentrum, City
country life [ˈkʌntri ˌlaɪf]	Landleben
busy road [ˈbɪzi rəʊd]	stark befahrene Straße
busy [ˈbɪzi]	belebt, verkehrsreich
traffic [ˈtræfɪk]	Verkehr
air [eə]	Luft
better [ˈbetə]	besser
after [ˈɑːftə]	nach
old-fashioned [ˌəʊldˈfæʃnd]	altmodisch
excitement [ɪkˈsaɪtmənt]	Aufregung

5 D
Read the text again and underline the comparative forms.

Lesen Sie den Text noch einmal und unterstreichen Sie die Komparative.

5 E
worse [wɜːs]	schlechter, schlimmer

6
A tale of two towns [ə ˌteɪl əv ˈtuː ˈtaʊnz]	Eine Geschichte über zwei Städte

7 A
Compare two of the paintings.

Vergleichen Sie zwei der Gemälde.

painting [ˈpeɪntɪŋ]	Gemälde, Bild
colourful [ˈkʌləfʊl]	farbenfroh
romantic [rəʊˈmæntɪk]	romantisch
realistic [ˌrɪəˈlɪstɪk]	realistisch

8 B
Check the drawing.

Überprüfen Sie die Zeichnung.

9
This is the key of the kingdom. [ðɪs ɪz ðə ˈkiː əv ðə ˈkɪŋdəm]	Das ist der Schlüssel zum Königreich.
key [kiː]	Schlüssel
kingdom [ˈkɪŋdəm]	Königreich
empty [ˈempti]	leer
basket [ˈbɑːskɪt]	Korb
sweet [swiːt]	süß

10
Find ten items in this unit that make you feel good.

Suchen Sie in diesem Kapitel zehn Dinge, die Sie in gute Stimmung versetzen.

feel [fiːl]	(sich) fühlen

11 B
page [peɪdʒ]	Seite

12
In this unit, find:

Suchen Sie in diesem Kapitel:

a preposition containing ...	ein Verhältniswort, das ... enthält
preposition [ˌprepəˈzɪʃn]	Verhältniswort
contain [kənˈteɪn]	enthalten
adjective [ˈædʒɪktɪv]	Eigenschaftswort

V

UNIT 15

1A

Complete the table.	Vervollständigen Sie die Tabelle.
country of origin [ˈkʌntrɪ ˌəv ˈɒrɪdʒɪn]	Herkunftsland
perhaps [pəˈhæps]	vielleicht
Greek [griːk]	griechisch
That could be a man's name. [ðæt ˌkʊd biː ə ˈmænz ˌneɪm]	Das könnte ein Männername sein.
That must be a Spanish name. [ðæt ˈmʌst biː ə ˈspænɪʃ ˌneɪm]	Das muß ein spanischer Name sein.
I'm sure that's Scottish. [aɪm ˈʃɔː ðæts ˈskɒtɪʃ]	Das ist bestimmt schottisch.
Scottish [ˈskɒtɪʃ]	schottisch

2A

nickname [ˈnɪkneɪm]	Spitzname

3A

Listen and make notes.	Hören Sie zu und machen Sie sich Notizen.
He/She grew up in [hiː/ʃiː gruː ʌp ɪn]	Er/Sie wuchs auf in
grow up [grəʊ ʌp]	aufwachsen

4A

Do you know anyone who …	Kennst du / Kennen Sie jemanden, der/die …
anyone [ˈenɪwʌn]	(irgend)jemand
outside Europe [ˈaʊtsaɪd ˈjʊərəp]	außerhalb Europas
outside [aʊtˈsaɪd]	außerhalb
whose [huːz]	dessen, deren
abroad [əˈbrɔːd]	im Ausland
of foreign origin [əv ˈfɒrɪn ˈɒrɪdʒɪn]	ausländischer Ursprung

5

famous characters [ˈfeɪməs ˈkærəktəz]	berühmte Persönlichkeiten
famous [ˈfeɪməs]	berühmt

5A

about 1210 [əˈbaʊt ˈtwelv ˈten]	um das Jahr 1210
for certain [fə ˈsɜːtn]	mit Sicherheit
certain [ˈsɜːtn]	sicher
poor [pɔː]	arm
married [ˈmærɪd]	verheiratet
girlfriend [ˈgɜːlfrend]	Freundin
popular [ˈpɒpjʊlə]	beliebt
legend [ˈledʒənd]	Legende
B. C. (= before Christ) [biː siː (bɪˈfɔː ˈkraɪst)]	v. Chr. (vor Christi Geburt)
northwestern France [ˌnɔːθˈwestən ˈfrɑːns]	Nordwestfrankreich
fought against [fɔːt əˈgeɪnst]	Verg.-Form v. *fight against*: kämpfen gegen
fight [faɪt]	kämpfen
Roman army [ˈrəʊmən ˈɑːmɪ]	römische Armee
Joan of Arc [ˌdʒəʊn əv ˈɑːk]	Jeanne d'Arc *(Jungfrau von Orléans)*
hero [ˈhɪərəʊ]	Held
they say [ðeɪ seɪ]	man sagt
when I woke up this morning [wen aɪ ˈwəʊk ʌp ðɪs ˈmɔːnɪŋ]	als ich heute morgen aufwachte
woke up [wəʊk ʌp]	Verg.-Form v. *wake up*: aufwachen
wild rose [waɪld rəʊz]	Wildrose
sailor [ˈseɪlə]	Seemann
away [əˈweɪ]	*hier:* nicht zu Hause
hair [heə]	Haar
strong [strɒŋ]	stark

6

Each person asks a question in turn.	Alle stellen nacheinander eine Frage.
in turn [ɪn tɜːn]	nacheinander
century [ˈsentʃʊrɪ]	Jahrhundert
successful [səkˈsesfʊl]	erfolgreich
rich [rɪtʃ]	reich
die [daɪ]	sterben
politician [pɒlɪˈtɪʃn]	Politiker
die naturally [daɪ ˈnætʃrəlɪ]	eines natürlichen Todes sterben
naturally [ˈnætʃrəlɪ]	natürlich

7

review [rɪˈvjuː]	Rückblick, Wiederholung
Can you put them into different categories?	Können Sie sie in verschiedene Kategorien einordnen?

8

and all of the rest [ənd ˈɔːl əv ðə ˈrest]	*etwa:* und all die anderen
like best [laɪk ˈbest]	am liebsten mögen

PREVIEW E

PREVIEW E

1 bookworm ['bʊkwɜ:m]   Bücherwurm

2 course magazine   Kursmagazin,
[kɔ:s ˌmægə'zi:n]   Kurszeitschrift

Personal and place names   Personennamen und Ortsnamen

Dieses Verzeichnis enthält alle englischen Namen, die in BRIDGES 1 NEU vorkommen und die nicht schon auf der Cassette oder im Kapitel-Verzeichnis erwähnt werden. Hier finden Sie auch einige Namen, die in Englisch anders ausgesprochen werden.

1/3A	Yorkshire ['jɔ:kʃə]			Portman ['pɔ:tmən]
	Leeds [li:dz]			Athens ['æθɪnz]
1/9A	Jonathan Marks ['dʒɒnəθən 'ma:ks]			Singapore [sɪŋə'pɔ:]
Pr.A/2A	Pat [pæt]			Sydney ['sɪdnɪ]
4/5B	Webster ['webstə]			Ascot [æskət]
	Jenkins ['dʒenkɪnz]			Grange [greɪndʒ]
4/8	Shakespeare ['ʃeɪkˌspɪə]			Windsor ['wɪnzə]
	Foyle's [fɔɪlz]			Berks (= Berkshire) [ba:ks ('ba:kʃə)]
	London ['lʌndən]		**Pr.C/1D**	Piccadilly Circus [ˌpɪkə'dɪlɪ 'sɜ:kəs]
	Wiscasset [wɪs'kæsɪt]			Max [mæks]
	Maine [meɪn]			Frank [fræŋk]
	Toronto [tə'rɒntəʊ]			Friendship International
	Canada ['kænədə]			['frenʃɪp ɪntə'næʃənl]
5/4	Finland ['fɪnlənd]		**10/7A**	Ruth Lawrence [ru:θ 'lɒrəns]
6/5B	Ann [æn]			Nunn [nʌn]
	Stephen ['sti:vn]			Oxford University ['ɒksfəd ju:nɪ'vɜ:sətɪ]
	Tom [tɒm]			Kansas ['kænzəs]
	Rebecca [rɪ'bekə]			Ray Kroc ['reɪ 'krɒk]
6/7C	Thomas Hood ['tɒməs 'hʊd]			MacDonald's [mək 'dɒnəld]
6/9A	Billy Connolly ['bɪlɪ 'kɒnəlɪ]			Grandma Moses ['grænma: 'məʊzɪz]
7/1	New Delhi ['nju: 'delɪ]		**10/8**	Liverpool ['lɪvəpu:l]
	Indian ['ɪndɪən]		**11/2C**	Turkey ['tɜ:kɪ]
	Highland Gardens ['haɪlənd 'ga:dnz]		**11/4**	Durham ['dʌrəm]
	Brenda Reeves ['brendə 'ri:vz]			Ann Arbor ['æn 'a:bə]
	Hollywood Drive ['hɒlɪwʊd 'draɪv]			Michigan ['mɪʃɪgən]
	Los Angeles [lɒs 'ændʒəli:z]		**11/7**	Fort Worth [fɔ:t 'wɜ:θ]
	California [kælɪ'fɔ:njə]			Gloucester ['glɒstə]
7/3A	Aimee ['eɪmi:]		**11/8A**	Banks Road ['bæŋks 'rəʊd]
7/5A	Martin ['ma:tɪn]			Rochester ['rɒtʃɪstə]
	Caroline ['kærəlaɪn]			Kent [kent]
	Ian ['i:ən]			Angela Frewin ['ændʒələ 'fru:ɪn]
	Peggy ['pegɪ]		**11/9A**	Paris ['pærɪs]
	Alec ['ælɪk]		**14/4**	Teresa [tə'ri:sə]
	Edna ['ednə]		**14/5A**	Wood [wʊd]
8/2A	St. Mary's [sənt 'meərɪz]			Moira Wardlaw ['mɔɪrə 'wɔ:dlɔ:]
	Lord Street ['lɔ:d stri:t]			Moffat ['mɒfət]
	Nelson ['nelsn]		**15/1A**	O'Brian [əʊ 'braɪən]
	Red Lion ['red 'laɪən]			Llewellyn [lu:'əlɪn]
	Queen [kwi:n]			Lesley ['lezlɪ]
9/1	Bristol ['brɪstl]			Tranter ['træntə]
	Jill Baynes ['dʒɪl 'beɪnz]		**15/5**	Julius Caesar ['dʒu:ljəs 'si:zə]
	Designs [dɪ'zaɪnz]			Napoleon [nə'pəʊljən]

one hundred and ninety-three

Alphabetical word list Alphabetisches Wortregister

Jeder Eintrag ist mit dem Verweis auf die entsprechende Kapitel- und Schrittnummer des ersten Vorkommens versehen.

Wörter und Wendungen, die in der TELC-Liste enthalten sind, sind mit einem Punkt (•) gekennzeichnet.

A
- a 1/7B, 2/8A
- about 2/4B, 3/1A, 3/5A
- above 3/7C
- abroad 11/5
- absolutely 12/2
  act out 2/8C
  add 4/5A
- address 4/2
- ad(vertisement) 5/2A
- afraid 11/4B
- after 14/5C
- afternoon 1/6A, 3/1A
- again 4/3C
- against 12/3A
  age 7/2A
- ago 13/5
- agree 11/4B
- agree with 11/4B
- air 14/5C
- all 6/1B, 11/10A
  all day 6/5A
  alligator 1/7A
  alone 9/3B
  aloud 1/4B
  alphabet 2/1A
- already 11/8A
- also 10/7A
- always 3/8A
- am 1/5A
- a.m. 3/1A
- America 1/2
- American 10/7A
- an 2/1A
- and 1/1
- announcement 13/2B
- another 7/9A
- answer 4/6A, 4/6B
- any 7/8C, 7/9A, 8/7B
- anyone 15/4A
  apartment building 14/5C
  appetite 13/7A
- apple 3/7A
- application 7/1
- April 6/7A
- are 1/4A

- area 6/3
  armchair 14/2A
- around 11/8B
- arrival 5/3A
- arrive 5/2A
- art 10/1A
  art gallery 12/7A
- artist 9/2
- as 10/9, 11/8A
- as usual 9/5B
- ask 2/6A
  ask about 11/8B
- ask for 8/4A
  aspirin 8/1A
- at 3/2A
- at home 5/6B
- at work 9/0
  atmosphere 13/1A
- attractive 11/1
- August 6/7A
- aunt 7/8C
- Austria 2/2A
- autumn 6/8
- away 15/5A

B
- back 6/5B
  bacon 3/4A
- bad 11/5
  bad at 10/2A
  bake 13/10
  baker's 8/6
  ballad 12/3A
  balloon 6/1A
- bank 8/1A
  baseball 10/5B
  basket 14/9
- bathroom 14/1A
  beach 6/4A
  bean 13/8A
- beautiful 6/5A
- because 1/5A
- because of 10/3A
- bed 14/2A
- bedroom 14/1A
- beer 1/8B
- before 12/9A
- begin 13/10
- behind 14/3
- Belgian 4/8

- Belgium 2/2A
- best 8/8A
- better 13/5E
- between 6/6B, 14/3
- big 4/5A
  bike 5/6A
- bill 13/3A
  bingo 4/1C
  biology 10/1A
- bird 6/7C
  birth 7/1
- birthday 7/8A
- bit 10/5B
- black 6/1A
- blue 6/1A
- boiled 3/4A
- book 2/8, 4/8, 12/1A
  bookshop 4/8, 8/2A
- border 4/8
- boring 10/2A
- born 7/1
- boss 9/1
- both 12/1C
- box 1/11
  Boxing Day 7/7A
- bread 3/6
- breakfast 3/2A
- brilliant 10/7A
- Britain 4/7A
- British 10/7A
- brother 7/5A
- brother-in-law 7/5A
- brown 6/1A
- building 9/3B
- bus 5/6A
  bus driver 9/3C
  bus service 8/7A
- business 10/7A, 11/6B
  business telephone number 7/1
- busy 14/5C
- but 4/5B
  butcher's 8/6
- butter 3/4A
- buy 8/1A
- by 5/2A
- bye 1/7C
  bye bye 1/7C
  B.C. 15/5A

C
- café 6/4A
- cake 3/7A
  calendar 7/8B
- call 2/5B, 7/3A
- camping 1/9A
- can 4/3B
- Canada 4/8
- can't 6/5A
- car 5/1A
  car ferry 5/2B
- card 1/7B, 6/4A
  carrot 13/2A
- cash 8/1A
- cat 12/2
- cellar 10/8
  Celtic 12/3A
- century 15/6
- certain 15/5A
- certainly 13/3A
- chair 14/2A
- change 14/5C
- cheap 6/5A
- check 1/4B
- cheese 3/6
  chef 13/5
  chemistry 10/1A
- chemist's 8/1A
- cheque 8/1A
  chess 10/7A
  chess player 10/7A
  chest of drawers 14/2A
- chicken 13/2A
- child 6/5A
- Chinese 12/4E
- chips 10/4A, 13/2A
- choose 2/8C
- Christmas 6/1B
  Christmas Day 7/7A
  Christmas Eve 7/7A
- church 4/5A
- cigarette 11/10A
- cinema 12/4A
- city 7/1, 11/5A
  city centre 14/5C
- class 4/9B
  classical 10/4B
- clean 10/8, 11/2A
  cleanliness 13/1A

- climate 11/2B
- clock 3/3
- close 8/5B
- closed 8/5A
- clothes 8/6
  clothes shop 8/6
- cloud 6/6A
- cloudy 6/2B
- club 12/7A, 14/5C
  coach 5/1A
- coffee 3/4A
  coffee table 14/2A
- cold 6/2A
- colleague 9/1
- collect 9/4B
- colour 6/1A
  colourful 14/7
- come 11/8A
  come from 14/5A
- common 3/8B
- company 11/1
- compare 2/9
  complete 1/5A
- computer 10/7B
- concert 12/3A
  contact 11/6
  contain 14/12
- continental 3/4A
- conversation 14/2B
  cooker 14/2A
- cool 6/2A
- corner 8/2A
  cornflakes 3/4A
  Corsica 6/2C
- correct 1/4A
- cost 5/2B
- could 10/7A
- couldn't 10/4B
  count 10/7A
- country 2/2A, 14/5C
  country life 14/5C
  country of origin 15/1A
  countryside 6/6A
- cup 8/1A
- cupboard 14/2A
  cycle path 12/7A
- Czech 2/2B
- Czech Republic, The 2/2A

D

  dairy product 13/8D
  dancing 12/1A
- Danish 2/2B
- dark 6/1A
- date 7/1
  date of birth 7/1
- daughter 7/1

- day 2/6A, 10/4B
- dear 6/5B
- December 6/7A
- decide 9/7A
- Denmark 2/2A
- dentist 9/4A
- department store 8/6
- departure 5/3A
- depend 11/4B
- describe 9/3B
  dessert 13/2A
- detail 11/7
  dialogue 1/4A
- die 15/5A
- diet 13/8D
- difference 6/6B
- different 2/8C
- difficult 10/5B
  dining area 14/1C
  dining table 14/2A
- dinner 3/2A
- directions 8/4A
- dirty 11/2A
- disappointing 13/6A
  disco 6/5A
- discuss 8/8A
- dish 13/2A
- divorced 7/1
- do 6/4A
- doctor 9/3A
  doctorate 10/7A
- dog 11/10A
- don't 2/4A
- door 14/3
- double 2/5A
- double room 2/8A
- draw 5/10
- dream 6/1B
- drink 3/8A, 8/1A, 10/2A
  drinking song 12/3A
- drive 10/7B
- dry 11/2A
- Dutch 2/2B

E

- each 6/9B
  eastern 6/2C
- easy 10/3A
- eat 3/8A
- egg 3/4A
- eight 2/3B
- eighteen 4/1A
- eighty 4/1A
- eleven 3/1A
- else 13/5
- empty 14/9
- end 13/5
- engineer 9/3C

- England 1/2
- English 1/8A, 2/2B
  English-speaking 11/5
- enjoy 11/8A
- enough 11/8A, 12/7A
  etc 2/5A
- Europe 11/1
- European 2/2
- even 4/10A
- evening 1/6A, 3/1A
  evening out 12/5C
- event 12/3A
- everything 13/5
- every 5/2A
- everybody 12/7B
- example 7/11
  except 6/7C
  excitement 14/5C
- exciting 10/5B
- excuse 8/4A
- exercise 12/1A
  exotic 12/4E
- expensive 6/5A
- experience 13/6C
- expert 13/8D
- expression 1/7B
- eye 10/8

F

- factory 11/1
- fairly 11/1
  false 10/5E
- family 7/1
  family name 7/1
  family tree 7/5A
- famous 15/5A
  fantastic 10/5B
- far 8/4A
- fast 12/3A
- father 7/4A
- favourite 10/2A
- February 6/7A
- feel 14/10
  feel good 14/10
  female 7/1, 15/1A
- ferry 5/1A
  festival 12/3A
- few 13/5
  fiddle 12/3A
  fiddler 12/3A
- field 6/6A
- fifteen 4/1A
- fifty 4/1A
  fight against 15/5A
- file 1/4C
- fill in 1/9B
  fillet 13/2A

- find 2/9
- find out 6/3
- fine 1/4A
- finish 13/5
- first 4/5C, 8/10, 14/5C
  first name 4/2
- fish 13/4A
  fitness club 12/7A
- five 2/3B
- flat 4/5A
  Flemish 2/2B
  flexible 9/1
- flight 5/2B
- flight attendant 9/2
  flight no. 5/3A
  flight number 5/2A
- floor 14/5C
- flower 1/8A
- foggy 6/2B
  folk 3/9A
  following 10/7A
- food 2/4A, 3/7
  footballer 9/2
- for 1/8A, 2/8A, 3/5A
- foreigner 14/5A
- forest 6/6A
- form 7/1
- forty 4/1A
- four 2/3B
- fourteen 4/1A
- France 2/2A
  free time 12/1A
- French 2/2B
- fresh 3/8A
- Friday 2/6A
- fridge 14/2A
  fried 3/4A
- friend 7/1
- friendly 9/1
- from 1/2, 3/2A, 5/2B
- front 12/2, 14/3
- fruit 3/4A
  fruit juice 3/4A
- full 3/4A, 13/5
  full of 13/10
  full-fat 13/8D
- furniture 14/1A

G

- garage 8/1A
- garden 4/5B
  gardener 10/5B
  gardening 1/8B
- garlic 13/8A
  geography 10/1A
- German 2/2B
- Germany 1/2
- get 5/2A

get here 5/6A
get petrol 8/1A
get to work 5/6B
- girl 10/3A
- girlfriend 15/5A
- give 11/6B
- go 6/4A
- go down 8/2A
- go for 6/4A
- go out 12/4A
- go to 5/2B
- good 1/6A
- good at 10/2A
- goodbye 1/7C
  goodnight 1/7C
  goods 8/1A
  grade 10/1A
- grandchildren 7/5A
- grandmother 10/5B
- grandparents 7/5A
- grandson 7/5A
- grapefruit 3/7A
- grass 6/1B
- great 6/5A, 12/4D
- Great Britain 2/2A
- Greece 5/2B
- Greek 10/7A, 12/4E
- green 6/1A
  greengrocer's 8/6
- ground 10/8
- group 1/4B
- grow up 15/3A
- guess 7/3C
- guest 2/8C

H
- hair 15/5A
  half past 3/1B
- hall 14/1A
- ham 13/2A
- happy 7/8A
- hard 12/3A
- harp 12/3A
- hat 2/4B
- hate 1/10, 6/9B
- have 3/2B
- have got 7/1
- he 1/3A
- headache 12/4E
- healthy 11/1, 13/8C
- hear 1/7B
- heavy 12/4E
- hello 1/1
- help 4/3B
- her 7/1, 7/4A, 9/7A
- here 4/6A
  hero 15/5A
- hi 1/1
- high 11/10A

- him 9/7A
- hire 6/4A
- his 7/4A
  historical 11/1
- history 10/1A
  hockey 10/5B
- hold 11/10A
  hold up 1/7B
- holiday 6/4A, 7/7A
  holidays 9/1
- home 5/6B, 6/5B
  home address 7/1
  home town 14/5B
  host family 11/8A
- hot 6/2A
- hotel 2/8A
- hour 9/1
- house 4/2
  house number 4/2
  household goods 8/1A
- housewife 9/4A
- how 1/4A
  how far 11/7
  how long 5/2B
  how many 3/7B, 7/2A
  how much 5/2B
  how often 5/2B
- hundred 4/1A, 11/10C
- hungry 13/5
- husband 7/4A

I
- I 1/1
- ice cream 13/2A
  I'd like 2/8A
- idea 2/3B, 12/4A
  I'll 13/3A
  I'm 1/1
- important 9/1
- impossible 10/5B
- in 1/4A, 3/1A
- in front of 14/3
- including 8/5B
- industrial 11/1
- industry 11/1
- information 5/2A
- inside 13/5
  institution 12/3A
- instrument 12/3A
- interested in 10/4B
- interesting 8/8A
- interview 5/6B, 11/6
- introduce 7/5B
- invitation 11/8A
- Ireland 2/2A
- Irish 7/3A

is 1/1
- island 11/5
- it 1/7B, 2/4C
- Italian 2/2B, 2/4A
- Italy 2/4A
  item 13/1A
  it's 2/4B

J
- jam 3/4A, 9/5
- January 6/7A
  jazz 1/9A
- job 9/1
  jogging 6/4A
- juice 3/4A
- July 6/7A
- June 6/7A
- just 8/4A

K
- key 14/9
  kidney 13/2A
- kilometre 4/8
- kind 8/4A
- kind of 12/3A
- king 13/10
  kingdom 14/9
- kiss 10/8
- kitchen 13/5, 14/1A
- know 2/4C

L
- lady 1/7A
- lamp 14/2A
- land 11/1
- language 2/2B
  language learning 11/6B
- large 11/1
- last 9/5B
- late 9/5B
  late for 9/5A
  later 1/7A
- leaf 6/7C
- learn 10/5B
- least 13/1A
- leave 5/3A
  leave from 5/2B
- left 4/7B, 8/2A
  legend 15/5A
- leisure 12/1A
  leisure activity 12/1A
  leisure facilities 12/7A
  lemon 13/8A
- let 12/4A, 13/3A, 13/7A
- letter 4/2, 11/8A
- lie 6/4A

lie-in 12/1A
- life 9/7A
- light 6/1A
- like 1/8B, 6/2C
- line 5/5A
- list 3/7C
- listen 1/4B
  listen to 3/9A
  litre 11/10A
- little 11/8B
- live 4/5A
- living room 14/1A
- local 11/1
- long 4/2
- look at 1/4C
- look forward to 11/8A
  look through 7/11
- lot 8/4A, 8/5B
- lot of 8/5B
- lots of 11/8A
- love 3/9A, 6/5B, 6/9B
- low 11/1
  low-fat 13/8D
- luck 10/8
- lucky 14/5C
- lunch 3/2A
  lunchtime 8/5B
  Luxembourg 2/2A

M
- machine 14/2A
- madam 5/7A
- main 13/2A
  main dish 13/2A
  Majorca 6/2C
- make 3/1C
  make love 12/2
  make notes 4/2
  make questions 4/9
- male 7/1, 15/1A
- man 7/8A, 8/7A
- many 3/7B
- map 6/2C
- March 6/7A
  marital status 7/1
- mark 4/12
  marks 10/3A
  marmalade 3/4A
- married 7/1
- match 1/7A
  mathematician 10/7A
  mathematics 10/7A
- maths 10/1A
- May 6/7A
  mayonnaise 13/2A
- me 4/3B

- meal 6/4A
- mean 6/2A
  meaningless 1/5A
- meat 13/4A
- meet 1/4A
  memo pad 1/2
- mention 11/6A
- menu 3/4A
- metre 4/8
  Mexican 12/4E
- middle 7/1
  middle name 7/1
- milk 3/7A
- million 11/11B
- mind 12/4C
- mine 13/5
  minus 10/1A
- minute 5/2B
- miss 10/8
  missing 4/1A
  mixture 13/5
- modern 4/5A
- moment 13/3A
- Monday 2/6A
- month 6/7A
- moon 6/1B
- more 8/7B, 14/5B
- morning 1/6A, 3/1A
- most 8/5A, 8/8A
- mother 7/4A
- motorbike 5/6A
- mountain 6/6A
- move 10/5B
- Mr, Mrs 1/6A
- Ms 11/8B
- much 2/8A, 9/3B
  muesli 3/7A
- museum 6/4A
- music 1/9B
- must 15/1A
- my 7/8C

N
- name 2/8A
- national 12/3A
- nationality 7/1
  naturally 15/6
- near 4/5B
- need 7/1
  negative 6/5A
- neighbour 2/2
- Netherlands, The 2/2A
- never 3/8A
- new 4/3B
  New Year's Day 7/7A
  New Year's Eve 7/7A
  newsagent's 8/1A
- newspaper 6/4A
- next 1/7C
  next door 6/5A
  next to 8/2A
- nice 1/4A, 4/7A
  nickname 15/2A
- night 13/5
  night train 5/7A
- nine 2/3B
- nineteen 4/1A
- ninety 4/1A
- no 2/3B, 4/6A
- nobody 12/7B
- noisy 4/5A
- nonsense 10/8
- normally 3/2B
- north 13/8B
- northern 6/2C
  northwestern 15/5A
- Norway 6/2C
- not 5/5A
  not so 13/8C
- note 4/2
- nothing 12/2
- notice 13/12A
- November 6/7A
- now 3/1B
  no. 5/3A
- number 2/3B, 3/3, 4/2
- nurse 9/4A

O
- o'clock 3/1A
- October 6/7A
- of 1/7B, 8/5B
- of course 2/8A
- off 13/5
- offer 11/1
- office 9/1
- often 3/8A
- oh 2/5A, 5/7A
- oil 13/8A
- OK 2/8A
- old 4/5A
  old-fashioned 14/5C
  olive 13/8A
  olive oil 13/8A
  omelette 13/2A
- on 2/4B, 2/8A, 14/3
  on time 9/5A
- once 12/1B
- one 1/7B, 2/3B, 11/8A
- only 6/3
- open 8/5A, 8/5B
  opera 14/5C
- opposite 4/7B, 8/2A
- or 3/4A
- orange 3/7A, 6/1A
- order 1/4A, 13/3A
- original 5/5B
- other 3/6, 6/3
- our 4/2, 7/6
  outdoors 6/1A
- outside 15/4A
- over 8/4A, 10/7A
- own 2/8C

P
- pad 1/2, 4/11A
- page 14/11B
- paint 10/7A
  painter 10/7A
  painting 14/7
- pair 4/7B
  panoramic 10/5B
- pardon 2/8A
- parents 7/5A
- park 4/5A
- part 11/1
- partner 2/7
- passport 7/1
- past 3/1B
- pasta 13/8A
- pay 9/1
  PE (physical education) 10/1A
  pea 13/2A
  pear 3/7A
- people 4/5C, 11/1
  per 11/10A
- per cent 12/2
- perhaps 15/1A
- person 4/5C
- petrol 8/1A
  petrol station 8/1A
  phone book 4/8
  phone call 2/5B
  phone number 2/5A
- photo(graph) 7/5B
  phrase 9/3B
  physics 10/1A
- piano 12/1A
- pick 12/4E
- picture 1/7A
  pie 13/2A
- piece 14/2
- pink 6/1A
- pipe 12/3A
- place 4/10A
  place of birth 7/1
  plaice 13/2A
- plan 6/4C, 11/8A
- plane 5/1A
  plant 14/2A
- play 6/4A
  playground 12/7A
- pleasant 11/1
- please 2/8A
  plus 10/1A
- p.m. 3/1A
- pocket 13/10
- poem 3/9A
- point 9/1
- Poland 2/2A
- policewoman 9/4A
- Polish 2/2B
- political 11/6B
- politician 15/6
- poor 15/5A
- popular 15/5A
  population 11/1
  positive 6/5A
- post code 4/3A
- post office 4/7A
- postcard 6/4A
- poster 6/9B
- potato 13/2A
- pound (£) 5/2B
- practise 2/1A
  preposition 14/12
- press 12/3A
- price 5/3A
- prison 10/5B
- probably 11/6, 15/1A
- product 13/8D
- pronounce 13/12A
  pronunciation 1/11
- proud of 10/5B
- pub 4/5A
  public transport 5/6C
- purple 6/1A
- purpose 7/1
- put 2/4B

Q
- quality 13/1A
  quantity 13/1A
- quarter 3/1B
- question 4/2
- quickly 10/9
- quiet 4/5A
- quite 10/5B, 11/4A

R
- radio 12/2
- railway 4/5B
  railway station 4/5B
- rain 6/1B
  rainy 6/2B
- rather 12/4A
- read 1/5A
  read aloud 1/4B

- read out 9/3C
- reading 1/8A
- ready 13/3A
- realistic 14/7
- really 10/5B
- reason 9/2
- record 4/8, 8/4D
- record shop 8/4D
- red 6/1A
- red meat 13/8A
- register 11/10A
- relative 7/9A
- relax 12/1A
- remember 4/10A
- repeat 4/3B
- report 2/3B, 6/4B, 10/1A
- rest 15/8
- restaurant 6/5A
- result 2/9
- return ticket 5/5
- return trip 5/11
- review 15/5A
- rhyme 2/1
- rice 13/8A
- rich 12/4E, 15/6
- ride 10/7B
- right 2/7, 8/2A
- river 6/6A
- road 8/2A
- roast 13/2A
- role play 5/9
- roll 3/4A
- romantic 14/7
- room 2/8
- rose 15/5A
- round 13/7A
- run 4/8

S

- sad 12/3A
- safe 9/1
- sailor 15/5A
- salad 13/2A
- same 3/7B
- Sardinia 6/2C
- Saturday 2/6A
- sausage 3/4A
- say 2/2A
- say about 8/2B
- school 8/7A
- science 10/1A
- Scotland 6/2C
- Scottish 15/1A
- sea 6/5A
- seafood 13/8A
- season 6/8
- second 4/5C
- secretary 9/2
- see 1/7C
- sell 8/1A
- sentence 1/3B
- separated 7/1
- September 6/7A
- series 14/5A
- serve 8/5B
- service 8/7A, 13/1A
- seven 2/3B
- seventeen 4/1A
- seventy 4/1A
- several 10/5B
- sex 7/1
- shall 12/4A
- she 1/3A
- shiftwork 9/3B
- shine 10/8
- shoe 8/6
- shoe shop 8/6
- shop 4/5A
- shop assistant 9/4A
- shopping 6/4A
- short 4/7
- show 7/5B
- signature 7/1
- similar 3/7B
- sincerely 11/8A
- sing 10/4B
- sing along 12/3A
- singer 10/3A
- singing 1/8B
- single 7/1
- sir 5/8A
- sister 7/5A
- sit down 13/5
- six 2/3B
- sixteen 4/1A
- sixty 4/1A
- skiing 1/9A
- sky 6/6A
- sleep 6/5A
- slow 12/3A
- small 4/5A
- smoke 11/10A
- snow 6/2B
- so 6/5A
- so many 10/4B
- sofa 14/2A
- some 6/4A, 8/5B
- someone 4/6B, 15/4A
- something 3/8B
- sometimes 3/8A
- son 7/1
- song 3/9A
- sorry 2/4C
- sound 5/11
- soup 13/2A
- south 13/8B
- southern 6/2C
- Spain 6/2C
- Spaniard 13/8D
- Spanish 10/7A
- speak 2/4A
- speak to 9/7A
- special 7/7A, 13/5
- spell 2/6A
- spelling 2/7
- spend 10/5B
- spicy 12/4E
- sport 10/10
- sporting 11/6B
- spring 6/8
- stamp 8/1A
- standard return 5/2B
- start 10/4B
- start work 9/5A
- starter 13/2A
- station 4/5A
- statistics 11/10
- stay 11/5, 11/8A
- stay with 11/8A
- steak 13/2A
- step 10/9
- still 6/4C
- stop 13/5
- story 9/7A
- street 4/2
- street name 4/2
- strong 12/3A
- student 2/1B
- study 10/7A, 13/5
- subject 10/1A
- submarine 6/1B
- successful 15/6
- sugar 3/7A
- summer 6/8
- Sunday 2/6A
- sunny 6/2B
- supermarket 3/7C, 8/1A
- sure 11/2A
- surname 4/2
- surprising 11/10
- Sweden 6/2C
- sweet 14/9
- swim 10/5B
- swimming 2/4A
- swimming pool 12/7A
- Switzerland 2/2A
- syllable 3/10A
- symbol 6/2B

T

- table 13/5, 14/2
- take 2/4C, 5/2B
- talk 12/3A
- talk about 8/7A
- tea 3/4A
- teacher 3/2
- telephone number 2/8A
- television 12/2, 14/2
- tell 12/4E
- ten 2/3B
- tennis 6/4A
- tennis court 12/7A
- terrible 6/5A
- text 7/3A
- than 11/6, 14/5C
- thank 2/8A
- thank for 11/8A
- thank goodness 6/5B
- thanks 1/4A
- that 2/2A
- the 1/4A
- theatre 12/5A
- theatre group 10/5B
- their 4/3B
- them 3/7B, 8/5B
- then 8/11, 10/4A
- there 9/7A, 13/3A
- there are 6/6B
- there's 6/5A
- they 3/4D
- thing 8/1A
- think 2/2A
- think of 2/7
- third 4/5C
- thirsty 13/7A
- thirteen 4/1A
- thirty 4/1A
- this 1/1
- those 10/5B
- thousand 4/8, 11/11B
- three 2/3B
- Thursday 2/6A
- tick 3/7C
- ticket 5/5
- tie 1/8B
- till 8/5B
- time 3/1A, 9/5A, 10/5B
- times 12/1B
- timetable 5/3A
- title 9/7A
- to 3/1B, 3/2A, 5/2B
- toast 3/4A
- today 7/8A
- together 12/3A
- toilet 14/1A
- tomato 3/4A
- tonight 12/4A
- too 1/2
- touch 6/1B

V

- tourism 11/1
- tourist 11/1
  tourist attraction 12/3A
  tourist information centre 8/1A
- town 4/5B
- tradition 12/3A
- traditional 13/8D
- traffic 14/5C
  traffic jam 9/5A
- train 5/1A
- tram 5/6A
- translate 3/4B
- travel 5/2A, 9/3B
  travel agent 9/4A
  travel agent's 5/4A
- travelling 1/9A
- tree 6/6A
- trip 5/4
- true 10/5E
- try 9/4B
- Tuesday 2/6A
- turn 2/7
- TV 12/1A
- twelve 3/1B
- twenty 3/1B
- twenty-five 3/1B
- twice 12/1B
  twin town 11/6A
- two 2/3B
  typical of 13/8B

U

- uncle 7/8C
- underground 5/6A
  underline 3/7B
- understand 2/4A

- unit 5/10
  United States 7/1
- upstairs 10/8
  USA 7/1
- use 2/8C, 10/7B
- used to 12/9A
- useful 8/5D
- usual 9/5B
- usually 8/5B

V

- vegetable 13/2A
  verb 10/7A
- very 2/8A, 6/2A
  video rental shop 12/7A
- view 6/5A
- villa 14/5C
- village 8/7A
  visa 7/1
- visit 7/1, 11/5A
- visitor 8/5D
  vowel 7/10

W

- wages 11/1
- waiter 9/4A
- wake up 15/5A
- Wales 1/9B
- walk 5/6B, 6/4A
- walk around 11/8A
- want to 5/4A
  wardrobe 14/2A
- warm 6/2A
  wash dishes 10/5B
- washing machine 14/2A
- watch 12/1A

- waterfall 11/10A
- way 1/4A, 7/2A, 13/5, 13/12A
  way in 5/5A
  way out 5/5A
- we 2/2A
- weather 6/2A
  weather report 6/4B
- Wednesday 2/6A
- week 1/7C
- weekday 8/5B
- weekend 8/5B
- welcome 4/3B
  welcome to 1/6A
- well 6/5B
  western 6/2C
- what 1/8A, 12/4D
  what about 3/5B
  what for 5/5A
- when 1/7B, 5/2B, 10/4A
- where 5/2B
- which 2/2A, 8/8A
- white 6/1A
- who 7/5A, 10/3A, 15/4A
- whole 12/3B
- whose 15/4A
- why 7/8A
  widowed 7/1
- wife 7/4A
- wild 15/5A
- win 10/3A
- window 14/3
- windy 6/2B
  wine 1/9B
- winter 6/8
- with 3/1A, 6/5A

- without 1/5A
- woman 8/7A
- wonderful 10/3A
  woods 4/5B
- word 1/11
  word map 5/10
- work 5/6B, 9/3B
  work with 9/3B
  working hours 9/1
- world 4/8
- worry 10/7A
- worse 14/5E
- worst 10/5B
- would like 5/8A
- write 1/3B
  write down 4/9A
  write in 14/1A
  write music 10/7A
  writer 9/4A
- wrong 2/7

Y

- year 6/7A, 7/1
- yellow 6/1A
- yes 2/8
- yesterday 12/6
- yet 13/3A
  yoghurt 3/4B
- you 1/2, 1/4A
- young 4/8
- your 2/5A
- yourself 2/4B
  youth club 12/7A

Z

- zero 4/1A

TAPESCRIPTS

UNIT 1

Step 1

Bruce: Hello! I'm Bruce and this is Linda.
Linda: Hi! I'm Linda and this is Geoff.
Geoff: Hello! I'm Geoff.

Step 3

Bruce: I'm Bruce. I'm from Leicester. This is Linda. She's from Amarillo.
Linda: This is Geoff. He's from Leeds.

Step 4 B

- Hello, Pat. How are you?
- Fine, thanks. And you?
- I'm fine. By the way, this is Helga. She's from Germany.
- Hello, Helga. Nice to meet you.
- Nice to meet you.

Step 5 B

I am
because
you are.
Without "you are"
"I am"
is meaningless.
Without "I am"
"you are"
is meaningless, too.

Step 6 B

- Good evening.
- Good evening.

- Good morning, Peter.
- Good morning, John.
- How are you?
- Fine, thanks.

- Mrs Irving? Good afternoon. Welcome to Berlin. I'm Harry Adler.
- Nice to meet you, Mr Adler.
- Nice to meet you.

Step 7 B

1. Bye bye love, bye bye happiness.
   Hello loneliness, I think I'm gonna cry.
2. … You say goodbye and I say hello
   Hello hello
   I don't know why you say goodbye
   I say hello …
3. Goodnight ladies, ladies goodnight …
4. … Irene goodnight, Irene
   Irene goodnight
   Goodnight Irene, goodnight Irene
   I'll see you in my dreams …
5. See you later, alligator.
   After a while, crocodile …

Step 7 C

Student 1: Bye. See you next week.
Student 2: Goodbye.
Student 3: Goodnight.
Student 4: Bye bye.

Step 9 B

Derrick: Hello, I'm Derrick. I'm from Wales and I like wine. And this is Heinke. She's from Tübingen. She likes reading.
Heinke: Hi, I'm Heinke, and this is John. John's from Toronto and he likes flowers.
John: Hi, I'm John and I like flowers. And this is Elizabeth. She's from Minnesota and she likes music.
Elizabeth: Hello.

Step 11 B Pronunciation

- hi, dialogue, fine, goodnight, I'm, like, nice, wine, write
- this, English, music, in, is, listen, pictures, singing

UNIT 2

Step 1 A

a b c   One, two, three
d e f   Hi, I'm Geoff
g h i   Hello, goodbye
j k l   How do you spell …?
m n o   Yes and no
p q r   Here we are
s t u   How are you?
v w x   Rhymes with sex
y, z or z   She and he

Step 3 A

Auszüge aus folgenden Sprachen:

1. English (GB)
2. French
3. Danish
4. English (US)
5. Dutch
6. Polish
7. German
8. Italian
9. English (Austr.)
10. Czech

Step 6 B

1. ❏ When's the next English class?
   ○ I think it's on Tuesday.
2. I don't like Monday.
3. Ah! Sunday.
4. ❏ What's the English for *Mittwoch*?
   ○ Wednesday.
5. … on a Saturday night with you …
6. See you on Friday!
7. How do you spell Thursday?

Step 8 B

❏ Good morning, Park Hotel.
○ Good morning, I'd like a double room for Friday evening, please.
❏ Yes, of course. What's your name, please?
○ Szkopiak, John Szkopiak.
❏ Pardon?
○ Szkopiak.
❏ How do you spell that, please?
○ S-Z-K-O-P-I-A-K.
❏ OK, and what's your telephone number, please?
○ Dover 7654382.
❏ Thank you very much. See you on Friday. Goodbye.
○ Thank you. Bye.

UNIT 3

Step 3

1. ❏ When's breakfast?
   ○ At about quarter past seven.
   ❏ OK.
2. ❏ Excuse me, when's dinner?
   ○ Dinner's at eight o'clock, sir.
   ❏ Thank you.
3. … and the time is now exactly half past seven and it's time for …
4. It's ten to one. Is lunch ready?
5. ❏ By the way, what's the time?
   ○ It's about twenty past six.
6. ❏ Excuse me, what's the time?
   ○ It's twenty-five to four.

Step 4 C

1. I normally just have toast and marmalade for breakfast, and a cup of tea.
2. I like muesli and tea for breakfast.
3. We like a full breakfast with bacon and eggs, toast and marmalade and coffee.
4. I only have a cup of tea in the morning.
5. We have rolls and jam and lots of coffee.

Step 7 C

Our fruit and vegetable department today has a special offer of Italian pears only 40 pence a pound and English Golden Delicious apples only 90 pence for 3 pounds …

… Try our delicious pork sausages. Just the thing for your weekend barbecue …

… Don't miss out on our new bakery offering a wide selection of cake and bread from all over Europe …

Step 9 A

It's Pronoun Love

I like rock and folk songs
You think Mozart's great.
May the first's my birthday
You never know the date.

She likes wine and coffee
He drinks tea and beer.
Can she and he be they one day?
Can you and I be we?

Step 10 A Pronunciation

- lunch, twelve, likes, tea, rolls, juice
- dinner, evening, often, seven, hotel, always, coffee
- sausages, tomatoes, marmalade
- continental

Step 10 C Pronunciation

Two syllables:
- dinner, evening, often, seven, always, coffee
- hotel

Three syllables:
- sausages, marmalade
- tomatoes

UNIT 4

Step 1 B

14 - 15 - 87 - 27 - 17 - 80 - 19 - 60 - 13 - 63

T

Step 3, A + C 21
- ❏ Hello.
- ○ Hello Pat, this is David. Have you got a minute? I've got one or two problems with my address book – can't read my own writing. Can you help me, please?
- ❏ Yes, of course. If I can.
- ○ Thanks. Well, the first thing is Susan and James Wilson. I know they're in Brighton now, but ... what's their new address?
- ❏ It's 69 Granby Street.
- ○ Granby. How do you spell that, please?
- ❏ G-R-A-N-B-Y.
- ○ G-R-A-N-B-Y, thanks very much. And what's the post code?
- ❏ BN2 2BE.
- ○ BN2 2BE. Great, now the other problem is MT Travel in Cambridge – can you tell me their telephone number?
- ❏ Just a moment, yes ... it's 0223 467451.
- ○ Sorry, can you repeat that, please?
- ❏ Of course, 0223 467451.
- ○ 0223 467451. Well, that's all, Pat. Thanks very much.
- ❏ You're welcome.

Step 5 C 22
1. I live in a flat in the centre of town. It's an old flat but it's big and I like it. The street's very busy so it's rather noisy.
2. We live in a small house near a park. It's very quiet and the park's great for the children. It's a modern house but it's small, very small.
3. I live in a small modern flat near the station. I'm very near all the shops but the street's quiet. It's nice. I like it.

Step 11 B Pronunciation 23
- flat, pad, thanks, apple, match
- half, garden, park
- day, take, name, later

Step 12 Pronunciation 24
What's your address?
What's their new address?
What's the post code?
Is it big or small?
Can you help me?
Can you repeat that, please?
Do you live near here?
Do you like Italian food?
Do you speak English?
Do you understand French?

UNIT 5

Step 1 B 25
1. ferry 2. coach 3. car 4. plane 5. train

Step 3, A + B 26
- ❏ Birmingham European Airways, good morning, can I help you?
- ○ Good morning. I'd like some information about flights to Vienna, please.
- ❏ I'm sorry, madam, but there are no direct flights from Birmingham to Vienna. First you have to fly to Amsterdam, and then on to Vienna.
- ○ Oh, how long does it take?
- ❏ About four hours including the stopover in Amsterdam. The flight leaves Birmingham at eight thirty in the morning and arrives in Amsterdam at ten fifty.
- ○ And when does the flight leave for Vienna?
- ❏ An hour later, at eleven fifty. It arrives in Vienna at thirteen thirty-five.
- ○ ... Leaves Amsterdam at eleven fifty and arrives in Vienna at thirteen thirty-five. OK. And how much does it cost?
- ❏ £99.
- ○ Fine, thanks for the information.
- ❏ You're welcome.

Step 4 B 27
- ❏ Good morning, do you speak English?
- ○ Yes. How can I help you?
- ❏ I'd like to go to Germany.
- ○ Would you like to go by plane or by ferry?
- ❏ Well, by ferry, I think.
- ○ I see, when would you like to leave?
- ❏ About June the first, if possible.
- ○ Let me see. Err ... the ferry leaves every Tuesday and Friday. You can leave on June the second, that's a Tuesday.
- ❏ Hmm, what time does it leave?
- ○ It leaves Helsinki at 1 p.m. and arrives in Travemünde on Wednesday at 5 in the afternoon.
- ❏ Sorry, when does it arrive?
- ○ The next day at 5 p.m.
- ❏ The next day!?
- ○ Yes, 28 hours at sea, but you'll love the trip. The ship's very comfortable. There are three restaurants, pubs, a swimming pool ...
- ❏ That sounds nice, but how much does it cost?
- ○ That depends, prices start at about 900 Finnmarks per person.
- ❏ 900 Finnmarks? Mmh, ... and by plane?
- ○ Sorry?
- ❏ How much does a flight cost?

Step 7 B 28

- ❏ British Rail, Glasgow Central. Good afternoon.
- ○ Good afternoon. I'd like to go to London. When does the night train leave?
- ❏ Twenty-three fifty from Glasgow Central.
- ○ Twenty-three fifteen?
- ❏ No, madam. Twenty-three fifty.
- ○ Oh, twenty-three fifty. Thank you.
- ❏ You're welcome.

Step 8 B 29

- ❏ British Airways. Good morning.
- ○ Good morning. I'd like to go to Dublin.
- ❏ When, sir?
- ○ Sorry?
- ❏ When would you like to go?
- ○ On Monday morning. When does the first flight leave?

Step 11 Pronunciation 30

railway, reading, report, results, return, ferry, arrive, breakfast, Greece, Friday, three, price, train, tram, travel, public transport, return trip

Step 12 Pronunciation 31

I like reading.
I'd like to go to Dublin.
I like gardening.
I'd like to go to London.
I like London.
I'd like some information.

UNIT 6

Step 1 B 32

1. We all live in a yellow submarine …
2. Again I'll touch the green, green grass of home …
3. Purple rain, purple rain …
4. I'm dreaming of a white Christmas …
5. Blue moon …
6. Lady in red …

Step 4 B 33

This is Radio Monaco and here is today's weather for the French Riviera. It'll be cool and rainy; only 17 degrees on the coast and even cooler in the mountains, with a strong north wind. The sea's cold for this time of the year, too; between 16 and 18 degrees. But the bad weather will get better overnight and tomorrow should be warm and sunny.

Step 7 B 34

January, February, March, April, May, June, July
January, February, March, April, May, June, July
August, September, October, November, December
August, September, October, November, December
January, February, March, April, May, June, July
January, February, March, April, May, June, July
August, September, October, November, December
August, September, October, November, December
January, February, March, April, May, June, July
January, February, March, April, May, June, July
January, February, March, April, May, June, July
January, February, March, April, May, June, July
January, February, March, April, May, June, July

Step 8 35

1. autumn   2. spring   3. winter   4. summer

Step 10 A Pronunciation 36

I'd like to go skiing in February.
I don't like skiing.

We can't sleep – there's a disco next door.
You can go to the disco and sleep later.

Why do you go for a walk every day?
I don't go for a walk every day.

I'd like to play tennis with Karen.
She can't play tennis.
Yes, she can.

I'd like to go swimming.
But the weather is terrible.
I'd still like to go swimming.

UNIT 7

Step 2 A 37

- ❏ Are you stopping over in New York or going on to L.A.?
- ○ Well, I'm spending a couple of days in New York. I fly on to Chicago next week.
- ❏ On business?
- ○ Well, the weekend in New York is a kind of vacation. My wife and I are meeting our son there, but I have to go to Chicago for a business conference next week. By the way, my name's Allan Smith.
- ❏ Nice to meet you. I'm Faith, Faith Desai. So your son lives in New York?

two hundred and three 203

○ That's right. He moved there from our home in Denver about five years ago.
❏ Oh, how old is he?
○ Robert? He's twenty-four now. And how about you?
❏ I live in Scotland.
○ Oh, whereabouts in Scotland?
❏ In Glasgow.
○ Got any children?
❏ Yes, two. A son and a daughter. Philip's five and June's eight. Oh, look, here comes the food!

Step 4 B 38

Bruce: My father's name is Alec. My wife's called Peggy and my son's name is Martin.

Linda: My mother's name is Lena. My husband's called Immo and my daughter's name is Hillery.

Step 6 A 39

Children

We are the
Sons and daughters of
Our parents.

Our parents are the
Sons and daughters of
Our grandparents.

Our grandparents are the
Sons and daughters of
Their parents.

We are all
Sons and daughters.

We are all
Children.

Step 10 Pronunciation 40

1. son - husband - mother - daughter - brother
2. surname - first - birth - divorced
3. Wednesday - evening - Texas - hello - ten
4. beer - here - thirty - near - we're
5. pears - where - their - there - ferry

Step 12 Pronunciation 41

surname, first name and middle name
first name, surname and middle name
middle name, first name and surname

sons, daughters and grandchildren
daughters, sons and grandchildren
grandchildren, daughters and sons

UNIT 8

Step 4 B 42

Dialogue 1

○ Excuse me?
❏ Yes?
○ Is there a garage near here?
❏ Yes, just go down this street. It's not far. It's on the left.
○ Thanks a lot.
❏ You're welcome.

Dialogue 2 43

○ Can I help you?
❏ That's very kind of you. Where's the town museum, please?
○ Oh. That's in Minster Road, just over there on the right.
❏ Of course, I can see it now. Thank you very much.
○ Not at all. Goodbye.
❏ Bye.

Step 7 A 44

Where I live we've got a good baker's and a very good grocer's, and a newsagent's, and a couple of pubs, but there aren't many shops in the village now. When I was young it was different, but they've closed a lot of them down 'cos of course these days people get into their cars and drive into town and do their shopping in the supermarket. They closed the school down as well a few years ago, 'cos they said it wasn't economic, and now the children have to go to school in town. We haven't got any restaurants or cafés or anything like that, but I suppose if you want to go out for a meal you can always go into town. We've still got our station and the trains run about every hour, so that's quite a good service I suppose, and the bus service is all right, too.

It's quite a good place to live … We've got some good shops, you know, butcher's, grocer's, baker's, clothes shops and that. We've got our own school that all the children go to. There are one or two nice pubs and cafés. It's a quiet place, really, there isn't much traffic. Most people don't work here, they go into town. We haven't got any trains, 'cos the station was closed a few years ago. Most people in the village have got cars of course, so it's not too bad, but it's a bit difficult especially for the older people, 'cos the bus service isn't very good.

Step 10 Pronunciation

can, at, a: You can cash cheques at a bank.
there, a: There's a post office near here.
to, the: It's next to the bank.
are: Some pubs are closed in the afternoon.

Step 11 Pronunciation 46

1. museum – Museum
2. Garage – garage
3. restaurant – Restaurant
4. cheque – Scheck
5. Bank – bank
6. café – Café
7. Information – information
8. aspirin – Aspirin
9. tea – Tee
10. beer – Bier
11. post – Post
12. Station – station
13. Supermarkt – supermarket

UNIT 9 47

Step 2

My work isn't always very interesting and the pay isn't very good, either. But I like the job because I have regular working hours and I never work at the weekends. That means I can spend lots of time with my four children and that's very important.

A lot of boys want to be footballers, and I was the same. But now I don't like the job very much. Only the best players get really good money, but for other players like me the pay isn't very good at all and it's hard work seven days a week.

I think it's a great job. Much better than sitting in an office all day. I love travelling. Sure the working hours are long and I'm often away from home for three or four days, but that's not really a problem. I haven't got any family or children yet.

You know, people often think that we teachers have got an easy life – long holidays, short working days, etc – but it's not like that at all. I work in the evenings and at the weekend. Not only that, the money's not very good either. But I don't mind. I still like the job because I love working with children.

Painting was always my hobby and now it's my job. I work at home, not in an office and, of course, I have flexible working hours. I sometimes work seven days a week from morning to night, but I usually work three or four days a week.

Step 8 B Pronunciation

important
holidays
regular
colleagues
interesting
cassette
footballer
evenings
sentences
engineer
assistant
secretary
terrible
arrived
minutes

Step 9, A + B Pronunciation

I'm fine, thanks. And you?
How do you spell that?
Of course.
Can you help me?
How much does it cost?
What's the weather like?
I'd like to book a flight.
Do you work in an office?
You can go swimming.

UNIT 10

Steps 1 B + 3 A

(The lyrics of this song cannot be printed here for copyright reasons.)

Step 4, A + B

❒ I'm talking to Bruce about things he liked when he was younger, what he liked at school and so on – Bruce, what were your favourite subjects at school?

○ My favourite subject was English actually, closely followed by German.

❒ So you liked languages?

○ I don't know. You see, I loved German but I didn't like French.

❑ I see, and what were the most boring subjects for you?
○ I think the only subjects that really bored me were music and art. Today I'm very interested in art and I love all sorts of music, but music at school was, well, it wasn't any music that I liked, it was mostly classical music which they wanted us to like but I didn't, I just thought it was, well, boring. And art was boring, too.
❑ And what subjects were you good at?
○ Well, I was good at English and German, probably because I liked them, and I was very bad at music. As I said, I didn't like the music the teachers played, I never learned to read music and I couldn't sing, and I still can't.
❑ When you were 15, what was your favourite food?
○ Chips. No doubt about it, fish and chips, sausage and chips, egg and chips. I really liked chips, and I loved eggs. I ate three or four eggs a day. I don't eat so many now. They say too many eggs are bad for you. And I don't like chips very much. English chips are terrible.
❑ What about drinks?
○ When I was young I drank a lot of tea but I don't like it very much now. I usually prefer coffee. Of course, when I was fifteen I was starting to go to pubs and drink beer. I still do.
❑ And what about your taste in music?
○ When I was 15?
❑ Yes.
○ Well, as I said, I didn't like classical music, but we're talking about 1964, 1965 and the rock music was great, the Beatles, Rolling Stones, and so on. And I must say, I still like a lot of those old songs.

Step 5 A

Interviewer: Let's think about school for a minute.
Jonathan: Hm …, I'm surprised, I really can't remember much. Mostly I liked it.
John: Well, I'm afraid I didn't. The high school I went to in Toronto was incredibly big, there were about 2,500 pupils and I didn't like it very much. I spent most of my time playing hockey and baseball.
Linda: I remember one fantastic teacher, everybody loved him, but otherwise it wasn't very exciting.
Heinke: I remember the school theatre group, the school newspaper, things like that, and friends.
Derrick: I remember changing schools quite often: because of my father's job my parents moved several times and I went to several different schools. It was a bit difficult sometimes. The worst move was from Wales to England.
Interviewer: What about other things you've learned?
Heinke: I learned to swim quite late – when I was twelve – and I'm very proud of my running dive. I thought I would never learn it.
Linda: I learned to drive a car when I was 16. In the States you get your driving licence at 16. We had lessons at school.
John: I did that at 16, too. That's normal in Canada. One thing I'm really proud of is learning German. I started when I was about 22 or 23 and I'm proud of it because I was never good at languages at school and I thought German was impossible to learn.
Interviewer: What about jobs?
Heinke: My first job was teaching.
Linda: My first job was in my father's office. It was very boring. My best job was teaching English in a prison. I learned quite a lot of things there which you don't learn in the outside world.
Derrick: My first job was washing dishes in an Italian restaurant.
Interviewer: And holidays?
Jonathan: I've got very strong childhood holiday memories. We usually spent our holiday in Paignton in Devon, which is where my grandmother lived. And she had this fantastic house up above the town with a panoramic view of Torbay – the English Riviera it's called – and a beautiful garden. She was a great gardener. Those were really happy times. And of course it was always hot and sunny and it never rained because that's what it was like in those days as I'm sure other people remember too.

Step 8

1. It was in the month of Liverpool
   In the city of July
   The moon lay thick upon the ground
   The snow shone in the sky
   The flowers were singing sweetly
   The birds were in full bloom
   I went down to the cellar
   To clean an upstairs room

2. Said she to me, "Was that you?"
   Said I, "Who?"
   Said she, "You."
   Said I, "Where?"
   Said she "There."
   Said I, "When?"
   Said she, "Then."
   Said I, "No."
   Said she, "Oh ..."

3. I remember – I remember well –
   The first girl that I kissed.
   She closed her eyes, I closed mine,
   And then – worst luck – we missed!

Step 10 Pronunciation

sport - history - boring - favourite - worst - thought - information - world

Step 11 Pronunciation

1. At school he didn't like classical music but today he's very interested in it.
2. At school he thought art was boring but he likes it now.
3. When he was at school he couldn't sing and he still can't.
4. When he was young he ate three or four eggs a day but he doesn't eat so many now.
5. When he was fifteen he started drinking beer and he still likes it now.
6. When he was fifteen he liked rock music and he still likes the old songs.

UNIT 11

Step 3, A + B

It's a small country.
There are a lot of visitors here in summer.
The weather's not always good in summer.
A lot of people from this country went to live in America.
There aren't many large towns.
It's not an industrial country.
They drink a lot of beer.
It's an expensive country.
Some people speak two languages.
It's a very green country.
It's …

Step 6, A + B

❑ Ms Ford, which of the twenty-six towns and cities was Coventry's first contact?
❍ That was with Stalingrad, later called Volgograd. We started in 1942 and it became a twin city in 1944.
❑ And the newest twin town?
❍ Jinan in China. We've had contacts with other towns in other countries in the last few years but these aren't real twin towns.
❑ Have you got any plans for more?
❍ Well, we're thinking of a town in Nicaragua but I don't think we can have many more. It's just too much work.
❑ So how many people have you got in your office to help with all this work?
❍ There are many different offices in Coventry that help us but my office has only three people: myself, my assistant and another lady who is our secretary. So we're really very small.
❑ That means you need a lot of help from the people of Coventry. Is that right?
❍ Yes, indeed. We really need their help. And I also think that this is one of the most important aspects of our work. To get as many people in Coventry working with us as we can. For example, we hope that they'll take guests into their homes and then be guests in the homes of people from the other towns. For us it's very important that the people of Coventry take an active part.
❑ It must cost a lot of money.
❍ Yes, that is a problem. We can't have full contacts with all of them. We don't have enough people and money for that. What we do is to look for something that's similar in Coventry and in each of the twenty-six towns. For example, in Britain we learn French and German as foreign languages, so we organize school contacts with St. Etienne in France and Kiel in Germany. In the same way, the people in St. Etienne and Kiel want to learn English. Another example's sport. Many contacts in Eastern Europe, for example Kecskemet in Hungary and Ostrava in the Czech Republic, come from sporting contacts. Sport's very popular in Eastern Europe and so we make contacts with sports clubs here in Coventry. Sometimes there are business contacts, for example with Dresden, or political contacts, for example the new contact with Nicaragua.

❏ Are there contacts for young people?
○ Yes. We have a schools department for contacts between groups of people. At the moment a good place for younger people is Bologna in Italy. We often have groups of young people under twenty-five going there. It is important that the young people don't think of it as a holiday but as a way of learning about other countries and people. We always organize a programme to show them what life in the other cities and countries is like. And very often they learn the language at the same time.
❏ Ms Ford, thank you very much.

Step 9 B

1. In Dublin's fair city
   Where the girls are so pretty
   I first set my eyes on sweet Molly Malone.

2. When it's spring again, I'll bring again
   Tulips from Amsterdam.

3. I love Paris in the springtime.
   I love Paris in the fall.
   I love Paris in the winter – when it drizzles,
   I love Paris in the summer – when it sizzles.

4. I belong to Glasgow,
   Dear old Glasgow town.
   Oh, what's the matter with Glasgow?
   For it's going round and round.

5. London Bridge is falling down, falling down, falling down
   London Bridge is falling down, my fair lady.

Step 10 B

- The person with the most first names lives in Barrow Hill in England. Tracey Nelson has 140 names because her parents did not know which name they wanted to give her, so they gave her all the names in the book.
- Berlin is the city with the most dogs in Germany. 74,991 dogs were registered there in 1988.
- The highest waterfall in Europe is near Lourdes in France and is 421 m high.
- The people of Cyprus smoke more cigarettes than any other people in the world: 4,050 cigarettes per person per year.
- The largest wine barrel in the world is in Heidelberg and holds 221,000 litres.
- The person with the longest first name in the world is Dr. Brahmatma of New Delhi. It takes him about three minutes to say all the 1,478 letters of his name – on a good day!

Step 11 A

a) 480 (four hundred and eighty)
b) 626 (six hundred and twenty-six)
c) 18,037 (eighteen thousand and thirty-seven)
d) 4,050 (four thousand and fifty)
e) 7,223 (seven thousand two hundred and twenty-three)
f) 16,995 (sixteen thousand nine hundred and ninety-five)
g) 47,991 (forty-seven thousand nine hundred and ninety-one)
h) 220,100 (two hundred and twenty thousand one hundred)
i) 34,518 (thirty-four thousand five hundred and eighteen)
j) 1,695,040 (one million six hundred and ninety-five thousand and forty)

Step 12, A + B Pronunciation

1. life
2. love
3. attractive
4. wife
5. live
6. enough
7. view
8. leave
9. expensive
10. ferry
11. have
12. very
13. travel
14. Coventry
15. over
16. village
17. visit

UNIT 12

Step 3

Talking all the day
With true friends who try to make you stay
Telling jokes and news
And singing songs to pass the time away
We watched the Galway salmon run
Like silver, darting, dancing in the sun
Living on your western shore
Saw summer sunset, asked for more
Stood by your Atlantic sea
And sang a song for Ireland

Drinking all the day
In old pubs where fiddlers love to play
Saw one touch the bow
And he played a reel that seemed so grand and gay
Stood on Dingle beach and cast
In wild foam we found Atlantic bass
Living on your western shore
Saw summer sunset, asked for more
Stood by your Atlantic sea
And sang a song for Ireland

Step 4 B

- ❐ George, let's go out tonight.
- ○ That's a good idea. Shall we go to O'Reilly's?
- ❐ Well, I'd rather go to the cinema. It's always so noisy at O'Reilly's.
- ○ OK, let's go to the cinema, then.

Step 4 D

- ❐ What shall we do at the weekend?
- ○ Well, there's a music festival in Dublin.
- ❐ Great! Let's go to that, then.
- ○ Shall we go on Saturday or Sunday?
- ❐ I don't mind. What about you?
- ○ Well, I'd rather go on Saturday, then we can have a lie-in on Sunday.

Step 10 Pronunciation

a) We haven't got any discos in our town.
b) I played football at school.
c) I didn't play tennis when I was younger.
d) We haven't got enough bicycle paths.
e) Let's go for a walk.
f) I started school in 1955.
g) Eighteen million people watched the football on TV last night.
h) I waited at the station for four hours.
i) I worked for ten hours yesterday.
j) Tennis isn't too expensive in England.
k) Did you have a nice weekend?

Step 11 Pronunciation

1. We haven't got many discos where I live.
   We haven't got any discos in our town.

2. I played a lot of football when I was at school.
   I played tennis.

3. I'd like to go out tonight.
   Well, I'd rather stay at home.

4. I started school in 1955.
   Did you? I started in 1953.

5. I waited for four hours.
   I waited for five.

PREVIEW D

Step 4

1. Er … Where do you want the sofa?
   In the living room, please …

2. Well, what shall we have?
   I'd like steak and kidney pie with boiled potatoes and carrots. And a soup to start with.

3. My father's German and my mother comes from Denmark, but I was actually born in Hamburg and we lived there for many years.

4. Excuse me. Can we have the menu, please?
   There you are.

UNIT 13

Step 2 B

We'd like to inform our customers that our new restaurant is now open for lunch and snacks. Today's special menu is tomato soup, fried plaice or steak and kidney pie, ice cream or apple pie. Enjoy your meal!

Step 3 B

1. ❐ Excuse me. Can we have the menu please?
   ▽ Oh, I'm sorry … there you are.
   ❐ Thank you.

2. ❐ Well, what shall we have?
   ○ I'd like steak and kidney pie with boiled potatoes and carrots. And a soup to start with.
   △ I think I'll have an egg mayonnaise and then plaice with chips and peas. What about you, Christine?
   ▷ Er … I'd like steak and kidney pie, too, with boiled potatoes. No starter. And you, Richard ?
   ❐ Let's see … ah, chicken, my favourite! I'll have that. And soup for me, too.

3. ▽ Are you ready to order yet?
   ❐ Yes, please. We'd like two soups and one egg mayonnaise, and then, er … one plaice, two steak and kidney pies, and one chicken.
   ▽ Thank you. And the vegetables?

4. ❐ Can we have the bill, please?
   ▽ Certainly. One moment, please.

Step 11 Pronunciation

1. I think I'll have a steak.
   I think I'll have a steak, too.

2. It's my round.
   No, it's not, it's my round!

3. This pie's really good.
   Hm, I like apples, but I don't like apple pie.

4. I'll have a cheese omelette.
   I think I'll have a ham omelette.
5. Which is the healthiest diet in the world?
   Well, the Spanish diet is one of the healthiest.

Step 12 A Pronunciation

liked   lived   started

Step 12 B Pronunciation

- liked, watched, stopped
- lived, moved, rained, stayed, played, studied, ordered
- started, visited, wanted, decided

UNIT 14

Step 1 B

1. bathroom
2. living room
3. kitchen
4. bedroom
5. toilet
6. hall

Step 2 B

- ❒ Er ... Where do you want the sofa?
- ○ In the living room, please, and the armchair and ...
- ❒ Just a minute; the sofa and the armchair first Joe, OK?
- ○ ... and then the coffee table, and the television ...
- ❒ ... coffee table and the TV ...
- ○ ... and the lamp and the plant go in the living room, too.
- ❒ What about the chest of drawers?
- ○ That goes in the bedroom, please.
- ❒ Did you get that, Joe? Anything else for the bedroom?
- ○ Yes ... the wardrobe and this picture.
- ❒ Does this table go in the kitchen?
- ○ Er ... no, can you put it in the living room, under the window?
- ❒ OK ... this goes in the living room.
- ○ And the fridge, the washing machine and these cupboards go in the kitchen.
- ❒ Joe and Frank, you take the fridge. We can carry the washing machine ...
  Right, that's the lot.
- ○ Oh, wonderful, thank you! Would you like a drink? There's some beer in the fridge.
- ❒ In the fridge?! That's why it was so heavy!

Step 11 A Pronunciation

television   fridge

Step 11, C + D Pronunciation

- television, usually, leisure
- fridge, page, Germany, language, June, geography

UNIT 15

Step 3 A

1. My father's German and my mother comes from Denmark, but I was actually born in Hamburg and we lived there for many years. I met my husband when I was twenty-five. He's Danish and comes from a small town near Copenhagen. I've now got a Danish passport, and I actually feel Danish. Of course I speak both German and Danish, but I speak English and French too.

2. I was born and grew up in Moscow. My mother's Russian but my father's German. His ancestors moved to Russia about 1800. We got German passports and moved to Bremen in 1988. I speak German and Russian but I feel more German.

3. I came to England in 1956 with my parents. We came here from Jamaica because there was no work there and we were told there were jobs in Britain. I was only three when we came here so I can't remember much about Jamaica. I went to school here in Britain, I work here in Britain, I have a British passport, my children were born here, my wife was born here and I really feel I'm British.

4. You won't believe this but my mother's Swiss, my father's Irish and I grew up in Germany. I've got both an Irish and a Swiss passport. I can speak English, French and German. I live in Ireland but I don't really feel Irish, Swiss or German. If anything, I suppose I'm a European!

Step 8 Pronunciation

There's Dick and Diana
And Sally and Sam
And friends like Joanna
And Peter and Pam

There's Christopher, Cathy
And Mary and Mike
There's all of my family
And others I like

There's Mark and there's Mandy
And all of the rest
But only one Sandy:
The one I like best!